RELIGION AND POLITICS IN IRAN

RELIGION AND POLITICS IN IRAN

Shi'ism from Quietism to Revolution

edited by

NIKKI R. KEDDIE

YALE UNIVERSITY PRESS
New Haven and London

Published with assistance from the Mary Cady Tew Memorial Fund.

Designed by Nancy Ovedovitz and set in VIP Times Roman type by Coghill Composition Co.
Printed in the United States of America by Murray Printing Company, Westford, Mass.

Library of Congress Cataloging in Publication Data
Main entry under title:
Religion and politics in Iran.
  Bibliography: p. 237
  Includes index.
  1. Shī'ah—Iran—Addresses, essays, lectures.
2. Islam and politics—Iran—Addresses, essays,
lectures. 3. Iran—Politics and government—Addresses,
essays, lectures. I. Keddie, Nikki R.
BP192.7.I68R44 1983   297'.82'0955   82–17351
ISBN 0–300–02874–1

10 9 8 7 6 5 4 3 2 1

*To Albert Hourani and Ernest Gellner
with friendship and gratitude*

CONTENTS

ACKNOWLEDGMENTS

This volume had its origin in a conference in the summer of 1980 organized by the Berlin Institute for Comparative Social Research. Kurt Greussing, Jan Grevemeyer, and Jochen Blaschke did most of the organizational and preparatory work for the conference and Carsten Colpe and I were co-conveners. The German edition of the conference, with a few additional papers, was edited by Kurt Greussing, while the present English edition was independently edited with a somewhat different selection of papers. Kurt Greussing and I exchanged editorial suggestions for each paper, and his editorial work and proposals were very useful in the preparation of this volume. Thanks are due to the conference organizers and participants for invaluable help at all stages.

In order to produce an English edition dealing with closely related topics, it was decided to both.add to and subtract from the contents of the original conference. As a result, the present volume includes four revised conference papers; two papers proposed for the conference by authors who were unable to attend, but who later wrote for publication; and four papers commissioned by this editor.

Suggestions regarding several of the papers were also made by Ervand Abrahamian, Juan Cole, Roy Mottahedeh, Abdulaziz Sachedina, and Andrew Whitley; and additional help came from Mangol Bayat, Adele and Amir Ferdows, and Martin van Bruinessen. Eric Hooglund and Andrew Newman gave assistance in putting the manuscript in final form that went far beyond the call of duty. Special thanks go to Robert Bellah for reading and commenting upon the manuscript on extremely short notice.

We have used a simplified system of Persian transliteration, without diacritics. Arabic transliterations are used in chapters concerning the Arabs, and throughout for terms better known in Arabic than in Persian forms (chiefly Islamic terms). Words that have entered English are generally given their dictionary spellings, and names habitually transliterated by a system other than ours are left in their familiar forms. Foreign terms not in most English dictionaries are italicized only upon their first use in each chapter. If an author expressed a strong preference for one of two legitimate transliterations of a foreign term, we have followed that preference.

Parts of the chapter by Azar Tabari appeared in *Khamsin* and much of the chapter by Willem Floor appeared in the *International Journal of Middle East Studies,* both of which are thanked for permission to reprint.

I also wish to thank Charles Grench, Mary Alice Galligan, and Robert Brown, to whom Yale University Press entrusted this volume, for their consistent cooperation and helpfulness.

Los Angeles, October 1982

CHAPTER ONE

Introduction

NIKKI R. KEDDIE

For reasons not yet explained, Iranian culture seems often to have been one of extremes. Before Islam, the good god and his evil adversary among the Zoroastrians evolved in part into the Manichaean extremes of good spirit and evil matter, and Manichaeism went into the communistic good-evil rebellious doctrine of the fifth-century B.C. Mazdakite sect. In politics, traditions of despotism have been punctuated by decentralization and by frequent revolts and rebellions that often, both in pre-Islamic and Islamic times, had a strong religious and often messianic coloring. These revolts, which were often temporarily successful in taking over parts of Iran, frequently expressed the grievances of the rural poor, or of uprooted and alienated urban classes. Their religious ideologies rarely mirrored the ruling orthodoxy but were often socially oriented and syncretic; in the early days of Islam these ideologies combined Mazdakism or other pre-Islamic ideas with Muslim notions, frequently from the minority, Shi'i branch of Islam. As Shi'i doctrines became better established, rebellious groups in Iran often identified with them: notably with one branch of the (Sevener) Isma'ili Shi'is pejoratively known to some as the Assassins from their alleged use of hashish. They carried on their revolts partly by the use of individual assassination of powerful men (whence our word *assassin*). The other main Shi'i group, the Twelvers, were for a long time largely quietist. In the fifteenth century an unorthodox activist branch of the Twelver Shi'is coalesced, however, and they used rebellious Iranian and Ottoman tribespeople to conquer Iran in the early sixteenth century. Afterward, this Safavid dynasty became orthodox Twelver rulers of a nonrevolutionary type. Sudden swings from revolt to stability, from centralization to decentralization, and from unorthodoxy to orthodoxy are hence not unique to post–World War II or post-1973 Iran, but have precedents in Iranian history. On the other hand, it seems likely that Iran's transformation since 1978–79 into a revolutionary, desecularizing, ideologically egalitarian, anti-American, nonmodernizing society in which almost the only consistent feature with the period of Mohammad

1

Reza Shah seems to be arbitrary rule, is a more extreme and rapid change than were those of the past. Even the changes brought by the Islamic conquest were more gradual, while the destructive Mongols cannot be said to have wrought a cultural or social transformation.

In trying to explain changes and conditions like those in recent Iran, scholars have resorted to many methodologies. One is historical, which includes many subtheories, and which tries to trace recent developments to roots or causes in the past. Almost no one objects to such a method when the past discussed is very recent; when one says, for example, that the classes disfavored by the late shah, such as the bazaaris, new urban migrants, and the ulama, participated heavily in the revolution of 1978–79 largely because of their alienation, economic grievances, and discontent. A problem, rarely methodologically discussed, arises, however, when one tries to consider seriously how far back in time one can find events and trends that had an important effect on the recent Iranian revolution. The opening paragraph of this essay assumes that traits found among Iranians as early as pre-Islamic times have some relation to today's Iran. (It does not, however, assume that Iranians have a consistent "national character" or "pattern of thinking" as it says nothing about causation—it could be Iran's contrasting geography or sparse and scattered settlement patterns that most influence similar patterns of thought and social organization.) Regarding the Iranian revolution, one important question in using a historical methodology is: Can we learn more about the revolution by tracing trends in Twelver Shi'i thought and action as far back as possible, or by studying the totality of conditions in Iran, with emphasis on economic, social, and cultural change since, say, 1953? Along with many others I would feel that the latter is more important if our primary aim is to understand the revolution and other recent events. On the other hand, the Shi'i ideologies of the revolution have part of their roots in the Shi'i past.

This book, dealing with religion and politics, is not intended to be about the development of religious doctrine and movements in the abstract, but about their development out of, and interaction with, a variety of social and political conditions. These interactions are stressed in the papers on contemporary events and thinkers; most strikingly in William Beeman's survey of economic and cultural developments in the shah's last years and America's relation to them, and in Mary Hegland's study showing how the ideological and practical significance of the myth of the Shi'i martyr Husain's death became radically transformed with changing village circumstances and the rise of Iran's revolutionary movement. Willem Floor ties ulama ideology and action more closely to their power, prestige, and economic interests than most scholars have done, while Azar Tabari gives a centuries-long survey showing the interaction of Iran's economy and politics with the ulama's position, concentrating most on recent events. Yann Richard's paper on Ayatollah Kashani, a sometime ally of Mosaddeq, concentrates rather on revising the distorted picture of this man that was current before 1979, but he too shows Kashani's relations to more general Iranian politics, stressing his lifetime hostility to the British, who were the main imperial power in Iran for most of his life. Shahrough Akhavi on Ali Shariati and Homa Katouzian on Sadr and Bani Sadr stress their thought, but show how Shariati's interpretation of Islamic sociology and Sadr's and Bani Sadr's views of Islamic economies support definite political positions, often influenced by Western thinkers. Gregory Rose stresses the idea of alienation from Islamic roots and the need to overcome this in the thought of Khomeini.

With all the attention given to political, social, and cultural factors in these papers, however, it remains true that religious leaders and ideas are given greater weight than if the aim had been to weigh each factor in the revolution according to the author's estimate of its importance. This is so because this book is about religion and politics, and because the religious component both of the revolution and of Iranian history is less well understood than, say, the socioeconomic or antiforeign components. This is partly because research on the latter can be done more or less adequately without access to difficult Persian and Arabic texts and knowledge of the history of doctrines, which is not true of research on religious thought. Also, the religious component in Iranian politics was underrated until recently, and is more unusual and harder to understand than the sociopolitical one. Not since Savonarola's Florence and Calvin's Geneva has the world seen such direct rule by severe fundamentalist clerics; and no previous revolution has been won after events like a year-long series of demonstrations by huge unarmed crowds, several times shot upon, followed by mass strikes, largely carried out in the name of an absent religious leader. The socioeconomic and cultural background of the revolution was not similarly unique and hence could be understood more easily.

For all the contributing importance of historical background, it can be argued that revolutionary conditions came into being mainly in the 1970s. Several large oil-exporting countries, as well as those like Egypt receiving massive outside funds, have seen similar trends to those in Iran since World War II and especially since the 1973 oil price rise, such as huge technological and consumer imports; import substitution industries catering to the wealthier classes; mechanization and commercialization of agriculture (along with population increase) resulting in huge rural-urban migration and massive alienation of the new urban poor; luxury building and consumption along with spreading slums; a massive influx of usually bad Western films, TV, and fads; and a growing cultural gap between those educated in, and rich enough to afford, Western ways, and the traditional classes. In the Eastern hemisphere the important oil exporters in OPEC all have Muslim majorities. Some of the above problems, ironically hastened by the "boon" of oil, have contributed to unrest in Muslim countries other than Iran, and also to a growing, and sometimes violent, series of Islamic movements. Such movements exist also in the non-oil-exporting countries of the Middle East where they have other causes (including opposition to minority Alawite rule in Syria, to minority Sunni rule in Iraq, and to secularism in Turkey).

In many Muslim countries anti-Western and anti-imperialist sentiment has grown since World War II, partly due to the association of Israel with the West and the United States, and partly because Western-oriented economic policies were seen to increase income distribution gaps and various other problems for the disfavored majority. Most people resented identification with either superpower, both of which were seen as using Muslim peoples for their own strategic and economic ends. Many intellectuals as well as ordinary people have increasingly rejected, at least in theory, ideology and culture coming from the disliked West and turned to militant and often utopian strains in Islam. Some aimed at major reforms and others at a revolutionary reorganization of society.

While some Muslim countries, including Egypt, are often pointed to as possible sites of future Islamic revolutions, it seems unlikely that such revolutions, if they occur, will take the form found in Iran, with leaders in the ulama directly ruling all branches of government. In the nineteenth and twentieth centuries the independent power of the Sunni ulama of the Middle East decreased while that of the Iranian Shi'i ulama, with a hiatus in the years of Pahlavi dictatorship, grew. This leads us to a point where the long-term view of history can give vital information not available from simply looking at the twentieth century. While it is not true, as some would have it, that the Shi'i ulama were nearly always antigovernmental, reformist, or revolutionary (see Floor and Tabari), or were more moral than the clergy of other religions or the Sunni ulama, it is true that the ulama had powers and pretensions which generally grew over the centuries, and that their history prepared them to play a unique role in modern politics.

II

In tracing historically religious themes with sociopolitical implications in Iran, it is possible to take at least two broad approaches. One is to look upon Iran as an entity, and trace religious ideas and organization and their ties to social movements back as far as one can into pre-Islamic Iranian history, showing what connections, if any, exist between these early movements and later Islamic ones. Such an approach is suggested by the opening paragraph of this introduction, and it could certainly be carried out far more than it has. (One of the few very good works partially exemplifying this approach is Alessandro Bausani's *Persia Religiosa* [Milan, 1959], which unfortunately has too little on the interconnections of the brilliantly analyzed religious thought with sociopolitical events.) In Islamic times, this approach would deal with Sunni, Sufi (mystical), and heretical movements as well as with Shi'ism, which became the predominant religion in Iran only when the Safavid dynasty made it the state religion and imposed it, often forcibly, from the early sixteenth century on. If one were writing a general history of religion and politics in Iran, such a consideration of a variety of religions and trends and their interconnections and differences would be necessary.

This book, however, concentrates heavily on Shi'i thinkers and movements in modern, and especially contemporary, times. While it would be possible to find some background even for some of these persons and movements in non-Shi'i Iran, their chief intellectual background is to be found in Shi'ism, beginning even when Shi'ism was primarily an Arab, not an Iranian, trend. Hence, the two chapters herein that cover premodern history, those by W. Montgomery Watt and Juan R. Cole, summarize developments in premodern Shi'ism, whether Iranian or not, that have significance for modern Iranian Shi'is. This does not mean that the authors or the editor hold the outmoded view that Shi'ism is peculiarly Iranian, or that non-Shi'i trends have not had a modern impact, but only that a choice was made of what seemed most important to cover in the necessarily brief historical background section. The study of Shi'i history has only in the last few decades begun to emerge from ignorance and mythology, and the Montgomery Watt and Cole chapters, basic as they may seem, in fact incorporate much new research and original conclusions. Montgomery Watt in his chapter, as at greater length elsewhere, shows that Twelver or Imami Shi'ism was not, during the lifetime of the imams (leaders descended from Muhammad's cousin and son-in-law Ali), a single party that recognized and followed the imams' rule and rulings. Montgomery Watt's writings suggest that it was a wealthy individual at the court of the Abbasid caliphate who put forth the fundamental doctrine that the Twelfth Imam went into hiding on earth and would return as the messianic Mahdi. For some time this was a doctrine that prevented serious conflict between the Imami Shi'is and the Sunni Abbasid caliphs, as an absent imam could not speak out or give instructions to his followers that might contravene the rulings of the caliph or, later, of temporal princes or sultans. As Cole's paper shows, the institution of the *mujtahid* who exercised *ijtihad* (individual judgment in interpreting religious law and doctrine) was very slow to develop among the Imami Shi'is, who at first rejected ijtihad. And it was only under the later Safavids, in the seventeenth century, that a minority of mujtahids began to claim that rulers should follow their advice on many important questions. The very rationale of the mujtahids, that they were better qualified than lay believers to interpret law and doctrine, and hence lay believers must follow them, was even rejected by the dominant seventeenth- and eighteenth-century school of *akhbaris*. The akhbaris said that believers should only follow Muhammad, the Qur'an, and the imams, and not fallible mujtahids; the way to follow the imams was to follow and interpret the Traditions *(akhbar)* regarding the imams' sayings and acts, as well as the imams' writings when these existed. Had the akhbari school won out, there would have been scant ideological basis for the sociopolitical claims and leadership of the mujtahids which grew under the Qajar dynasty (1796–1925).

The contrary mujtahidi or usuli school, however, gained strength and finally won out in the course of the eighteenth century, owing in part to sociopolitical factors: (1) With the early eighteenth-century Sunni Afghan invasion, followed by Nader Shah's further persecution of Shi'is, many Iranian Shi'i leaders fled to the Shi'i shrine cities of Ottoman Iraq, and they, like those who remained in Iran after Nader Shah, faced something of a vacuum in temporal power that encouraged Shi'i mujtahids to put forth increasing claims to power over their followers—claims that were not easily refuted or repressed by the weak temporal rulers. Hence a combination of apparently disastrous victories for Sunnism and decentralization in Iran were turned to good account by the mujtahids. (2) This same combination of circumstances weakened, and in some parts of Iran for some time ended, the appointment and other close ties of the Shi'i ulama with government that had existed in most of the Safavid period. Again, this might look like a loss for the ulama, but it provided the basis for a gain in Qajar times, when the ulama were less closely tied to the government, and only a minority of ulama had governmental appointments with actual duties, although the Qajars wished to demonstrate their piety through contributing to pensions and *vaqfs* (inalienable religious endowments). In the eighteenth and nineteenth centuries the mujtahids built up their actual power and following, and their independent power encouraged usuli doctrine, which stressed that each believer must follow a living mujtahid, just as ties to the state or local rulers encouraged akhbari doctrine, which kept the mujtahids from being rivals for power with temporal governments by denying them any real power or legitimacy.

As indicated, the independent power of mujtahids, a dramatic feature of nineteenth- and part of twentieth-century Iran, does not go back to the first centuries of Shi'i history. Though some mujtahids claimed it in the seventeenth century, they were a minority, and the mujtahidi doctrine won out only in the late eighteenth century, while the political strength of mujtahids, partially tied to the mujtahidi (usuli) doctrine, grew especially in the nineteenth century under the Qajar dynasty. The Qajars lacked the religious pretensions of the Safavids, who early claimed divine power and forged a descent from the Seventh Imam. Increasing political and economic subservience to Russia and Great Britain, along with minor Qajar efforts to modernize and strengthen the government, hurt the ulama, and Qajar tariff limits and extraterritoriality granted to Western countries hit the ulama's bazaar allies. There thus developed a sporadic but growing ulama-bazaar alliance that occasionally acted against the government, in embryo in the successful demand for the cancellation of the all-encompassing concession to the British subject Reuter and the dismissal of the prime minister who favored this concession in 1872–73; in a mass movement that forced the cancellation of a Tobacco Concession to a British subject in 1891–92; and especially in the constitutional revolution of 1905–11 (see Tabari). In the latter two, and especially the last, of these movements, a small group of modernizing, reformist intellectuals were also involved. They too had ties with merchant communities, and partly in their behalf promoted constitutional, economic, and legal reforms that could, among other things, have brought a modernization of Iran's economy that would have helped to strengthen the merchants and centralize the country.

Iran, however, has long had problems that make the country far harder to centralize and modernize than others with stronger agrarian and urban economies, less arid and rugged terrain, and hence fewer semi-independent nomadic, provincial, and ulama leaders—such as Egypt and Turkey. Those countries were able to centralize and modernize significantly in the nineteenth century, whereas Iran was not. Among other things, this meant that centralization and modernization were more gradual processes in Egypt and Turkey and, at least until very recently, less suddenly upsetting to old ways of life than was the rapid modernization from above in just fifty years in Pahlavi Iran (which accelerated further after 1973, with benefits concentrated on the richer classes).

Another consequence of Iranian decentralization was that it gave scope for growing ulama independence, especially as the ulama had not only their own effective tax system, but also their own private armies of students and retainers, so that they commanded considerable areas of what we might call government, including much of the legal and nearly all of the educational and welfare systems. This does not mean that, until post-1962 speeches and writings by Ayatollah Khomeini, there is any record of the ulama's believing they could rule directly—an idea not really part of Shi'i theory. Rather, most of them felt strongly that the government should not cut down on their prerogatives, should withdraw, rather than extend, concessions to the infidel West, and should heed the ulama's advice.

Recent antiroyalist acts by the ulama along with their participation in earlier oppositional movements have probably led to too great an emphasis on the ulama's "revolutionary" role or potential. As Floor indicates, most ulama, particularly the higher ones, were more conservative than revolutionary in their opposition; they wished to stop imperialist and Westernizing innovations, not create a new system of rule and society. As in many third-world societies, including non-Muslim ones, liberal nationalists, radicals, and traditionalists often combined to fight Western imperialism, and many of them also fought Western ways in favor of either neotraditionalism or radical new interpretations of local ways. What was special in Iran was that the leaders of "orthodox" religion, and not always nationalists and reformers, often took the leading role. A concatenation of circumstances favored this unique development: the economic strength and political power of the ulama; a doctrine which said that believers must follow a leading member of the ulama on nearly all points; Qajar weakness and Iran's decentralization; the unusually close ties of the ulama with actively dissatisfied and strong bazaar classes; the location of the leading ulama in Iraq, where the shahs could not control them; and the shahs' lack of any effective army, which allowed unarmed, ulama-led struggles to be effective. Most of the ulama, however, even if they went along with a Western-style constitution in 1906–07, were expecting it to increase, not decrease, their power, and especially to decrease the strength of their main power rival, the shah. This does not mean that many leading ulama, then and now, were not sincerely concerned over issues like poverty, welfare, and Iranian independence, but, as their own traditional handling of their own and vaqf peasantry suggests, their notions of welfare and justice were of a traditional type centering on charity for the poor, and they had, with very few exceptions, no program for social reorganization.

Also, some scholars have tended to underrate the degree to which many ulama cooperated with the government, openly or implicitly, both in Qajar and Pahlavi times. In the first half of the nineteenth century such backing far outweighed opposition. It was shown in many ways, but most dramatically in the ulama-governmental alliance against the Babi religion, which began when a young merchant, Sayyed Ali Mohammad, declared himself to be the gate or "Bab" to the hidden Twelfth Imam expected by the Shaikhi movement (see Cole). Babi movements were put down forcibly by the government with ulama approval in the late 1840s (although a minority of ulama joined the Babis); and both ulama and government backed the execution of the Bab in 1850 and later attacks on the Babis and the Baha'is (who developed out of the Babis).

Although the majority of ulama did not accept direct government appointments, they did accept pensions, funds, and vaqf land (as late as the late 1970s), and these helped to keep most of them as rather quietist, implicit supporters of the ruling powers except in the times of crisis mentioned above. After the Tobacco Protest, the ulama were quieted for some years largely by giving them money. Even during the constitutional revolution the ulama were increasingly put off by what they saw as threats to their power or ideas; when Mohammad Ali Shah brought back the "reactionary" Amin as-Soltan as his prime minister, the latter soon saw that it would be possible to make an alliance with relatively conservative ulama leaders in the parliament, especially Sayyed Mohammad Behbehani. Neither the shah nor the far left would tolerate this, however, and both plotted for Amin as-Soltan's assassination, which occurred in 1907. After the shah's coup d'état in 1908, for a time only the city of Tabriz resisted, and there most ulama were against the popular forces, as they were in several provincial cities. By the time of the second majles the ulama leaders occupied a largely conservative position, although many of them continued to support the constitution as a bulwark against arbitrary royal power, which had hurt them and their allies. Although many leading ulama in the Iraqi shrine cities supported the constitutional movement throughout, some did not.

An important nineteenth-century development strengthening the ulama which has received less notice than some factors mentioned above was the development of the institution of the *marja'-e taqlid* (source of imitation). This began with the eighteenth-century usuli school which said that every believer must choose a trained mujtahid to follow in law and doctrine. In the early nineteenth century there developed the notion that, ideally, there should be one marja'-e taqlid who could issue *fatvas* (decrees) binding on all believers. The first prominent single *marja'* was Shaikh Mortaza Ansari in mid-century, who did not participate in Iranian politics (see Cole). The decree that helped determine victory in the Tobacco Protest by outlawing all dealings in, and use of, tobacco by believers was, however, political and emanated from a later top marja', Ayatollah Shirazi. Although there has not always been a single universally recognized marja' (and there is not one today), this ideal, along with the development of binding rulings by mujtahids (whose older and more influential ones came to be called ayatollahs, and, at the top, great ayatollahs), created a kind of fluid hierarchy and organization among Iranian Shi'is stronger, more independent of government, and more influential than that found in Sunni countries. This hierarchy is neither appointive nor elective, but based on factors such as learning and consensus.

The years of heavy foreign intervention, war, and local rebellions (1912–21) saw some participation in these rebellions by lower religious figures, but no concerted activity by the ulama, except for nationalist ones like Sayyed Hasan Modarres and Ayatollah Kashani (see Richard).

III

With the coming to power of Reza Khan in a 1921 coup, and his rule as Reza Shah (1925–41), the role of the ulama began to be undermined. The government built up armed forces and a centralized secular bureaucracy; schools, courts, and most welfare services were similarly secularized; some support was given to greater equality and a more modern role for women through girls' education, and coeducation at the new university, although Reza Shah's decision to outlaw the veil, enforced from 1936 on, making Iran the first country forcibly to unveil women, could only backfire. While still prime minister in 1924, Reza Khan supported a campaign for a republic on the model of Ataturk in Turkey. Interestingly, the activist ulama, led by the most courageous among them, Sayyed Hasan Modarres (today regarded as a hero of the Islamic Republic), opposed a republic as un-Islamic, while their descendants in the recent revolution opposed monarchy as un-Islamic and saw a republic as Islamic. In both cases, the reasons are not far to seek, as current circumstances largely determined lofty theories. The Iranian ulama in 1924 associated a republic (as did Reza Khan) with the secularist Ataturk, who had first deposed the sultan and soon thereafter abolished the caliphate (both were in the hands of the same person in the Ottoman Empire). Ataturk also took other secularist, anticlerical measures, so it was easy to equate republicanism with secularism and anticlericalism. The ulama may have hoped to keep on the throne the weak Ahmad Shah Qajar, while a republic would surely mean a Reza Khan dictatorship. In fact, however, the ulama "victory" in forestalling a republic became a defeat, as Reza Khan was content to let republican propaganda drop and then have a stacked assembly depose the Qajars and declare him founder of the Pahlavi dynasty. In power he brought vaqfs under greater government control, limited those who could be certified as mollas, jailed a few recalcitrant ulama leaders, improved the position of religious minorities, and limited the ulama's judicial, educational, and welfare roles.

His son, Mohammad Reza Shah (1941–79) continued strongly secularist policies, especially after he achieved dictatorial powers following the 1953 anti-Mosaddeq coup. Secular education spread, women got more equal rights as in the 1967/75 family protection law, and the ulama were admonished to keep out of politics, sometimes suffering jail and even torture if they did not.

Even before the Pahlavis, many nationalist intellectuals developed ideas that blamed Iran's decline on the Arabs and Islam, and sought inspiration in idealized versions of Iran's great pre-Islamic empires and religions. While some of these intellectuals looked to radicals like Mazdak, when this type of ideology was picked up by Reza Shah and his son emphasis was placed on the great pre-Islamic emperors like Cyrus and Darius, and this monarchist nationalism was embodied in such things as the vastly expensive and mythomaniac celebrations at Persepolis in 1971. Naturally, as monarchy became increasingly a symbol against Islam and for dictatorship and subservience to foreigners, the ulama became increasingly antimonarchical, although for a long time their activists limited themselves to demands for a return to enforcement of the 1906–07 constitution, which was designed to create a very limited constitutional monarchy and included an ulama veto power over laws deemed contrary to Islamic law.

Rapid modernization from above, with increasing Western participation, helped create "two cultures" in Iran: those with Western-style education and employment who mimicked Western ways; and the peasants, nomads, bazaaris, urban migrants, and ulama who profited little if at all from this type of modernization, for whom traditional ways were functional, and whose resentments against the regime were best expressed by traditional religious symbols, such as the struggle of Imam Husain against the tyrant Yazid. After Mosaddeq's overthrow, both the left and secular nationalists were often jailed or forced underground or abroad, but it was harder to crush the religious opposition, which could express itself symbolically in mosques, processions, and religious circles held in homes. The well-organized ulama network and organizations for charitable and other purposes created a basis of political organization shared by no other group in the 1970s; and the ulama were far closer to the masses of the population than were the secularists. Also, many secularists held government jobs or had ties to the government, and for this they might be regarded with suspicion.

Increasingly the West and its ways were associated with imperialism and support for the shah, as well as with the corrupt upper classes and royal family. Until about 1960 most implicitly critical or antiregime writings were secularist, but then began a change, sometimes in the very people who had followed a secularist or even communist position. The best-known author embodying this change was Jalal Al-e Ahmad (d. 1969), a well-known author and essayist. A molla's son early attracted by communism and then by progressive secularism, Al-e Ahmad wrote a famous essay, *Gharbzadegi* (Westoxication), a word he borrowed and made famous. He criticized the blind, superficial imitation of Western consumerism and other Western ways, implicitly (because of censorship) criticizing the regime's Westernist and pro-American policy—for which reason his book was banned. The book is not religious, but in the last years of his life Al-e Ahmad expressed a desire to return to Islam, and made a pilgrimage to Mecca. What he wrote about this experience, criticizing Westoxicated and venal religious figures, leaves some doubt whether his return to Islam was wholly successful, but he seems to have believed that there was a true, progressive Islam, as expressed by the young Islamic reformer Ali Shariati, whom he admired. His evolution from communism to secular progressivism to reform religion—retaining his opposition to the regime and to the venal ulama in all stages—was echoed by many students and young intellectuals in the 1970s.

The more influential lay religious ideologist Ali Shariati (1933–77) seems to have borrowed some ideas from Al-e Ahmad, including the basic idea of an official, stagnant, "Safavid [read Pahlavi] Shi'ism," which supported blind imitation and not progress, in opposition to the true Shi'ism of Ali, which called for individual judgment and activity for social progress. Son of a progressive, nationalist preacher, he became a Paris-trained intellectual fond of citing Western thinkers in his definitions of Islam. Shariati was a charismatic speaker, most of whose works are transcribed talks that do not always come across clearly in their written form (on Shariati see Akhavi). He filled a position appropriate to the late 1960s and the 1970s, when secular oppositional leadership could not speak out. Young people, largely from traditional backgrounds but receiving Westernized educations, sought an ideology both progressive and indigenous that did not simply follow either the Western reformism or pre-Islamic Iranian nationalism largely co-opted by the shah, or the conservative, self-serving interpretation of Islam of many of the ulama, whom Shariati attacked. Shariati had and still has tremendous influence over students and intellectuals who wish to find progressive roots in Iran and Islam, and he appealed to bazaaris who might read little else. With the revolution his works were widely printed and sold, and it became a highly political issue whether, if he were still alive, he would approve of the regime. Certainly his criticism of the ulama both for their behavior and their interpretations of Islam, and the criticism by many leading ulama of him as a distorter of Shi'ism with little formal religious education, suggest that he represented a different stream of thought from that of most ulama. Before the victory of the revolution, when many political currents cooperated, Shariati's portrait was often carried beside that of Khomeini, but evidence is that Khomeini had had little use for him. Among Shariati's strongest admirers were and are the leftist Muslim guerrilla group, the *Mojahedin-e Khalq,* who enjoyed a brief period of legality and growth after the revolution's February 1979 victory, which they helped bring about. It is hard to imagine Shariati as anything but an opponent of the post-1979 superliteralist interpretations of Islamic law and punishment, the outlawing of leftist and democratic groups, direct and total rule by the ulama, and the ousting in June 1981 of President Bani Sadr, whose ideas are not too different from Shariati's.

The Mojahedin-e Khalq, partly influenced by Shariati, and characterized by the shah as "Islamic Marxists" and by the present regime as
"Marxists" or "Hypocrites," have had a more radical, activist, and
directly political position than Shariati's. A secret guerrilla organization
in the years before the revolution, they helped win the revolution,
especially by armed struggle at the end, together with the Marxist
Fedayan-e Khalq. Composed mainly of young people, they have no single
ideologist or head, although Massoud Rajavi, who tried to run in the first
presidential elections, and hid Bani Sadr and escaped with him to France
in July 1981, is their most prominent leader. Their positions may be
gleaned from their books and pamphlets. They often try to reconcile
Islam with socialism, and use some Marxist phraseology and concepts.
For a short time in 1975 a purely Marxist wing took over, but they were
ousted and formed a separate Maoist group (*Paikar*). The current Mojahedin, which has a sizable youthful following in several cities and especially
in the more leftist north, continues its Islamic socialist propaganda and
organization, and strongly opposes the Islamic Republican Party government, in alliance with Bani Sadr, the Kurdistan Democratic Party, and
others. For a time the Fedayan-e Khalq took a similar position, but it split
in 1980, with the majority emulating the Tudeh (communists) in an
essentially pro-Islamic Republican Party and pro-Khomeini position. In
1982, Iran was thus in the ironical position of having the two main secular
leftist groups supporting the "Islamic" government of the mollas, while
the main "Islamic" leftist group (along with some smaller secular leftist
ones) opposes that government. Mass government executions of Mojahedin preceded the fatal June 1981 bombing of Islamic Republican Party
headquarters, which killed seventy-four IRP leaders. Executions became
far more widespread and indiscriminate thereafter, although no responsibility for the bombing was proven, and the Mojahedin undertook a
countercampaign of killings. The Iran-Iraq war and reports of United
States aid to exile groups make attacks on the government seem foreign-
inspired to many Iranians.

Another important non-ulama religious leader, who like Al-e Ahmad
and Shariati had a clerical father, is Abol Hasan Bani Sadr. Although
neither his economic nor his political thought is above criticism (see
Katouzian), he was for a time important as a bridge between Khomeini
and the secularists and as a man who expressed mass desires for democracy and anti-imperialism. His fifteen-year absence from Iran in Paris, his
semianarchist disdain for political organization, and his understandable
unwillingness to let the Islamic Republican Party use their 1980 parliamentary electoral victory to strip him of all power, rapidly left him in a
very weak position, despite the 75 percent popular vote he received as
president. In the last months before his ouster as president and his July

1981 escape from Iran, he tried to put together a heterogeneous coalition of most of those who opposed the regime—military men, liberals, and leftists, including the Mojahedin-e Khalq, to whom he drew close in 1981. But, for all the personal popularity of lay Muslims like Shariati and, for a time, Bani Sadr, it is the Khomeinist wing of the ulama, who have had the organizational network and public standing that enabled them to emerge as the single party ruling all branches of government. By 1982, however, not only had most of the Great Ayatollahs made criticisms of Khomeini or his allies, but there were bitter splits in the IRP over such issues as land reform, which Khomeini and others wanted but most did not; over succession to Khomeini; and over cultural, legal, and foreign-policy questions.

The key figure in this development is Ayatollah Khomeini, who began to attack the Pahlavis in a 1944 work, and emerged as a public leader in 1963–64, attacking the government over votes for women, capitulations to the United States and Israel, and illegitimate autocracy. Exiled to Turkey in 1964, he went to Iraq in 1965. His lectures published in 1971 as *Islamic Government* are the first clear Twelver Shi'i statement that monarchy is illegitimate. He also wrote that all legislative power lies with God, so that assemblies can only pass rules to apply divine law. From Iraq other tracts and tapes from Khomeini attacked the reformist Family Protection Law of 1967 and continued to attack the monarchy and its ties to the United States and Israel (see Rose).

From the 1950s on, other mujtahids were taking a more moderate oppositional position, with many calling for a real return to the constitution of 1906–07, which would greatly limit the powers of the shah and give veto power over legislation to a committee of mujtahids. Among the ulama taking this position was the relatively progressive Mahmud Taleqani (1910–79), of whom it is said that his long years as a political prisoner, which brought him into contact with Mojahedin and other progressive thinkers, opened his mind to their views. In 1955 he republished, with an introduction by himself, a long forgotten proconstitutional tract written during the constitutional revolution by Ayatollah Na'ini, which gave an Islamic basis for supporting a largely secular and Western-style constitution. Later he participated in a congress after the 1961 death of the conservative single marja'-e taqlid, Ayatollah Borujerdi—a congress that tried to reform Shi'i institutions to be more in accord with contemporary needs. He was one of the authors of the book emanating from this congress in which writers suggested a council to lead Shi'ism. Along with the lay Muslim Mehdi Bazargan, he was active in the Freedom Movement, which was a bridge between religious and secular liberals. A man of tremendous popularity and charisma, he criticized some acts by the Khomeini regime in the first months of 1979, but after his own children were abducted, apparently with official sanction, in the spring of 1979 he, for some reason, silenced his criticisms. As leader of the huge Friday prayers on the Tehran University campus in Ramazan, 1979, he echoed the regime's attacks on the Kurds, for whose autonomy he had earlier evinced sympathy, and on the left. The day before he died of a heart attack in September 1979, he mildly criticized himself and the regime for attacking the Kurds. His lifetime record, however, is as perhaps the most socially conscious of the major ulama.

A prominent ayatollah who differed even more from Khomeini, although not in a left direction, is Kazem Shariatmadari, often considered the most learned of the ulama. Shariatmadari supported a return to the 1906–07 constitution, and was evidently willing to go along with Shahpour Bakhtiar, named prime minister by the shah in January 1979, in his plan for a constitutional monarchy, in which the king would be only a ceremonial ruler. Once this proved impossible, Shariatmadari felt it would be better to keep the old constitution minus the monarchy than rush into a new one, which was bound, given Khomeini's views, to increase the direct political power of the clericals, which Shariatmadari did not support. He criticized or boycotted various election and referendum plans, and also criticized the warfare against the Kurds that began in 1979. He refused, however, those who asked him to lead or openly support any opposition movement or party, and, after autonomist movements in his native Azerbaijan in late 1979, he has been muzzled and kept under a kind of house arrest in Qom. Shariatmadari, unlike many of the men discussed above, is no radical; in many ways he may be considered a "traditionalist," upholding an old clerical idea that the ulama should advise rulers, that on certain key points the rulers should have to take their advice, but that the ulama should not rule directly. On questions like the status and abilities of women and family law he is quite traditional. While he is very popular in Azerbaijan and Khorasan, some Iranians consider him to be a socially conservative representative of wealthy bazaar and other elements, however politically liberal he may seem. At one time American media gave the impression that he was virtually an Azerbaijani separatist, but this is untrue, and he refused support for the main postrevolutionary movement that put forth autonomist demands for Azerbaijan. He wants to reduce greatly the role of clerics in politics and supports constitutional government; hence he appealed to many liberal and leftist secularists in 1982. His potential appeal, especially if Khomeini were to depart from the scene, may have caused accusations against him as failing to report antigovernment plots in the spring of 1982.

Several elderly and learned clerics who, like Shariatmadari, are considered Great Ayatollahs, rarely speak out directly, but most are said increasingly to oppose Khomeini and the Islamic Republican Party regime on various grounds. Wholesale executions on vague charges without proper trials are against Islamic legal tradition, and these and other violations of legality, along with the increasingly despotic and arbitrary nature of the regime, are among the causes of opposition by the Great Ayatollahs, most of whom are rather conservative and traditionalist.

More noted in the foreign press are younger and less learned ulama who have less religious respect but much political power. These include men like the late Ayatollah Beheshti (d. 1981), an able and clever politician, and Ayatollah Montazeri, Khomeini's possible successor as *faqih,* although 1982 events suggested succession by a council is a likely alternative. This group included many students or disciples of Khomeini and largely shared his approach. Those who have escaped assassination organized into dominant factions or groups, which half tolerate in practice, if not theory, the support of secular leftists (the Tudeh and the Fedayan Majority), while trying to keep them without influence, and try to suppress both liberal and leftist oppositionists. For a time Khomeini tried to maintain a balance between the clericals and his lay religious supporters—chiefly Bani Sadr, and earlier Mehdi Bazargan, Ibrahim Yazdi, and Sadeq Qotbzadeh—but the American-embassy hostage crisis removed all but Bani Sadr from power, and by June 1981 Khomeini ratified the majles's removal of Bani Sadr as president. Both the lay and clerical groups of early Khomeini backers had, in 1978, a populist appeal as anti-American, anti-Zionist, antimonarchical, and apparently egalitarian leaders. Partly because of the effective preexisting ulama network and hierarchy, and the respect the ulama had among the masses, who know little of the lay exiles, only the Khomeinist ulama were able to construct an effective political organization, supported by the powerful revolutionary guards (*pasdaran*). Bani Sadr, in part because of his semianarchist beliefs, did not even try to construct an organization before 1981, when he joined a coalition with Rajavi, Kurdish leaders, and others. Until mid-1981 the lay leaders also feuded and jockeyed for power with each other more than the clericals did; rivalries within the Islamic Republican Party were kept more behind the scenes.

Those with some kind of religious posts and training in Iran are said to number about 180,000, and, though the figure seems inflated, many of them form an effective cadre to promote ulama rule. The very rapid time period of less than fifty years in which the Pahlavis had reduced ulama power meant there were many alive who could still remember the former situation and how it worked. Both from conviction and self-interest there was a postrevolution rush to reestablish ulama prerogatives; the Family Protection Law was ended and Islamic law and judges reestablished; there was a campaign to Islamicize education, including a stress on Arabic and the Qur'an and then a closing of the universities until they could be Islamicized; all this meant new jobs and respect for formerly low-status ulama. The provision of food and other necessities to the poor and unemployed was organized largely under ulama auspices on what was considered to be an Islamic basis. In addition to gaining back their old positions, many ulama occupied new official positions of a type they had never had before, so in a sense they had more than recouped their pre-Reza Shah position. This is one of the extreme swings discussed at the beginning of this introduction, yet it seems doubtful that a clerical class, innocent of economics and arousing much opposition at home and abroad, can stabilize their rule unless, perchance, they attract allies with Westernized training and either moderate their program or become strong enough to crush opposition. Many observers expect a conservative "Thermidorian Reaction," and though this seems probable it is unclear what form it will take.

The popular classes for whom Persian is a first language (a slight minority in Iran) still seem partly, if often passively, to support the government, despite grumbling, as there is little change in their poverty (and much of that can be blamed on the Iran-Iraq War) while their cultural sensibilities, religious feelings, and hostility to Western incursions have been assuaged. Also, war against Iraqi invaders identifies the government with self-defense. There are, however, many oppositional groups. Many in the Westernized middle and upper classes have suffered losses, and many have fled abroad. Among religious minorities Jews, and especially Baha'is, whose leaders were executed in large numbers from the spring of 1981, are apprehensive and many of them have also fled. The large border ethnic minorities that are either partly or wholly Sunni and have related groups across the border—the Arabs (mostly Shi'i), the Baluchis, the Turkomans, and especially the Kurds—have been rebellious and autonomist in varying degrees for varying mixtures of ethnic and religious reasons. Even Shi'i linguistic minorities, whether large and settled like the Azerbaijanis or small and largely nomadic, like the Qashqa'i and some other tribes, have some autonomist aims. The Kurdish autonomy struggle has been the longest, most sustained, and best politically organized, and large parts of Kurdistan, as of some other minority regions, have de facto autonomy in 1982, as the government cannot control or conquer them. Some Iranians fear Kurdish separation and association with Iraq.

Special is the position of Iranian women. As Tabari's paper notes, the proposal to grant votes to women in 1962 was a key point in arousing the open opposition to the government of Khomeini and other ulama leaders. Later, Khomeini wrote severely against the Family Protection Law of 1967, saying that those divorced under it were not really divorced and, if they remarried, their children were illegitimate. Even Ali Shariati put forth the fashionable argument that in the West women were sex objects, an argument that ignores women's role as sex object in the Muslim world—an exclusive sex object in an arranged marriage for her husband,

who himself is sexually quite free. Before the revolution, as more oppositionists joined the religious opposition many women donned the *chador*
and conformed to traditional forms of sexual seclusion in order not to
offend the truly traditional, and as a sign of their opposition to the
Westernism and Western ties of the shah's regime. It is doubtful that
many oppositionists realized how seriously Khomeini and the ulama
around him took traditions regarding women and the family. Many
women expected to take off the chador and return to their former ways
once the revolution waś won, especially as Khomeini made general
statements about women's equality. While it is true that Khomeini
changed his earlier position against women's voting, on other matters he
remained obstinate; the Family Protection Law was ended, as were
coeducation, mixed bathing, and many other forms of mixing the sexes.
Khomeini's first attempt to enforce *hijab* (covering all but the face and
hands) at work was withdrawn after protest, but later it was reinstated.
With all this it should be realized that many women, especially from the
popular classes, gained new self-respect by taking independent public
action for the first time during the revolution, and to a degree this has
continued. Also, many of these women already wore the chador, observed sexual segregation rules, and often did not benefit from the Family
Protection Law. Official pressures, however, have reduced the profes-
sions and ways in which women can work, and the proportion of working
women. Unquestionably, the direction of women's rights has changed,
and even if prerevolutionary legislation only significantly helped a minority, the movement was in the direction of greater legal equality, and
liberals and leftists hoped to extend this, not restrict it as is still happening
in segregation, education, work, and legal and family rights.

The chapters herein shed new light on how Iran's unique religious
evolution and revolution occurred, and how Iranian aspirations for
greater independence and a better life became channeled toward religious
leaders better qualified to lead and orchestrate the toppling of an unpopu-
lar regime than to set up a new regime that might bring equitable
development, political participation, and cultural satisfactions to the great
majority of Iranians.

THE HISTORY OF SHI'ISM
AND POLITICS

CHAPTER TWO

The Significance of the Early Stages of Imami Shi'ism

W. MONTGOMERY WATT

A system of religious doctrines may serve different purposes in the life of a society. More or less the same system may in one case be the opiate of the masses and in another case the focus of emergent social forces, such as those campaigning for justice or organizing a revolution. Those who believe in the system are not necessarily fully conscious of the social ends it is achieving, though sometimes they may be. These considerations are particularly relevant to the study of the early development of Imami Shi'ism.

Students of the early stages of Shi'ism have a particular difficulty to face in that later Shi'i apologists made assertions about early events which critical history cannot accept as true, though it is of course an important historical fact that such assertions were made and widely believed. In what follows I accept the general standpoint of critical history and discuss particular issues where that is relevant.[1]

In a sense the fixed point from which the investigations begin is the fact that it was only between 874 and about 920 that Imami Shi'ism took definite shape. It stands to reason that there could not be an Imami or "Twelver" form of Shi'ism before the death of the Eleventh Imam and the disappearance of the Twelfth. To understand, however, what happened at this time—the period of the Lesser Occultation—it is necessary to look at the earlier stages of the development. These will here be brought under two headings: Proto-Shi'ism under the Umayyads; and Proto-Shi'ism under the Abbasids. Meanwhile, attention may be called to certain of the dominant ideas in Shi'i thought. First there is the idea of charisma, either

---

1. Since this study is a piece of interpretation rather than of primary research, detailed footnotes are out of place. For the period up to about 925 full references to the sources will be found in my book *The Formative Period of Islamic Thought* (Edinburgh: Edinburgh University Press, 1973).

personal or familial or divinely bestowed, attaching to particular leaders. The most distinctive characteristic of Shi'ism in general is indeed the cult of the charismatic leader. Second, there is the idea of the Mahdi. It is to be noted that this differs from Judaeo-Christian conceptions of the Messiah or Sunni conceptions of the Mahdi, in that no one knows the identity of the Messiah or Mahdi until he actually makes the claim. For the Imami Shi'is, on the other hand, the identity of the Mahdi is known but he is in concealment or occultation (*ghaibah*), and it is the time of his reappearance which is not known. Third, there is the idea of the transmission of authority by designation, an idea which appears to be closely associated with the belief that the ideal form of rule is autocratic.

Proto-Shi'ism under the Umayyads[2]

Apart from the loyalty evoked in individuals by the personal qualities of Ali, the chief early manifestations of Shi'i ideas were various revolts under charismatic leaders or under men who claimed to act on behalf of members of "the family" or to represent their interests. The best known of these instances of activism was Husain's abortive bid for the caliphate in 680, which ended at Karbala. The most successful was that of al-Mukhtar at Kufa in 685, allegedly in the interests of Muhammad ibn al-Hanafiyya. In the half-century after the failure and death of al-Mukhtar in 687 there were no revolts that were in any sense Shi'i; but the last dozen years or so of the Umayyad dynasty saw some potential and actual revolts of Shi'i inspiration, including that which brought the Abbasid dynasty to the caliphal throne in 750. For the first few decades of the Abbasids there were also revolts against them which owed something to Shi'i ideas.

The details of these revolts and the associated sectarian movements do not concern us here, but it is important to try to appreciate the underlying ideas and attitudes. The phenomena are brought together under the heading of Proto-Shi'i because they do not conform exactly to later Zaidism, Imamism, or Isma'ilism; but they have in common some feeling for the presence in certain members of "the family" (of Muhammad) of special qualities of political leadership or spiritual guidance, in short, of charisma. This charisma differed, however, from that later ascribed by the Imamis to their imams. For one thing it was not restricted to these imams, but might be found in almost any member of Muhammad's clan of Hashim. In the years round 750 it was claimed for Ali's brother Ja'far and Muhammad's uncle al-Abbas. The Umayyads even seem to have tried to include themselves in "the family" by extending it to the descendants of Hashim's father, Abd Manaf; but this was not generally accepted. Even those who took a more restricted view of the occurrence of charisma had

2. *Formative Period*, chap. 2, pp. 38–59.

sometimes a different account of the succession of imams and made Muhammad ibn al-Hanafiyya follow Husain and be succeeded by his own son Abu Hashim. The original Abbasid claim to legitimacy was that Abu Hashim had transferred the imamate to the grandfather of the first two Abbasid caliphs and that he had been succeeded by his descendants. All these facts show that up to 750 the Proto-Shi'i idea of charisma was in an extremely fluid state.

The first persons to be attracted to this idea were mainly Arabs from nomadic tribes. A relatively large proportion of these came from South Arabian tribes, and this might conceivably be linked with the long tradition of kingship in South Arabia. These men were probably attracted to Proto-Shi'ism because they felt insecure as a result of the rapid transition from nomadic desert life to that of camp-cities and raiding expeditions. One of the common human reactions to insecurity is to look for a man with charisma who can lead his people to a better state of things. Since Arabs believed that the potential for noble deeds and wise counsel was transmitted through the tribal stock, it would be natural to look to some member of the clan of Hashim for deliverance from insecurity.

Besides these activists among the Proto-Shi'is there were also quietists, who did not contemplate revolt but consoled themselves with messianic ideas. The first man to whom such ideas were attached seems to have been Muhammad ibn al-Hanafiyya (d. 700). He is mentioned by the poet Kuthayyir as being not dead but in concealment, and it is confidently expected that he will return as the Mahdi to set right all wrongs and establish justice on the earth. About the same time (early eighth century) other men held that Ali was not dead but would return as the Mahdi. The attraction of this conception of the Mahdi is that it gives a measure of hope to men in circumstances which they feel to be almost intolerable, and yet does not require them to take the risks involved in trying to remedy particular abuses. Some believers in a concealed imam seem to have held that in his absence it was wrong to use force to promote justice, but that, when he appeared, it became a duty to take up the sword. This seems to indicate a strong link between belief in the Mahdi and political quietism.

Proto-Shi'ism under the early Abbasids[3]

Some, perhaps much, of the support by means of which the Abbasids were able to replace the Umayyads came from men who were Proto-Shi'i in outlook. There had been an element of deception, however, in the

3. Ibid., pp. 157–62; also pp. 162–66 (Zaidis); pp. 186–89 (Hisham ibn-al-Hakam).

propaganda of the Abbasids. Their general Abu Muslim had not said he was acting on their behalf but merely that the cause was that of "him of the family of Muhammad who shall be approved." When it transpired that this was to be an Abbasid and not an Alid, many were presumably disappointed, but few were prepared to take to arms in support of any Alid. It is indeed possible that for the better part of a century many who supported the Abbasids did so on Proto-Shi'i grounds. This may explain the change that was made under the caliph al-Mahdi (775–85), whose messianic regnal name is itself not without significance. Abbasid rule was now legitimized on the basis of the assertion that Muhammad had transferred the imamate to his uncle al-Abbas, who had handed it on to his descendants, the Abbasids. Gradually, however, it would seem that men of Proto-Shi'i sympathies came to be more and more exclusively concerned with the descendants of Ali.

To bring this matter into a clearer perspective, let us consider the persons described as Rafidis by Sunni writers on sects and heresies. Rafidis is a nickname, roughly meaning "deserters," and was given to them by Sunnis because they "deserted" Abu Bakr and Umar and regarded Ali as the rightful successor of Muhammad. Because of their attitude to Ali they belong to the Proto-Shi'is. Indeed later Imami writers (after 900) regarded them as Imamis, but it is doubtful if they themselves used the name, though they may have employed the term *Ahl al-Imama,* "people of the imamate," or some similar phrase. One of the best known names among them is that of Hisham ibn al-Hakam (d. about 805). The first to give a theological exposition of the doctrine of the imamate is said to have been Ali ibn Mitham, who lived about the same time.

The fact that such men are claimed as Imamis might suggest that they recognized the series of imams up to their own day, but there are grounds for thinking that this is impossible. Both the men named took part in a symposium on love, imitating that of Plato, held in the salon of Yahya ibn Khalid al-Barmaki; and they can hardly have been friendly with the vizier if they believed that an Alid was the rightful ruler of the empire. The same conclusion follows from the statement that another man defended Imamism against Zaidism in the presence of the caliph al-Ma'mun himself. Ali ibn Mitham is said to have argued that on Muhammad's death Ali was *afdal an-nas,* "the most excellent of men," as well as having been designated by Muhammad, and that those who recognized Abu Bakr and Umar were thus in error (though he did not accuse them of sin). It is to be noted, however, that there is no mention of Ali's designating a successor. We must also take into account the general consideration that if the Abbasids had any suspicion of a plot against themselves, they would quickly have got rid of the rivals; but the most they did in this line was that Harun ar-Rashid imprisoned Imam Musa al-Kazim for a time.

If men like Hisham ibn al-Hakam, then, were not plotting to set up an Alid as caliph, what were their political aims? Their basic principle seems to have been that authority must come from above and can not be conferred by the votes or acclamation of ordinary people. This means that authority can only be conferred by someone who already has authority, and so the method of appointment of an imam must be designation by his predecessor, as Muhammad had designated Ali. This conception was not necessarily restricted to the series of Alid imams, but seems to have been held as a general principle; for example, a friend of Hisham ibn al-Hakam called as-Sakkak wrote a "refutation of those who deny the necessity of the imamate by designation." Thus it would appear that the Rafidis who were friendly with the viziers and caliphs were saying that the actual caliphate should be regarded as having absolute autocratic authority. In particular this would mean that the caliph ought to be a divinely inspired and guided man, capable of speaking the last word on any disputed question of God's law; the last word should not belong to the ulama.

There is admittedly some speculation in this account of the political attitudes of the Rafidis, but there is also much evidence to support it. It has to be seen in the context of the political tensions within the caliphate from about 785 to 850. Within the heartland of the caliphate, even, there were many diverse interest groups, and these appear to have arranged themselves—without any formal organization, of course—in two composite blocs. On the one hand there was the autocratic or absolutist bloc; and in this we find not only Rafidis and perhaps other Proto-Shi'is, but also the "secretaries," who performed the detailed work of administration under the caliph, and many Persians and Yemenite Arabs. On the other hand there was what may be called the constitutionalist bloc, which possibly reflects the tradition, found especially in northern Arab tribes, whereby decisions were taken in an assembly of all the adult male members of a tribe and ancestral practices were generally upheld. Members of northern Arab tribes tended to be found in this bloc, but the most notable group in it was the ulama, who claimed to be, and were to some extent recognized as, the authoritative exponents of the divine law as contained in the Qur'an and the *sunna* or normal practice of the Prophet. One of the practical questions was whether the caliph and his administration could overrule the ulama, or whether, when the ulama were agreed on a point of law, the caliph was bound to accept this.

The caliph al-Ma'mun in particular seems to have been very much aware of the tension between the two blocs, and some of the measures he adopted are apparently aimed at reducing it. His own sympathies may well have been with the absolutists, but he also knew that the ulama had strong support from the ordinary people. One of his measures, taken in 817, was to designate as heir to the caliphate Ali ar-Rida, the Eighth Imam of the series of twelve, though probably not recognized as such by many people at this time. What the outcome of this move might have been we cannot tell, for Ali died in the following year. Another measure was the establishing of the so-called Inquisition (*mihna*), by which important ulama and others were required to profess in public that they believed the Qur'an to be the created, not the uncreated, speech of God. This was not theological hairsplitting, but a political move to weaken the ulama. If the Qur'an is God's uncreated speech, it expresses his character and so cannot be altered; but if it is created, God might have created it otherwise, and so there is not the same objection to its being altered by a divinely inspired imam.

Besides taking these particular measures al-Ma'mun and his advisers held religio-political views designed to reduce tension. These may be described as a form of Zaidism, though they are not identical with the Zaidism of the writers on sects or later Zaidi writers. Al-Ma'mun allowed that Ali was the "most excellent" (*afdal*) of the Muslims after Muhammad, but insisted that he had accepted the rule of Abu Bakr and Umar. This was essentially the Zaidi principle of the "imamate of the inferior" (*al-mafdul*, the one surpassed, *sc.* by others). In designating Ali ar-Rida as his heir, al-Ma'mun had in fact asserted that he was the "most excellent" of the Muslims, and he may have had the idea that in future the caliph should be the "most excellent" among the Alids and Abbasids jointly. He presumably held that he himself was the "most excellent," and he certainly acted as if he had personal authority. He was the first Abbasid to use the term *imam,* and he had, of course, fulfilled the Zaidi requirement of vindicating his claim to the imamate by force of arms.

By the time of the accession of al-Mutawakkil to the caliphate in 847, the failure was clear of the attempt to reduce tension between the two blocs by some form of compromise. Within a year or two measures were taken that effectively made Sunnism the official religion of the caliphate. It was possibly because of this change that Zaidism faded away in Iraq and continued to exist only on the periphery (Dailam and the Yemen). The establishment of Sunnism was doubtless also one of the factors leading to the organization of Imami Shi'ism.

The Significance of the Lesser Occultation[4]

Hasan al-Askari, the Eleventh Imam of the series, died on or about 1 January 874. Either at that time or a year or two afterward his son Muhammad mysteriously disappeared; the date is often given as 878, but the whole matter is very obscure, and even the Imami sources are not unanimous. Up to this time even the pro-Alid wing of the Proto-Shi'i

4. Ibid., pp. 274–78.

movement had contained many different elements. One writer describes fourteen groups with varying attitudes following the death of the Eleventh Imam, and another writer names twenty groups, while the position had been almost as complex throughout the previous century. With such divisions Proto-Shi'ism could have little political influence. It is thus not altogether surprising that during the next half-century a group of skillful politicians put forward a theory—Imamism—which was accepted by most of the pro-Alid Proto-Shi'is.

It is presumably a fact that the Eleventh Imam had a son who disappeared in mysterious circumstances. Imami theory, however, goes beyond the fact to an interpretation of it, namely, that the disappearance was a voluntary going into concealment or occultation, and this had the further implication that in this state the Twelfth Imam was not subject to mortality but would at an appropriate time return as the Mahdi. The idea of a Mahdi, alive but concealed, was, of couse, not new. Apart from the instances under the Umayyads mentioned above, some Proto-Shi'is had applied the conception to the Seventh Imam, Musa al-Kazim, who probably died in 799. To propound such a theory about the Twelfth Imam was clearly a deliberate political act, especially when it was also claimed that he was represented on earth by a *wakil,* "agent," who was presumed to be in contact with the imam (though the evidence for this is not clear). There was in fact a succession of four agents, the last dying in 940, and the time up to that date is known as the period of the Lesser Occultation (*al-ghaibah as-sughra*). After 940, when there is no wakil and no contact with the imam, it is the period of the Greater Occultation (*al-ghaibah al-kubra*), and this still continues.

The intellectual formulation of Imami theory appears to have been chiefly the work of Abu Sahl an-Naubakhti (d. 923), one of a powerful and wealthy family, of whom another member became second wakil. The other wakils seem to have been men of a similar standing. Some of their reasons for adopting and propagating Imamism are fairly clear. It got rid of the endless bickering between rival claimants to the imamate, of whom there had often been several, and offered the possibility of creating a united movement. It transferred the control of this movement from imams, who were politically incompetent, into the hands of a group of men with wide knowledge of affairs and considerable political skills. It virtually freed the movement from all suspicion of plotting against the Abbasid dynasty while enabling it to be slightly critical of Abbasid policies. It may well have followed the men a century earlier who were claimed as Imamis in wanting the office of caliph to be thought of in autocratic or absolutist terms, but clear evidence is lacking. When one further takes into account the fact that the Imamis thought of themselves as "the elite" (*khassa*) and of the Sunnis as "the common people" (*amma*), it seems probable that the Imami sect constituted something like a political party whose purpose was to promote the interests of certain wealthy groups within the community.

The Significance of the Greater Occultation[5]

The death of the fourth wakil in or about 940 marked the passage from the Lesser to the Greater Occultation. Once again, this can hardly have been something which just happened, but was almost certainly a deliberate political act. The problem for the modern scholar is to discover what this change meant in actual political terms. Even if the decisive date is 940, however, it must be presumed that the new form of Imamism was felt by its adherents to be suitable in the situation after 945 when effective rule over the central lands of the caliphate passed into the hands of the Buyid dynasty. Indeed, since there were no political changes affecting Imamism until the time of Shah Isma'il Safavi in the early sixteenth century, those who professed it must have continued to find it satisfactory, at least as a form of religious belief.

The political situation in 940 was very different from that in 874 or 878, when the Twelfth Imam had disappeared. The reign of the caliph al-Mu'tamid from 870 to 892, when control was mostly in the hands of his brother al-Muwaffaq, was a time of stability and good government; and the first sixteen years of the caliphate of al-Muqtadir (908–24) were somewhat similar. Apart from these periods, however, there had been since 862 an almost continuous struggle for power at the center. In particular, the generals in charge of the Turkish guards on whom the caliphs relied had often shown that they had power to make and unmake caliphs. In the course of this turmoil the power and authority of the caliphs began to dwindle. Governors of distant provinces demanded that they should be succeeded by sons or other relatives, and the caliphs were forced to agree to the appointments demanded of them. Finally, in 936 the caliph ar-Radi found no alternative but to nominate the governor of Basra, Ibn-Ra'iq, as "chief emir" (*amir al-umara*) to be in charge of the army, police, and civil administration at the center of the caliphate. As is well known, the Abbasid caliphs continued in office in Baghdad after this until 1258 as titular heads of the caliphate, without political power but with certain ceremonial and spiritual functions, especially in respect of the legal system. Effective power was in the hands of a varying number of military commanders, each of whom was nominally appointed by the caliph as governor of a province or group of provinces.

After 936 the struggle for power continued in Baghdad, though now as a

5. Louis Massignon, *La passion d'al-Hallaj*[2] (Paris: Gallimard, 1975), Vol. 1, pp. 354–68; cf. my *The Majesty That Was Islam* (London: Sidgwick & Jackson, 1974), pp. 212–14.

struggle for the position of chief emir. In 945, however, that position, in fact if not at first in name, passed into the hands of the family or dynasty of the Buyids, already securely established as rulers of western Persia. Though they never held much more than Iraq and western Persia, they had special importance as rulers of Baghdad and the center of the caliphate, and maintained themselves there until 1055. They are often said to have been Imamis, but for reasons to be given presently this can hardly have been the case. They were certainly sympathetic to Shi'ism in a broad sense, however. Mu'izz ad-Daula, the first Buyid ruler in Baghdad, improved the position of the Alids there. Then in 962 he gave orders for the cursing of Mu'awiya, the first Umayyad caliph, who defeated Ali, and those who had oppressed the family of the Prophet, and in the following year encouraged the celebration of the mourning for Husain and the feast of Ghadir Khumm, commemorating Muhammad's designation of Ali, ceremonies which later became distinctive of the Imamis. On the other hand, it has to be noted that about twenty years later the Buyid ruler of the day suppressed these ceremonies because of the rioting occasioned by them between Sunnis and Shi'is.

Despite these marks of sympathy for Shi'ism, a little reflection shows that the Buyids could not have been Imamis in the strict sense. The Imamism of the Lesser Occultation would have been quite impossible for them, since it would have meant acknowledging the superior authority of the wakil of the time. Yet the Imamism of the Greater Occultation was not much better. To profess it would have implied rejecting the nominal authority of the Abbasid caliph. This would have been politically danger-ous, since for many—perhaps the majority—of their subjects the Buyids were legitimized by the fact that they held appointments from the caliph. If they were to depose the Abbasid caliph and set an Alid in his place, they laid themselves open to the danger forseen by one of their advisers, who is alleged to have said, "no one seriously believes in an Abbasid caliph, and no one would object if you ordered his execution; but men would believe that an Alid caliph was divinely inspired, and would obey *him* if he ordered *your* execution." Another danger in such a case was that some rival might set up an Abbasid caliph in his own capital and have the advantage of legitimizing himself in this way. There was always the possibility, too, of the reappearance of the imam in occultation or someone claiming to be the imam; and this again would threaten Buyid power. Thus the Buyids, despite Shi'i sympathies, were not Imamis, and still less Zaidis or Isma'ilis. They made no effort to convert their subjects to Imamism, and do not appear to have used Imami arguments in their propaganda against the Fatimids, the Isma'ili dynasty that established itself in Egypt in 969 and claimed to be rightful rulers of the Islamic world.

In the light of this situation in the middle decades of the tenth century, what can be said about the political aims of those who proclaimed the doctrine of the Greater Occultation? Insofar as it put an end to the office of wakil it may be surmised that this office had proved in practice not to have the advantages originally envisaged. This again could have come about for one of two reasons. On the one hand, it might have been the case that, even in favorable circumstances, the wakil had less influence than had been expected. Moreover, there had at times been rival claimants to the office, so that the movement was no longer united. On the other hand, the office might have been affected by the fact that military commanders had replaced the caliph as effective rulers. A claimant to the office of wakil, who was still alive in 945, is said to have been put in prison by the Buyids. Apart from that, some of the wealthy Imamis were financiers involved in the money affairs of the caliphate; and financial breakdown went along with the decline of caliphal power.

Another point to be considered here is that with the assumption of power by military commanders religious doctrines lost much of their political relevance. The commanders certainly accepted Sunnism, but primarily as a legal system. They presumably did not tolerate interference by ulama in the detailed work of government, and paid little attention to religious doctrine except when the Abbasid caliphate had to be defended against Fatimid propaganda; but this last was more a concern of the Seljuq dynasty, which succeeded the Buyids. If the Imamis gave up trying to influence policy by their doctrines, they would be in much the same position as the Sunnis, especially since during the first third of the tenth century they had begun to work out their own system of law, notably through al-Kulaini (d. 939).

Leaving aside the question of the success or failure of the office of wakil, it is to be noted that there was a quietist strain in Shi'ism which had been manifested during the Umayyad period in the application of messianic ideas to Ali and his descendants. The doctrine of the Greater Occultation may also be regarded as a reassertion of this quietist strain. The Imamis, while they waited for their imam, were prepared to tolerate and partially support whoever might be their ruler, but without any deep involvement in politics. It almost looks as if Imamism had become an apolitical "personal" religion, such as the West has had for the last two or three centuries. Certainly religious beliefs marked off the Imamis from other Muslims as an elite community, and membership of this community was doubtless an important part of their identity.

One result of the proclamation of the Greater Occultation, probably unforeseen, was that leadership among the Imamis passed to their ulama from the group of men from whom had come those who held the office of wakil. Over the following centuries the leaders of whom we hear are scholars like Shaikh Saduq and Shaikh Tusi.

Conclusion

In the period up to the end of the tenth century Imami Shi'ism developed out of the earlier indefinite Proto-Shi'ism. In the course of this development we have traced a number of different stages. In some of these Shi'ism was linked with political activity, in others with an apolitical quietism. In some early activist stages revolts were led by members of "the family" or in their name, but none of these revolts is closely related with Imamism. Under Harun ar-Rashid and al-Ma'mun, however, the forerunners of Imamism were actively advocating a more autocratic conception of the caliphate; but about the year 850 the opponents of this policy—the constitutionalist bloc—were entirely successful and had Sunnism established as the religion of the caliphal empire. It was apparently in response to this establishment of Sunnism that some men who had previously belonged to the autocratic or absolutist bloc proclaimed the doctrine of the Lesser Occultation and so gave definite form to Imamism. The mark of this stage of Imamism was the existence of the office of wakil, and it was presumably hoped that the wakil would be able to influence caliphal policies in favor of the Imamis. These hopes were either never realized or else ceased to be realized after the loss of political power by the Abbasids. In these circumstances some of the leaders proclaimed the Greater Occultation, and in so doing seem to have depoliticized Imamism. This was in a sense a return to the quietism manifested in the messianic Shi'ism of the first Islamic century. From the proclamation of the Greater Occultation until the fifteenth century, Imamism seems to have been a "personal" religion linked with a distinctive legal system.

Since its repoliticizing about the fifteenth century, Imamism has again passed through several stages, and this study of the early period may help in the understanding of these. It suggests the existence of a tension or even a contradiction between the activist and quietist strains in Imamism. How can an apolitical quietist doctrine become the basis of an actual state? To a state, Imamism could certainly contribute a system of law covering most of the matters covered by law in the West: personal status (marriage, inheritance, etc.), criminal acts, commercial transactions. It could also contribute a system of philosophical theology. In these fields, then, the ulama could adequately represent the imam. There is an area, however, where the ulama had no qualifications for giving guidance, namely, the higher reaches of governmental administration. Until very recent times no Imamis have given much thought to this area. What seems to have happened in the past usually and to be happening now is that the Imami tradition of autocratic, absolutist rule has taken over. Indeed, in Iran at the moment one might say that, instead of there being a single wakil, many people have arrogated to themselves some aspect of the office of wakil and are interpreting it in an autocratic fashion. Because of this inherent contradiction (as it would seem), it is difficult to see how Imamism can solve the problems of Iran today except in the unlikely event of a leader's arising with unusual gifts of imagination and insight, a leader who could formulate policies that would be both realistic and in conformity with Islamic ideas.

CHAPTER THREE

Imami Jurisprudence and the Role of the Ulama: Mortaza Ansari on Emulating the Supreme Exemplar

JUAN R. COLE

Recent political developments in Iran have changed the way contemporary scholars view Imami Shi'ism and its religious institutions. In the Pahlavi period, when the influence of the ulama in Iran seemed to be on the wane, few Western scholars devoted much attention to the history of traditional Shi'i scholarship and law in Iran, particularly that of the postclassical period.[1] However, the ascendancy in 1981 of the ulama-dominated Islamic Republican Party, the continuing importance of the constitutionally sanctioned post of the *faqih* (supreme Islamic jurisconsult), and the increasing "Islamization" of various institutions and laws in Iran make it important to understand the history of Imami Shi'i law and religio-legal institutions.

In particular, the victory of the usuli school of jurisprudence in the eighteenth and nineteenth centuries takes on special importance. The usuli school taught that all Shi'is are divided into laymen and experts in religious law. It is the duty of all laymen, this doctrine holds, to emulate an expert, or *mujtahid*. This theory provides an ideology which certainly can be used to support the idea that the ulama should have a leading role in society, though the idea that the ulama should rule would have seemed heretical to most Shi'i mujtahids until very recently. Moreover, in the usuli school a practice grew up in the nineteenth century of recognizing one mujtahid as a supreme source for emulation (*marja'-e taqlid-e motlaq*). While the ulama remained a rather loose and unstructured body

---

1. Major exceptions here have been Nikki R. Keddie, *Religion and Rebellion in Iran: The Tobacco Protest of 1891–92* (London: Frank Cass, 1966); Hamid Algar, *Religion and State in Iran 1785–1906: The Role of the Ulama in the Qajar Period* (Berkeley and Los Angeles: University of California Press, 1969); and the first chapters of Denis M. MacEoin, "From Shaykhism to Babism," Ph.D. diss., Cambridge, 1979.

of experts, the institution of a supreme source for emulation introduced the possibility of a strong, centralized leadership.

Here, I wish to investigate some of the views on jurisprudence of the second scholar to be widely recognized as the supreme source for emulation among Imami Shi'is, Mortaza Ansari (1800–64). However, first it will be useful to review some of the basic developments in Shi'i law and religious institutions prior to this time. While this area has not been much studied, it is possible even now to summarize the main lines of the history of Shi'i jurisprudence, and to make some comments about the evolving role of the Imami ulama.

The early evolution of Imami Shi'i thinking on jurisprudence cannot be seen in isolation from Islamic law and practice as it developed in early Islam as a whole, even among those groups that eventually became the Sunnis. Serious thinking about law and its interpreters probably did not arise until after the passing of the Prophet Muhammad. Of course, the Qur'an was accepted by all as a source of law, but there is very little in the way of law in the sacred scripture of Islam. The next most important source of law to gain wide acceptance among Muslims was *ijma'*, the consensus of the community. This was the living tradition of Muslims who were still close to Muhammad in time.[2]

Also important early on was *qiyas,* or legal analogy. This was almost certainly a technique derived from rabbinical practice. For instance, grape wine was not prohibited in the Qur'an, but jurists outlawed it by analogy to date wine, which was. This practice of analogical reasoning to derive legal judgments not explicitly found in the Qur'an or in the community's collective memory of the Prophet's practice was called *ijtihad,* or individual endeavor. One who practiced ijtihad was a mujtahid.

Finally, some two hundred years after the hijra, oral reports attributed to the Prophet and transmitted by only one or two persons in each generation were put forward as a source of law. These individual reports (*khabar al-ahad*) gradually became more important in the theory of jurisprudence than *ijma'*, or the consensus of the community based on a collective memory of the practice of the Prophet and his primitive community (*khabar al-mutawatir*). Since analogical reasoning (ijtihad or qiyas) had also been important in obtaining this consensus, it too was eclipsed by the new emphasis on individual oral reports from the Prophet.

After ash-Shafi'i (d. A.D. 819), and the finalization of the four great schools of Sunni jurisprudence, two kinds of independent judgment or ijtihad were recognized. One was absolute ijtihad, such as ash-Shafi'i himself practiced, and the other was relative ijtihad. In relative ijtihad, the

2. Fazlur Rahman, *Islam* (Chicago: University of Chicago Press, 1979, rev. ed.), pp. 70ff.

jurisprudent worked within a particular school of law, using individual reasoning only in cases where a judgment had not already been derived. In actual practice, jurists were often not completely tied to the judgments of their schools. Sometimes they preferred judgments from other schools, and some figures, like Ibn Taimiyya, Jalal ad-Din as-Suyuti, and the Mujaddidi Naqshbandis in India like Ahmad Sirhindi and Shah Waliyu'llah argued for a less conservative approach to ijtihad in the postclassical period. The meaning of the word *ijtihad* often changed over time, as well. For many writers, such as al-Ghazali, ijtihad came to mean any effort put forth to arrive at the intent of the Qur'an and Sunna—a usage so general that it avoids the more controversial connotations the word bore in its technical sense.

Debates over ijtihad in Islamic jurisprudence might fruitfully be compared to arguments in the contemporary United States over the virtues of a strict constructionist approach to the Constitution versus an activist court. However, in Islamic law, unlike Anglo-Saxon law, court judgments do not constitute a precedent. The only precedent-setting judgments for Sunnis were those of the founders of the four great schools of jurisprudence in the early centuries of Islam.

Ijtihad, based on legal analogy, developed out of personal opinion (*ra'y*). Since ra'y had no agreed-upon conscious method it was even less likely to result in a consensus than ijtihad based on analogy. In the Sunni schools, analogy replaced personal opinion as a legal method. Some schools added a fifth principle of jurisprudence (the first four being the Qur'an, the Sunna, consensus, and qiyas), which was *istihsan,* or rulings made for the good of the community.

Among the schools of law that rejected personal opinion, ijtihad, and istihsan altogether were the Zahiri school popular in Muslim Spain, and the Imami Shi'i school. The problem of the sources of law was postponed for many Shi'is by the continued existence of charismatic Alid leaders. Only with the death of Ja'far as-Sadiq (A.D. 765) for the Isma'ilis and of Hasan al-Askari (A.D. 873/4) for the Imamis was the need for a routinization of this charismatic authority gradually recognized. It was at this point that collecting oral reports from the Imams and thinking on jurisprudence and dogma began in earnest among Shi'is.

One suspects that is was in imitation of the Sunnis that the Imami Shi'is also developed four sources of law. These are the Qur'an, the Sunna, consensus, and reason (*'aql*).[3] However, for Shi'is consensus was not the living practice of the community based on a collective memory of the

3. See Robert Brunschvig, "Les *Usul al-fiqh* imamites à leur stade ancien (Xe et XIe siècles)," in *Le shi'isme imamite* (Paris: Presses Universitaires de France, 1970), pp. 201–13; and Harald Löschner, *Die dogmatischen Grundlagen des ši'itischen Rechts* (Cologne: Carl Heymanns Verlag KG, 1971), pp. 67–174.

practice of the Prophet and the Imams. It was, rather, a consensus about what these holy figures had said, and its meaning. 'Aql is reason used to arrive at a decisive (qat'i) judgment through syllogism rather than analogy. This was contrasted to ijtihad, which is only the considered opinion (zann) of the jurist. The Shi'i tradition rejects any judgment deriving from mere opinion, no matter how considered. Indeed, Shi'i thinkers from the tenth through the thirteenth centuries rejected ijtihad and knew of no acceptable use for the word. Perhaps the first Shi'i thinker to use the word *ijtihad* in a positive sense to mean the application of individual effort to the derivation of a judgment on the basis of technical expertise was 'Allamah Hasan al-Hilli (d. A.D. 1326).[4]

That Shi'is have used terms like ijma' (consensus) and ijtihad in a radically different sense from the one intended by these words among Sunnis has given rise to much confusion. It is often stated, for instance, that the door of ijtihad was never closed for Shi'is. The closing of the door of ijtihad refers to the belief held by many Sunnis that absolute ijtihad was no longer possible after the death of ash-Shafi'i. But since Shi'is at first rejected personal opinion, ijtihad, and the validity of considered opinion (as opposed to a decisive judgment), their jurisprudents were theoretically far more constricted than those of the Sunnis. The door of ijtihad may not have been closed among the Shi'is, but the "ijtihad" they were allowed to practice was a far more narrow procedure than even the relative ijtihad of the later Sunnis, at least in this early period.

Nevertheless, the Shi'i jurisprudents had a definite role in helping shape ideal law in their specialized spheres of personal status and commercial law. (How much real effect they had on positive law is an open question. Most law is based on evolving custom, and is the result of thousands of individual decisions. Constitutional law and other forms of law from above, including revealed law, often have relatively little effect in the face of custom.)

In the eighth century, Shi'i jurisprudence probably began with arbitration efforts on the part of men close to the imams.[5] As time went on, a body of men grew up that knew the oral traditions of Muhammad and the imams, and was familiar with the legal reasoning employed by Ja'far as-Sadiq and his successors. As Roy Mottahedeh has pointed out, the ulama included professional scholars who taught or gave judgments to those who sought their opinions, as well as part-time scholars and even hob-

4. Mortaza Motahhari, "Ijtihad dar Islam," in S. Mohammad Hosain Tabataba'i, ed., *Bahsi dar bareh-ye marja'iyyat va ruhaniyyat* (Tehran: Intishar, 1341/1962), p. 41.

5. There are two oral reports from Imam Ja'far as-Sadiq in the tenth-century collection of such reports by al-Kulaini that urge Shi'is not to seek legal judgments from the non-Shi'i state, and one of these gives authority to make such judicial rulings to the relaters of the imam's oral reports. See Norman Calder, "Judicial Authority in Imami Shi'i Jurisprudence," *British Society for Middle Eastern Studies Bulletin* 6 (1979): 104–05.

byists.[6] The study of the oral traditions from the Prophet (and, in the case of the Shi'is, of the imams) was a central preoccupation of this group.

During the time of the Lesser Occultation, or soon thereafter, when the Shi'is were led by a series of four agents (*vakils*) of the Twelfth Imam, an oral tradition grew up giving the relaters of oral traditions the status of deputy (*niyabah*) of the imams. This was obviously a claim to leadership put forward by the *muhaddithun,* the experts in the oral traditions of the Prophet and the imams.[7] In later times, the "relaters of oral traditions" mentioned above came to be interpreted as mujtahids. However, the "relaters of oral traditions" orginally comprised a much broader group than simply the jurisprudents.

The collection and study of Imami oral traditions flourished under the Buyids in Baghdad, and that city served as a convergence point for Shi'i scholars from the old centers of Kufa and Qom.[8] However, the mid-eleventh-century victory of the Seljuq Sunnis over the Buyids tended to disperse Shi'i scholars, deny them state patronage, and force them into a low profile or even dissimulation (*taqiyya*). The intellectual efflorescence of the Imamis that had taken place under the Shi'i Buyids declined sharply.

It was not until the Mongol period that Shi'i jurisprudence became a well-developed specialty and major works were composed in this discipline. Earlier scholars tended to focus on studies of oral traditions and of dialectical theology (*kalam*). That jurisprudence developed so late is no doubt partly owing to the fact that the Shi'is were not in power and their law thus functioned in a more informal way for a much longer period of time than was the case with the Sunnis. Also, Shi'i scholarship on law was inhibited first by the presence of the imams (who made it seem unnecessary) and then by their absence. Early Shi'i thinkers after the occultation of the Twelfth Imam felt hobbled in many ways. Many argued that in the absence of an infallible imam, such functions as Friday prayers and the waging of jihad could not be carried out. This view persisted among Imami Shi'is of the akhbari school in India well into the eighteenth century, and may lie behind the lack of mosques and Friday prayers to this day among such heterodox Shi'i groups as the 'Alavis in Syria and Turkey. However, in the central Islamic lands most Shi'i ulama gradually took on Friday prayer functions, though not state-related ones like jihad. These early Imami thinkers would have considered the idea of a Shi'i state ruled by ulama in the absence of the Imam as an unthinkable heresy.

The establishment of the Safavid state in the early sixteenth century in

6. Roy Mottahedeh, *Loyalty and Leadership in an Early Islamic Society* (Princeton: Princeton University Press, 1980), pp. 135–50.

7. Abdulaziz A. Sachedina, *Islamic Messianism: The Idea of the Mahdi in Twelver Islam* (Albany: State University of New York Press, 1981), pp. 100–01, 107–08.

8. Ibid., pp. 32–33.

Iran radically changed the position of the Imami ulama. The Shi'i ulama within Iran suddenly found themselves key allies of the extremist Shi'i Safavids. Moreover, many Shi'i ulama were brought to Iran from Syria, Iraq, and Bahrain. The ulama gradually began to assert themselves, and tensions arose between them and the extremist Shi'i Turkomans, who saw the Safavid kings as manifestations of God or as the promised Mahdi.[9] But while they may have been appalled at the beliefs of the Safavid military, the ulama quickly became part of the state apparatus. They presided over the Islamic-law (*shar'*) courts while state functionaries were appointed to civil customary-law (*'urf*) courts. The ulama were represented at court by the state-appointed Sadr, who in turn appointed the Shaikh-al-Islam, or chief jurisconsult. Some Sadrs gained temporal power, maintaining their own armies.[10]

The power of the Shi'i ulama in Iran grew during the sixteenth century. The eminent Shi'i jurisprudent Ibrahim Qatifi wrote in 944/1537 that ijtihad was not originally permitted in the Imami school and only became permissible because of the exigencies brought about by the occultation of the Imam.[11] He held that one might emulate a mujtahid in a matter on which there is no consensus, as long as he lives. However, Qatifi warned that it is illegitimate to follow a dead mujtahid's rulings in controversial matters, because a new consensus might emerge after his death, or his argument might be found faulty. He was concerned lest the exaltation of the rulings of ijtihad reach a point where the Qur'an and the Sunna ceased being consulted. The results of ijtihad, he pointed out, are liable to error, and there were many who had misgivings about ijtihad itself, so that it varied with the school chosen by the jurisprudent.

A story about Qatifi related by al-Isbahani illustrates the independence of spirit some ulama had during the reign of the Safavid king Tahmasp (1533–76). The renowned jurisprudent is said to have been visiting the Shi'i shrines in Iraq when he met an opponent, Shaikh Ali Karki. At that time, Shah Tahmasp sent a gift to Qatifi in the way of patronage. Qatifi rejected it, proudly replying that he had no need for it. Shaikh Ali rebuked him, saying that what he had done was possibly forbidden in Islamic law, and was at the very least discouraged. He pointed out that the third Iman, al-Hasan, had accepted the patronage of the Umayyad usurper

9. Jean Aubin, "La politique religieuse des Safavides," in *Le shi'isme imamite*, pp. 235–44.

10. Roger M. Savory, "The Principal Offices of the Safawid State during the Reign of Ismai'il I," *Bulletin of the School of Oriental and African Studies* 23 (1960): 91–105; and "The Principal Offices of the Safawid State during the Reign of Tahmasp I," *BSOAS* 24 (1961): 65–85.

11. Mirza Muhammad Baqir al-Khwansari al-Isbahani, *Rawdat al-Jannat* (Tehran: Maktabat-e Isma'ilian, 1390/1970, 8 vols.), 1:25–29.

Mu'awiyah. He taunted Qatifi that he did not have a more exalted station than al-Hasan, and Tahmasp was not as bad as Mu'awiyah.

Perhaps as a reaction to the new-found power of the ulama, a school of jurisprudence grew up in the late sixteenth and early seventeenth centuries that attempted to reassert the primacy of the infallible guidance of the imams over the interpretive role of the later ulama. The akhbari school was founded by Mohammad Amin Astarabadi (d. 1624), and attained its greatest influence in the eighteenth century.[12] The akhbaris rejected consensus and reason as sources of Shi'i law, and accepted only the Qur'an and the oral traditions of the Prophet and the imams. Only the sayings of the imams, they felt, could offer an infallible interpretation of the Qur'an itself. They forbade the emulation (*taqlid*) of anyone not infallible, and maintained that all Shi'is are emulators of the imams. Astarabadi vehemently attacked the mujtahidi school of Shi'i jurisprudence, which allowed some legal reasoning on the basis of technical specialization, and charged that this school was an innovation dating from the time of al-Kulaini (fourth/tenth century). Akhbari ideas were widely approved and influential in the seventeenth century, and with the collapse of the Safavids in 1722 they became the reigning orthodoxy.

The eighteenth century was a particularly dark period for the Imami Shi'i establishment.[13] The Afghan conquest of the Safavids brought ravaging Sunni tribesmen into Iran, and Nader Shah's Sunni-Shi'i ecumenism threatened to transform Shi'ism into little more than a fifth school of Sunni jurisprudence. The new government pursued policies that often stripped control of pious endowments from the Shi'i ulama, leaving them impoverished. In the wake of all this, two challengers to akhbari supremacy grew up in the holy shrine cities of Iraq and spread to Iran. One was the Shaikhi school, which taught that there always existed in the world a perfect Shi'i, whose judgment should be sought on legal matters. The other, a resurgence of the mujtahidi school, was known as the usulis. It saw the collectivity of the mujtahids as sources for emulation in regard to the Shi'i laymen. It is the development of the usuli school that primarily concerns us here.

The major proponent of the usuli school of jurisprudence was Aqa Mohammad Baqer Behbehani (1705–91), who resided at the 'atabat, the Shi'i shrine cities of Iraq.[14] Behbehani and his students succeeded in

12. Ibid., 2:120–39.

13. See Hamid Algar, "Shi'ism and Iran in the Eighteenth Century," in Thomas Naff and Roger Owen, eds., *Studies in Eighteenth Century Islamic History* (Carbondale and Edwardsville, Ill.: Southern Illinois University Press, 1977), pp. 288–302.

14. Al-Isbahani, *Rawdat al-Jannat*, 2:94–98; Mirza Mohammad Tanakaboni, *Qisas al-Ulama'* (Tehran: Ketabforushi-ye 'elmiyyeh-ye Eslamiyyeh, n.d.), pp. 198–204; cf. Algar, *Religion and State in Iran*, pp. 33ff.

convincing a majority of their colleagues, both in Iraq and ultimately in Iran, to forsake the akhbari school for their own. Behbehani accomplished this partly through brilliant argumentation, and partly by setting thugs (*mirghazabs*) on akhbari rivals to beat them up and intimidate them. In his major work, a treatise on ijtihad and the oral traditions of the imams, Behbehani defined with greater clarity the meaning of ijtihad for usulis, and established the role of the mujtahid. He argued that lay Shi'is should emulate the mujtahids, and not only the imams, as in akhbari thought.

Within the ranks of the mujtahids, usuli thinkers had gradually come to believe that one scholar could be considered more knowledgeable than any of the rest, and that his judgments should be deferred to. He was considered the highest source for emulation. The first scholar so recognized was Mohammad Hasan Najafi (c. 1788–1850), author of the work on law entitled *Jawahir al-Kalam* (Jewels of Speech). Mortaza Ansari, who was residing in Iraq when Najafi died, developed this institution further, and it is said that his position as supreme source for emulation was recognized as far afield as Turkey and India.[15] The triumph of the usuli school and the emergence of the institution of the supreme source for emulation are as important in the history of modern Shi'ism as the victory for papal power at Vatican I was for modern Roman Catholicism. Under the Qajar dynasty, the ulama recovered much of the influence they had lost under Nader Shah. While Ansari himself tended to stay out of politics, the ideology and institutions of usuli Shi'ism provided a framework for an activist body of ulama with a clearly defined leadership.

Mortaza Ansari was born in 1214/1800 in Dizful into a family of scholars that had produced several ulama, though none of his eminence. In 1232/1817, at the age of seventeen, he went to the Shi'i shrine city of Karbala, where he studied for four years. When the Ottoman governor of Iraq conquered Karbala, the young Ansari fled with its other Shi'i inhabitants to Kazimain, and then returned home to Dizful. In 1240/1824–25, Ansari decided to set out for Mashhad on a pilgrimage to the tomb of the Eighth Imam, Reza. He also made a point of meeting with eminent scholars along the way. He stayed at Borujerd as the guest of Hujjat al-Islam Asadollah Borujerdi for a month, and then moved on to Isfahan. There, he met with Mohammad Baqer Behbehani's eminent student, Sayyid Mohammad Baqer Rashti, who was the leader of the Isfahani ulama. Ansari's pilgrimage took him through Kashan, and on to Mashhad, where he remained several months. On his return he stopped in Tehran, and took a position in the mosque of the shah's mother. He stayed there

15. Mortaza al-Ansari, *Zendegani va shakhsiyyat-e Shaikh Ansari* (Ahwaz [?]: n.p., 1380/1960–61).

for six years, during what were probably the last years of Fath Ali Shah's reign.

Ansari then returned to Dizful, where he stayed for a couple of years, and became the head of Khuzistan's Shi'i educational establishment. Ansari finally left Dizful when a local official attempted to pressure him into making a legal judgment favorable to a relative. Ansari was from all accounts an upright and cautious man, and he preferred to leave his homeland rather than remain in a position where the representatives of temporal authority could pressure him to compromise his principles.

In 1249/1833–34, Ansari returned to Iraq, where he settled in Najaf, and studied with the head of the Shi'i educational establishment there, Ali Najafi. Shaikh Ali died in 1254/1838, and was succeeded as the chief religious authority in Najaf by his brother, Hasan, and by Shaikh Mohammad Hasan, author of *Jawahir al-Kalam*. Hasan died in 1262/1846, and Shaikh Mohammad Hasan Najafi was recognized, not only as the head of Najaf's Shi'i community, but as the supreme source for emulation among many Shi'is in Iraq and Iran. Four years later, Shaikh Mohammad Hasan convened a gathering of the ulama of first rank in Najaf. At first, Ansari remained absent, but Shaikh Mohammad Hasan insisted that he be brought. He then appointed Ansari to be the source for emulation after him. In that same year, the author of *Jawahir al-Kalam* died, and Ansari became the leader of the Shi'i world. But Ansari first offered the post to Sa'id al-Ulama Mazandarani, then in Karbala, on the grounds that he had been more learned when they were students together. Mazandarani replied that since that time, Ansari had been teaching and researching in Najaf, while he himself had been "involved in the affairs of the people." The requirement that the supreme source for emulation be the "most learned" thus implied that a man who spent his life as a quiet scholar and teacher was more qualified than someone who had been active as legal adviser on commercial and personal status law to merchants and pilgrims.

Ansari's biographer and grand-nephew, for whom he was a namesake, argued that Shaikh Mohammad Hasan's step in appointing Ansari to succeed him was merely to make him better known among the ulama. He pointed out that a new supreme source for emulation need not be appointed by his predecessor.[16] This seems, however, an after-the-fact interpretation. The author of *Jawahir al-Kalam* may well have been attempting to formalize the selection of the new source for emulation, and to make that selection the prerogative of the preceding holder of the post. Shaikh Mohammad Hasan might have had a premonition of his imminent demise, and may have felt it extremely important to have a smooth transition at that time. In 1266/1849–50, Shi'ism was nearly being rent

16. Ibid., p. 74.

asunder by the question of how to react to Babism, a messianic movement begun in 1260/1844, which was claiming tens of thousands of converts. The young, weak Naser ad-Din Shah had just acceded to the Qajar throne, and violence had broken out in Mazandaran between Babis and Shi'is. The cautious and erudite Ansari thus inherited a troubled estate, and he opted for a neutral and quietist approach to heading up the Shi'is until his death in 1281/1864.

Ansari spent most of his fourteen-year term as supreme exemplar for the Shi'i world—teaching, writing, and administering. Although at the helm of a newly created institution that held within itself the potential for a powerful, centralized leadership of the religious institution, Ansari was concerned to develop strong Shi'i institutions at the local level. He encouraged the development of local centers of learning by ordering that the prescribed religious contributions, the *sahm-e Imam* (share of the Imam) be donated to local educational establishments rather than being sent directly to Najaf.

Through his writings and talks, Ansari helped to develop usuli ideology, defining the relationship between laymen and the mujtahids they were to emulate, and between the mujtahids and the supreme source for emulation. At this point it will be useful to analyze Ansari's positions on these issues as presented in a Persian manual on ritual practice that he wrote, entitled *Sirat an-Najat* (The Path of Salvation).[17] This particular exposition has the virtue that it was obviously intended for literate laypersons, and so is not simply a theoretical display for a handful of experts. In this brief survey, it will not be possible to deal in depth with some of the more technical issues Ansari raises here, but an attempt will be made to delineate his views on basic questions. Ansari's chapter on "Emulation" in *Sirat an-Najat* consists of forty-four "issues," which are not arranged in any obvious order, and this analysis will proceed on a grouping of related issues regardless of their original sequence in the text.

Ansari's manual on ritual practice is based on answers to questions asked of him by Mohammad Ali Yazdi. In his introduction to the book, Yazdi refers to Ansari as "the Imam's Chosen One and the Caliph in truth over all men in all judgments concerning what is permitted or forbidden, the Exemplar of both the experts and laymen."[18] While the use of the term "Caliph" *(khalifa)* may simply have been hyperbole on Yazdi's part, it indicates the magnitude of the claims being made for the supreme source for emulation only a few years after this institution became a recognized part of usuli practice. It should also be noted that Yazdi claimed that Ansari was a caliph in legal matters, but did not put forward claims of temporal sovereignty for him.

17. Mortaza Ansari, *Sirat an-Najat* (Iran: Hajj 'Ali Akbar, 1300/1883), pp. 1–5.
18. Ibid., p. 1.

Ansari defines taqlid as an action, but says that it is sufficient to learn the judgment of the mujtahid if one applies it when the need arises. That is, one is technically performing emulation only when engaged in a ritual act, but there is a broader sense in which learning the views of one's mujtahid constitutes emulation. Emulation of a mujtahid is a requirement: only when a layperson performs some ritual act (for instance, prayer) with the proper intention and in accordance with the view of a living mujtahid is the ritual act valid. Otherwise, it is void. Moreover, in matters requiring emulation, it is not sufficient for the layman to take a general judgment from the mujtahid; rather, he must take a detailed judgment (issues 1, 14, 20).

While it is often claimed that Islam has no clergy in the Christian sense of a body of persons specially ordained to perform sacraments, usuli ulama come very close to being clergy. As can be seen in the above points, the emulation of a mujtahid lends ritual validity to the religious practices of the laymen. Ansari goes so far as to urge a Shi'i layman who has no access to a mujtahid to emigrate from the place he is living to someplace where he could consult a living exemplar (issue 41).

Ansari explains that it is impermissible to continue to emulate one's mujtahid once he has died. The layman must emulate the most learned living mujtahid if this is at all possible. If he finds this impossible for some reason, then he may emulate a mujtahid who is not the most learned. The most learned mujtahid is the one who is most erudite in arriving at the proper ruling according to the law of God and in understanding it, through evidence based on Islamic law. In identifying the most learned jurisprudent the layman may depend on the advice of one just man who is himself an expert on the law; or he may, if he so wishes, depend on the advice of a group of experts. However, the layman must seek the advice of at least two just men who are experts should he wish to identify a mujtahid who is not the most learned. As for recognizing a just man, Ansari explains that justice is a quality whose external beauty makes it apparent, and it is required that one attain a considered opinion that the quality of justice inheres in the expert from whom one is seeking advice (issues 2, 3, 4, 39).

Ansari says that whenever a layman has out of necessity emulated a mujtahid who is not the most learned, and the situation changes so that he has access to the rulings of the most learned jurisprudent, then the layman must transfer his loyalty to the latter. However, it is impermissible to change from one living mujtahid to another except on the grounds that the second is more learned. Should two mujtahids be found equal in their knowledge of Islamic law, it is permissible, after a thorough investigation, for the layman to emulate either one. There are some qualities that would decide between two equal mujtahids. For instance, if two jurisprudents are equal in knowledge, the layman should emulate the more pious and cautious of the two, or the more dependable. However, knowledge remains the primary criterion. For example, a more knowledgeable mujtahid takes precedence over a more equitable colleague who is less learned. Should there be no such distinction between two mujtahids, the layman may emulate both. However, should they differ on any issue, and the layman chooses one ruling over another, he must continue to practice according to that ruling and may not change at will to the ruling of the other mujtahid (issues 5, 6, 7, 8, 9, 36).

Ansari categorizes the duty to emulate the most learned jurisprudent as an absolute duty. That is, it remains a duty whether or not the layman can actually gain access to or identify the supreme source for emulation. The layman may not proceed on the judgment of his own reason in subsidiary laws, but must take advice from a mujtahid who knows all the requirements and who is the most learned of all. The quality of being the most learned must be evident in the mujtahid at the time he makes his legal deductions, not simply at the time he actually gives a fatva, or legal ruling (issues 13, 27, 44).

There are, Ansari makes clear, conditions under which a layman may emulate a less learned mujtahid. For instance, if the supreme exemplar prefers not to rule on a given issue, but one of his junior colleagues has given a ruling on it, the layman is obliged to consult the latter. Also, if a layman knows for sure that a jurisprudent agrees with the most knowledgeable mujtahid on a particular question, he may emulate the less learned man. He may even emulate him if he does not know for sure that he is in disagreement with the most learned jurisprudent. However, if the layman has a general knowledge that the junior mujtahid opposes the most knowledgeable jurisprudent on many matters, then he may only emulate the former if he first investigates to make sure that in this instance the two are in agreement. Should the layman subsequently find out that his mujtahid actually disagrees with the most learned jurisprudent, then he must change his allegiance to the latter and the most cautious thing to do would be to repeat the ritual acts he performed wrongly. In essence, then, the layman may emulate a less learned jurisprudent only when, in doing so, he is ultimately emulating the supreme jurisconsult. Should a layman forget the ruling of the most learned mujtahid on an issue, and as an interim measure emulate a less learned expert, if he later finds that the latter is in contradiction to the most learned, the layman must return to emulating the supreme exemplar. However, his ritual acts in the interim are not invalidated. Once a layman has emulated a man he feels to be the most knowledgeable jurisprudent of all, he is not obliged to investigate the claims of others to be mujtahids. He should simply continue to emulate the most learned expert (issues 11, 12, 29, 30, 33, 22).

Ansari states that there are three ways to receive a ruling from a mujtahid. One may hear it directly from him, one may receive it through at least one just man who heard it with his own ears, or one may take it from a book of the mujtahid's rulings (on the condition that it be sound and free from any error—either certainly or according to the strongest possible considered opinion). Should two just persons contradict one another, or contradict a written ruling, as to the judgment of the jurisprudent on a particular issue, the layman should practice caution (ihtiyat) and suspend judgment. To practice caution is to learn the rulings of all the most eminent mujtahids on an issue and to choose the strictest one. Whenever a contradiction occurs between the writings of the mujtahid and what one has heard from him, the oral expression takes precedence. Moreover, a human reporter of what the mujtahid said takes precedence over the book of fatvas. If one hears two contradictory statements from the mujtahid, or finds a contradiction within his writings, the most recent takes precedence. In understanding both the written and the verbal ruling, it is sufficient for the layman to attain a considered opinion as to its meaning (issues 38, 40).

Ansari says that anyone whose old mujtahid has died, and who wants to know whether it is permissible or necessary to continue to follow a certain ruling of his, must consult on this with a living mujtahid who is the most learned of all. Whenever a jurisprudent goes mad, commits a major sin, dies, or changes his mind on an issue, and the layman emulating him does not realize this but continues to perform his ritual practice according to the former ruling, his rituals are valid. However, if this ruling was incorrect, the most cautious thing would be for the layman to repeat the ritual acts, this time in the right way. For the most part, however, whenever a mujtahid changes his view on a question, and the layman understands this, the rituals previously performed by the laymen emulating him according to the old ruling are considered valid. Where an agent of a mujtahid has guardianship over a child or a pious endowment, and so forth, should his mujtahid die, become insane, or commit major sins, the agent is automatically dismissed. A living mujtahid may affirm the ruling of a dead one on a different basis from the original ruling. This does not affect the validity of the layman's emulation, and it is not even incumbent upon the layman to know the meaning of "emulation" for the school of jurisprudence that his own mujtahid follows. However, the layman must assure himself that the school of his mujtahid does require the continuing practice of emulation. Should a layman who can emulate a living mujtahid prefer to continue to emulate a dead one, this will make his ritual acts invalid (issues 10, 23, 26, 31, 32, 28).

Most of the rest of the issues in the chapter have to do with situations under which one's ritual acts are invalid. This brief summary of some of the main points in Ansari's treatment of emulation and the supreme source for emulation reveals some basic elements of usuli ideology. A very strong emphasis is put on the role of the jurisprudents in legitimating

Shi'i worship and ritual. All lay Shi'is must emulate a jurisprudent, and if at all possible they must emulate the single most knowledgeable Shi'i jurisprudent. Without this act of emulation, the religious practice of the laymen is invalid. A very sharp line is thus drawn between the religious experts and the laymen, which was not drawn in akhbari jurisprudence. Even the consensus about which mujtahid is the most learned of all is built by the mujtahids themselves, and they transmit it to the laymen, at least according to this ideal schema.

The rigid requirements here laid down are remarkable in that they clearly provide for a very loosely structured organization. A layman could change from one mujtahid to another simply by claiming that his new choice was more knowledgeable, rather as if Roman Catholics could choose to be considered part of whatever diocese they wished, and under the authority of whatever bishop they felt was most qualified. A lesser mujtahid could perhaps increase the number of his emulators by claiming that his rulings accorded with those of the supreme exemplar. When there was a widespread consensus in favor of a very popular supreme source for emulation, a local mujtahid might jeopardize his own following by opposing him. On the other hand, when no consensus could be reached, the system would accommodate several top mujtahids all claiming to be equally learned. The keynotes here are charisma rather than formally derived power, compromise and negotiation rather than strict hierarchy. The Shi'i religious institution thus attained an ability to alternate between a Roman Catholic–type model wherein there was one supreme, recognized authority, and a more Eastern Orthodox model, wherein there were several almost coequal regional leaders.

Mortaza Ansari was responsible for much of the institutional and ideological elaboration of the role of the supreme exemplar (*marja'-e taqlid-e a'la*) in the mid-nineteenth century. He himself did not put that position to a political use, even though some of his followers were already beginning to refer to him as a caliph. However, the structure he helped erect had great potentialities for marshaling the Shi'i ulama and masses to support for a political cause. This was demonstrated very effectively by Hasan Shirazi, the supreme source for emulation who defied Naser ad-Din Shah and issued a ruling that the smoking of tobacco was forbidden after the shah had granted a Western tobacco concession. The idea that all Shi'i laymen owed allegiance to one Shi'i jurisprudent, and that the local ulama were to be judged on how faithful they were to the rulings of this supreme exemplar, provided an ideological underpinning for the social and political power of the ulama. When social and economic conditions allowed the ulama to assert that power, as in the Tobacco Revolt of 1891–92, or the Iranian Revolution of 1978–79, this ideology permitted them to present a united, powerful front.

CHAPTER FOUR

The Role of the Clergy in Modern Iranian Politics

AZAR TABARI

What have been the motivation and goals of the Iranian clergy, as a distinct social grouping, throughout their prolonged involvement in contemporary Iranian politics? The history of this involvement can be marked off by the prominent role the clergy played in nineteenth-century protests against economic and political concessions made to non-Iranian nationals, particularly their leading role in the Tobacco Protest of 1891–92. But already with the constitutional movement (1906–11), they seemed overtaken as leaders of national politics by modern parliamentary nationalists. Later, in Reza Shah's period (1925–41), the drive toward consolidation of a modern bourgeois centralized state greatly reduced their social significance and political weight. In the turbulent years of 1941–53, most of the clergy were overshadowed by Mosaddeq's National Front. It was only after the 1953 defeat and the eclipse of the National Front that new life surfaced in theological circles in Tehran and Qom. Starting in the early 1960s, new discussions, a reorganization, and a more intertwined hierarchy of the clergy began to take shape. Later the emergence of nonclerical Islamic thinkers, particularly Ali Shariati, and the increasing prominence of Khomeini and his clerical supporters indicated a revival of the clergy's independent role in oppositional politics, leading to their seizure of power in February 1979.

How can we understand this sustained political involvement of the clergy over the past century: its initial prominence, its subsequent ebb and marginalization, and its modern militant revival?

Shi'ism in Iran

Contrary to nationalist and anti-Arab mythologies, Iran has not been a Shi'i society ever since the rise of Islam. Prior to the Safavids in the sixteenth century, religious power in Iran was divided among several Islamic currents. Although Shi'is had scattered citadels of control (espe-

cially Qom) as well as congregations in most cities, the four Sunni schools
were more prevalent and most of the famous Iranian theologians, including Ghazali, were Sunnis.[1] It was only with the consolidation of Safavid
hegemony in the sixteenth century that Shi'ism was forcibly imposed as a
national religion. The creation of an elaborate Shi'i clerical apparatus with
a differentiated hierarchy and specific judicial and administrative strata
was an integral part of the construction of a centralized Safavid state.
Moreover, the preeminent role of the Shi'i clergy gave the Safavid polity
an ideological profile distinct from its Ottoman rival.[2] According to
contemporary sources, clerical and state power had become so intertwined that it was customary for Safavid shahs to marry the daughters of
the supreme Shi'i clergy.[3]

    In the first half of the eighteenth century, under the Sunni Afghans and
then Nader Shah (1736–47), the Shi'i clergy lost its position of power
within the state. Under Nader Shah, Shi'ism was demoted to the status of
a fifth orthodox school alongside the four Sunni schools. Prominent Shi'is
were persecuted and many of the clergy, under both the Afghans and
Nader Shah, fled to Najaf and other sanctuaries in Iraq. Yet, at the same
time, the weakening of centralized state authority throughout the eighteenth century allowed the local clergy "to assume the role of local
governors, arbitrators of disputes, executors at law, and so forth."[4]
Meanwhile, the settlement of a divisive theoretical dispute within Shi'ism
prepared the way for the clergy's resurgence in the nineteenth century.
The akhbaris, who contested the clerical prerogative of *ijtihad,* were
definitively defeated by the usulis, who supported clerical ijtihad. The
usuli victory had important political consequences. During the decades of
persecution the akhbaris gained a following based on the fear of clerical
social and political involvement that the power of ijtihad implied. Had
they continued to be the dominant current within Shi'ism, the legitimacy
of the clergy's political role would have been drastically reduced. Their
defeat, on the other hand, encouraged a revival of clerical social and
political leadership.[5]

    The return of relative political stability under the long reign of the

    1. Michael M. J. Fischer, *Iran: From Religious Dispute to Revolution* (Cambridge,
Mass., 1980), p. 28.
    2. For a detailed description of the Safavid state apparatus, see Vladimir Minorsky,
Tadhkirat al-Muluk (London, 1943).
    3. M. Ravandi, *Tarikh-e ijtima'i-e Iran* [A social history of Iran], vol. 3 (Tehran, 1978), p.
481.
    4. Hamid Algar, "Iran and Shi'ism," in Kalim Siddiqui, ed., *The Islamic Revolution in
Iran* (London, 1980), p. 5.
    5. For a fuller discussion of the theoretical issues involved in the dispute between the
usulis and the akhbaris, see Hamid Algar, *Religion and State in Iran, 1785–1906: The Role of
the Ulama in the Qajar Period* (Berkeley, 1969), pp. 33–36.

Qajars (1795 onward) stimulated economic growth and expansion. In particular, the increase in trade with a Europe eager to export manufactures gave an unprecedented impetus to commercial activities and urbanization. Sometimes supported by the Qajar shahs, the revitalized Shi'i clergy greatly extended its spheres of influence and range of administrative power. It reestablished control over the courts, *vaqf* lands, and innumerable other social and political functions. Each *mujtahid* was distinguished by his own retinue of *mollas* and gangs: the former transmitted the mujtahid's influence to the local population, while the latter, representing his executive power, were charged with collection of "religious taxes," *khums* and *zakat,* as well as the administration of religious punishments. Only the death sentence needed ratification by the shah.[6]

There was, however, an important difference between this revival of clerical power under the Qajars and the role of the Shi'i hierarchy in the Safavid state. Although the nineteenth-century clergy enjoyed power and influence derived from their control over many functions that in modern Western societies are under state administration, they were not a *formal* part of the executive as some of them had been under the Safavids. The semiautonomous position of Shi'i administrative and judicial institutions may have been more favorable to the conquest of social hegemony than their official status under the Safavids. For instance, discontented social layers could turn to the Shi'i clergy for assistance, and the clergy could deploy its ability to manage social discontent as a bargaining counter against the court and bureaucracy. Repeatedly in the nineteenth century it mobilized masses to thwart the state's attempts to undermine or restrict its power. After 1850 the areas of conflict between the clergy and state began to widen as the religious hierarchy opposed initiatives to modernize and strengthen the Qajar government. Clerical resistance to reforms in the state apparatus that might threaten their prerogatives was linked to the struggle against economic concessions to foreign non-Muslims. The traditional social imbrication of the clergy and the native merchant community acquired a new sociopolitical expression in the form of a clerically led movement against Western economic and ideological penetration.[7]

The clergy, however, did not enjoy a monopoly of influence over popular unrest. Increasingly they faced a new generation of reformers and modernizers. While sharing most of the clergy's apprehension about the subordination of the Iranian economy to world market forces, and opposing the Qajars' concessions to Europeans, the new Iranian reformers (like

6. For an intricate description of the social and administrative powers of the clergy under the Qajars, see ibid., pp. 11–21, 60–72; also Ravandi, *Tarikh-e ijtima'i-e Iran,* pp. 491–527.

7. Algar, *Religion and State,* pp. 131–36, 169–183, 224.

counterparts elsewhere in Asia) believed that national sovereignty could only be preserved by the adoption of European technology and forms of government.[8] They opposed the old regime from an opposite point of view to the clergy, seeking reforms at all levels to modernize the state structure and establish a constitutional government. After the failure of a series of halfhearted state reforms, this modernist component of the opposition abandoned hope of reforming existing organs of power. Although reformers and clergy were driven into joint opposition to the Qajars, their alliance within the constitutional movement was uneasy. Before examining the respective roles of reformers and clergy in the mass struggles that eventually overthrew the Qajar dynasty, I will survey socioeconomic forces that gave rise to the new political phenomenon of a modernizing reformism in Iran.

The Social and Economic Background to the Constitutional Movement

The accession of the Qajars coincided with a reversal of the epoch of decline and economic stagnation that followed the collapse of the Safavids. Like other Middle Eastern countries, Iran was profoundly affected by the vast expansion of international trade associated with the Industrial Revolution. Yet, the Iranian case differed from most other Middle Eastern countries because its strategic geographical location made it a principal terrain for the collision of British and Russian empire-building. It was never formally colonized by either, and Anglo-Russian rivalry had paradoxical consequences for Iran's development. On the one hand, it was deprived of some of the "positive" effects of colonialism, such as railroads and foreign investment in mines and agriculture. The central government was hindered from seeking relations with capitalist third parties or entrepreneurs by restrictive agreements extorted by Russia and Britain, which gave the two rival imperialisms veto power over Iran's economic relationships. On the other hand, the relative "neglect" of the country by foreign capital allowed native merchants more space for growth than in many parts of the Middle East. This led to the emergence of a considerable layer of wealthy merchants—engaged in wholesale trade and banking—with their own international networks. By the end of the nineteenth century, Iranian commercial colonies existed in Istanbul, Baghdad, Baku, Tiflis, Calcutta, Bombay, Marseilles, London, and Manchester. The dimensions of some of these trading operations can be gauged by the estimated wealth of the Amin az-Zarb family, put at 25

---

8. For a very instructive review of the intellectual changes in this period, see F. Adamiyat, *Andisheh-ye taraqqi va hokumat-e qanun* [The thought of progress and rule of law] (Tehran, 1972), esp. chaps. 1–4.

million tomans (1 toman equaled 10 francs, so this amounted to 250 million francs). This figure should be compared with the total annual government revenue of the same period—about 50 million francs.[9]

This expansion of Iranian commerce persisted even though the cash needs of the central government grew and its real income stagnated or fell. Two wars with tsarist Russia (1813 and 1828) not only cost Iran some of its richest northern provinces and made it yield major economic concessions, but also forced the government to seek foreign equipment and advisers. Moreover, expanded relations with Europe encouraged the later Qajar shahs and their entourages to make repeated visits abroad, which drained the meager treasury of further foreign reserves. The financial crisis of 1866 and the decline of the price of silver relative to gold aggravated the government's desperate situation. The exchange value of the Iranian silver *qeran* fell from 1 franc in 1864 to 0.5 franc by 1900, with corresponding losses for the national economy.

In response the central government tried to avoid financial disaster by a combination of two strategems: (1) the sale of state-owned land and the increase in the price of state offices (local governorships were auctioned to the highest bidder who would, in turn, collect mercilessly from the peasantry);[10] and (2) loans from Russia and Britain procured by major political and economic concessions. These measures hurt Iranian merchants and traders. They had to pay import taxes to exigent Belgian customs officers as well as new road duties to the government. They were also deprived of their function of being the exclusive moneylenders to the central government. The preferred tax status of foreign concessionaires, and the dumping practices supported especially by the Russians, increased the competitive advantages of foreign manufacturers, while attempts at the establishment of local factories by Iranian merchants ended in bankruptcies. As early as 1844 native merchants had formed a league "for the prohibition of European Merchandise," which demanded that the government prohibit such imports "on the ground principally of the ruin Persian manufacturers are reduced to by the constant and immense importation of foreign goods." This petition and other subsequent appeals went unheeded by a regime that had mortgaged national economic

9. See Charles Issawi, ed., *The Economic History of Iran: 1800–1914* (Chicago, 1971), pp. 43–48.

10. Ibid., p. 76. A consequence of these futile attempts to stop foreign competition and stimulate local manufacture was the movement of the accumulated wealth of merchants into land speculation. The government's desire to sell all state land to obtain instant cash found eager buyers, as merchants found it profitable to buy large plots of land to plant in such export crops as rice, cotton, dried fruits, and tobacco. This combination of large landed proprietorship with urban-based commercial interests emerged in this period and remained a prominent feature of agrarian relations in Iran until the land reforms in the early sixties.

autonomy in treaties with Britain and Russia. Thus began the long period of growing tension between the merchant community and the Qajar shahs, whom they blamed for allowing foreign fetters to be placed on the development of Iranian commerce and manufacturing.

Emergence of Political Opposition to the Qajars

Expanded relations with Europe brought more than matches and textiles; they also opened Iran to new ideas. In the nineteenth century, a very few government officials, merchants, and other members of the upper circles of society sent their sons and nephews to Europe to learn more about "civilization and modernization."[11] Naturally, they seized upon those institutions that seemed most connected to European economic superiority: modern systems of scientific education, chambers of commerce, and the like.

The specific world view of these modernizing strata is vividly revealed in an article in *Habl al-Matin* (a Persian paper published in Calcutta in the early twentieth century), addressed to "Honorable Merchants":

Today the world of commerce is linked together like a chain and is like a single factory. . . . If you do not carry on your trade according to contemporary practices and if you continue with the habits and customs of the tent dwellers of a thousand years ago, the supervisor of the trading machine—whose esteemed name is Science—will replace you. . . . Today the world is rotating on the pivot of science. In Europe there are schools for every position, high and low. Let us leave aside commerce—even for coachmen and cart-drivers there are schools. . . . How much more regrettable, then, that you merchants do not yet have a school of commerce! . . . You have not as yet established a chamber of commerce in Tehran and are not aware of its benefits. It is owing to the lack of a chamber of commerce that you are steadily regressing . . . in Tehran, Tabriz, Isfahan, and other cities European businessmen are constantly setting up shops, obtaining concessions, and opening bank branches—and trade is slipping from your hands.

The writer then details a long list of the damages that Iranian merchants suffered as Europeans made increasing inroads, and concludes: "Passengers between England and America during their six-day cruise can talk by wireless to their people whenever they want. Why is it that the honored post office of the eminent government of Iran is still conveyed by asses

11. *Tamaddon* (civilization) and *tajaddod* (renewal) became watchwords symbolizing Europe to the yearning Iranian mind. It became a point of honor to be in favor of tamaddon and tajaddod. Those against them were looked upon as enemies of the nation, of progress, and of development. It is a tragic irony of present-day Iran that these same two words have become derogatory labels hurled at intellectuals and anyone opposing the rule of the clergy. They are equated with unforgiveable adaptation to the West.

and camels as it was centuries ago? Because we lack knowledge and a chamber of commerce."[12]

Other writers placed priority on the reformation of the state bureaucracy. In 1886 an important government functionary and close confidant of Naser ad-Din Shah submitted a secret report warning that if Iran were to preserve its independence, it must emulate the example of Prussia, whose rationalized bureaucratism had elevated it from poverty and crisis to one of the major world powers. The shah was further advised that he should not hesitate to import foreign experts if learned Iranians could not be found.[13] Despite such manifestoes and reform proposals, the Qajars' attempt at internal modernization never got very far. The combination of Iran's semicolonial subservience to Anglo-Russian imperialism and the vehement opposition of the Shi'i clergy to "anti-Islamic" innovations severely constrained reform from the top. Thus, the main intellectual and material impetus for change was shaped outside and in opposition to the government in the merchant colonies of Istanbul and Calcutta, and nourished by Iranian students and intellectuals abroad.

In the period immediately before the constitutional revolution the reformers' strategy was mainly focused around constitutionalism, and a body of literature developed about this "secret" of European civilization. The reformers faced an autocratic government, with no effective way of changing its policies—an arbitrary government whose decisions often seemed to reflect only the whims of the shah. Against this despotic regime, some reformers posed the alternative of a parliamentary government.

The earliest known Iranian account of a European parliamentary system was the detailed account of the British Parliament in the memoirs of Mirza Saleh, who spent four years in England at the end of the Napoleonic Wars studying languages, natural philosophy, and printing.[14] A half-century later, another dignitary, Mostashar ad-Dauleh, on his return from Europe wrote an essay, *One Word* (*Yek Kalemeh*), that encapsulated the vision of subsequent reformers.

During this period [1866–67] I observed that progress in France and England was a hundred times more advanced than in Russia. . . . What could have been the reason behind such an unbelievable achievement . . .? The secret lies in one word [*yek kalemeh*], the *law*. . . . In France and other civilized countries, the citizens debate justice and injustice through their representatives; there will thus be no opposition to the law, because it is they themselves who rule and have made the

12. A fuller version of this article appears in Issawi, *Economic History*, pp. 67–68.
13. Fereidun Adamiyat, *Ideolozhi-ye nehzat-e mashrute-ye Iran* [Ideology of the Iranian constitutional movement] (Tehran, 1976), p. 17.
14. Abdul Hadi Hairi, *Shi'ism and Constitutionalism in Iran* (Leiden, 1977), p. 13.

law. . . . The will of the people and their approval are the basis of all governmental policies; this comprehensive principle is of paramount importance, the truthfulness of which cannot be questioned by any wise man.[15]

In another famous travelogue, an Iranian merchant from Istanbul attempted to summarize the problem of Iran. There are two mottoes, he wrote, for running the country: one, according to the old Iranian proverb, that the kings know the good of the country; another, that the people know the good of the country. If a country is run according to the first motto, there follows the state of affairs as in Maragheh, Isfahan, and Qazvin (different Iranian cities), while the second motto gives the modernity of London, Paris, Washington, and Berlin. In an interesting passage, he drew attention to the case of Japan. "The Japanese alphabet [sic] is a thousand times more difficult than ours. . . . Yet this nation, with these educational obstacles, in a brief time, has surpassed others in scientific education, industries, statesmanship, and the progress of civilization." In contrast to the massive efforts of the Japanese to industrialize, he bitterly complained that the Persian rich refused to form banks or corporations, preferring to bury their gold in safes. They tried to get rich quick through fraudulent trading methods, while foreigners monopolized the development of Iran's resources. Iranians speculated in land, instead of building factories. At the root of these problems he identified the "negligence of the state and the laziness of the nation." "A country can be considered civilized only if the state and the nation are not at conflict. . . . National and state affairs can only be put into order if the opinion of the nation is put into practice." He then traced the history of European political traditions from Greek democracy to the establishment of the English Parliament—"thanks to this Parliament, the wealth and the welfare of that country have increased constantly." Finally, he returned to Japan, which had achieved a constitution. Before that time, Japan "like Iran was an autocracy, an ignorant, unscientific nation, without concern for sciences of civilization and humanities. But now, thanks to a constitutional regime, it has reached the highest level, as any ignorant idiot knows."[16]

The Japanese case was a recurrent reference in Iranian constitutional literature. Japan's stunning defeat of tsarist Russia in 1904 was interpreted by Iranian reformers as decisive proof of the superiority and strength of a constitutional regime. As Nikki Keddie has noted, "Not only was Asian pride, hitherto battered by a continuous stream of Western conquests, bolstered by this victory, but the fact that the only Asian constitutional power defeated the only major Western nonconstitu-

15. Quoted in ibid., pp. 31–33.

16. Adamiyat, *Ideolozhi*, pp. 92–99. (The expression translated as "any ignorant idiot" in Persian is literally "my aunt"—a common, derogatory way of speaking.)

tional power strengthened the fight for constitutional government as the panacea for internal ills and the secret of Western strength."[17]

In the late nineteenth and early twentieth century the Shi'i clergy were turned to by all sides. Their power was based on their institutional influence as well as their sociological links with the urban classes. On the one hand, the ulama were still the religious and traditional cultural leaders of society, and the entire educational system was still based on clergy-run schools of the classical type. On the other hand, most ulama were connected through intimate family ties with the mercantile and artisanal strata who turned to them for leadership. As Gallagher has observed, "to the extent that the clergy as *shi'a* symbolized a vital aspect of Iranian national consciousness, they inevitably suffered from the spread of foreign influence in the nineteenth and early twentieth centuries, all the more because the urban bazaar classes on which they relied for a counterweight to the political power were hard hit by Western commercial intrusion."[18] The leading role of the *ulama* in the successful protest movement against the Tobacco Concession in 1891–92 greatly increased their influence and prestige. They were, thus, a central force, which could be allied with, manipulated, combated, but never ignored.

There were two kinds of reformers' responses to the role of the clergy. First there were the "nationalists of a modern type, with ideas still found in Iranian nationalism—rejection of Islam, anticlericalism, agnosticism, Westernism, anti-imperialism, glorification of the pre-Islamic past, and hatred of modern Iranian actuality."[19] The most prominent of these early secular nationalists were Akhundzadeh, Mirza Aqa Khan Kermani, and Talebov. They glorified a pre-Islamic Iranian past which was identified with national splendor and power. Akhundzadeh, for example—although opposed to all religions—wrote to a Zoroastrian friend that this religion should be preserved and protected, and efforts should be made not to let any Zoroastrian be converted to Islam.[20] Similarly, Kermani blamed Islam for the decline of the Persians, and anti-Arab, anti-Islamic chauvinism colored his major writings.[21] Talebov shared a part of these beliefs and advocated the secularization of law.

Nonetheless, the pressure of Islamic conformity was so strong that

17. Nikki R. Keddie, "Religion and Irreligion in Early Iranian Nationalism," *Comparative Studies in Society and History* 4 (April 1962): pp. 265–95.

18. Charles Gallagher, "Contemporary Islam: The Plateau of Particularism, Problems of Religion and Nationalism in Iran," *American Universities Field Staff Reports* (New York, 1966), p. 14.

19. Keddie, "Religion," pp. 287–88.

20. Hairi, *Shi'ism*, p. 27.

21. See Mangol Bayat Philipp, "The Concepts of Religion and Government in the Thought of Mirza Aga Khan Kirmani, a Nineteenth-Century Persian Revolutionary," *International Journal of Middle East Studies* 5 (1974): 381–400.

even these anticlerical nationalists had to make concessions and adapt
their discourse to popular piety.[22] Talebov, for instance, was once forced
to cloak his secular convictions in the following formula: "Whatever is
against civilization is perpetually forbidden in our noble religion which
will be the basis of law in Iran. Any Muslim, including the writer of these
lines, whose heart and tongue do not approve this fact is an infidel.
Neither are they Muslims who do not consider the law a supplement to
religion and a guardian for the enforcement of the religious law."[23] Even
the militant Kermani resigned himself to a utilitarian attitude toward the
clergy: "Since philosophy has no strength amongst the Iranian people,
and because they are all oppressed and in need of fanticism . . . one must
resort to certain means to reform their situation. . . . If we ask for very
limited assistance from this half-alive horde of mollas, maybe we shall
reach our aims faster."[24] Some anticlerical nationalists were completely
utilitarian in this regard and refrained from attacks against Islam or the
ulama. Malkam Khan, himself from an Armenian family, affirmed that it
was not possible to contest religion: "One should make allowances for the
fanatical people of the country; for success in reformation, the intelligent
young man must learn religious science as well as French law."[25]

A second, smaller number of nationalist thinkers, however, genuinely
tried to reconcile their religious beliefs with nationalism and constitutionalism. Mostashar ad-Dauleh, for example, attempted a synthesis of Islamic and modern juridical principles by painstakingly dividing all laws
into religious and nonreligious classifications: advocating the equality of
all citizens, regardless of faith, within the boundaries of nonreligious
law.[26] This second category of nationalist ideologues also shared many
common objectives with the proreform wing of the clergy.

22. See Algar, *Religion and State*, pp. 76–77.
23. Quoted in Hairi, *Shi'ism*, p. 47.
24. Quoted in Adamiyat, *Ideolozhi*, p. 30.
25. Quoted in Hairi, *Shi'ism*, p. 40. This utilitarian adaptation to Islam was not limited to
the nationalists. The tiny nucleus of social democrats included a faction called "The
Defenders of Islam Faction of Iranian Social Democracy." Here are the excerpts from a
leaflet they issued on the occasion of the declaration of the constitution in 1906: "Workers of
the world unite! We, Social Democrats, the true defenders of Islam, send our congratula-
tions to the freedom lovers of the world on this day of declaration of the Iranian constitution.
We salute all the clergy and the merchants who support the people, and all the Islamic
Mojahedin in Tehran, who have all sacrificed their wealth and lives to reach their sacred
goals. . . . We, the Islamic Mojahedin, who are the men of God, cannot stop at the gains
made so far. We must hoist the red banner of liberty." (Quoted in Pavlovich, Teria, and
Iranski, *Seh maqaleh dar bareh-ye enqelabe mashruteh-ye Iran* [Three Essays on the
constitutional revolution of Iran], Persian translation [Tehran, 1978], p. 38.)
26. Hairi, *Shi'ism*, p. 32.

Shi'ite Theory of Government and Constitutionalism

The rise of the constitutionalist movement posed a complex challenge to the Shi'i clergy. Prominently involved in the protests against the Tobacco Concession, they had also been influenced (like their Sunni counterparts) by the general antiforeign agitation of Jamal ad-Din Afghani and kindred figures. But the development of constitutionalist ideology presented a problem of a different order; it forced them to take a stance toward a new and growing political project.[27] At stake was no longer a particular reform, this or that concession or unjust act, but the very structure of power in Iranian society. Initially, the response of the clergy was ambiguous and ambivalent. On the one hand, they had their own grievances against the Qajar regime as well as being sensitive to the generally rebellious and oppositional mood throughout the country. On the other hand, they were highly suspicious of, if not inimical to, new foreign ideas. Such contradictory pressures culminated in a split between proconstitutional and anticonstitutional wings of the clergy.

It is important to see the ideological framework in which these political tensions within the ulama were articulated. Traditional Shi'i theories of government had divided history into two different epochs: (1) the period before A.D. 874 when the imams were present on earth, and, in theory, no governmental problems existed since the judgment of the imams was presumed infallible and unquestioned by true believers; and (2) the period following the "occultation" (disappearance into hiding) of the Twelfth Imam, when questions of governmental structure and the legitimacy of authority became controversial. The imam's absence allowed the proconstitutionalist clergy to advocate what amounted to a semisecularization of the Iranian polity. Their argument was that, in the absence of an infallible imam, a completely just Islamic government was impossible, and believers had to seek the best possible state. In their view, the superior government was one that maximized the participation of the entire Shi'i community (since no one is infallible and participation lessened dangers of error).

27. Many clergy did not concern themselves with this problem and simply went along with the constitutionalists. Sayyed Mohammad Tabataba'i, for example, one of the two most famous clergy involved in the constitutional movement, once said: "We ourselves had not seen a constitutional regime. But we had heard about it, and those who ·had seen the constitutional countries had told us that a constitutional regime will bring security and prosperity to the country. This created an urge and enthusiasm in us, so we strove to establish a constitutional regime in this country." (Quoted in Adamiyat, *Ideolozhi*, p. 226.) Later, when conflicts broke out between clergy and constitutionalists over articles of the constitution, and when over severe objections of the clergy a secular judiciary was voted into the constitution, the same Tabataba'i—feeling betrayed by his secular allies—is quoted as having said, "with the establishment of these judicial courts, what else is there left for the clergy to do?" (ibid., p. 419).

The one well-argued attempt to use Shi'i theology as the basis of an organic critique of absolutism was Ayatollah Na'ini's treatise, *The Admonition and Refinement of the People (Tanbih al-umma wa tanzih al-mella)*. It was published in the spring of 1909; the period known as the Brief Tyranny (June 1908 to July 1909), when Mohammad Ali Shah had dissolved the first parliament, and constitutionalist armies were fighting their way from Gilan and Isfahan toward Tehran. In this period the anticonstitutionalist clergy, led by Shaikh Fazlollah Nuri, increased their agitation for the establishment of an Islamic parliament based on the *shari'a*. Nuri called the constitutional revolution the "great sedition," which "consisted of three stages—(1) discourse and presentation; (2) writing and declaration; (3) practice and test. The call for the first stage was favorably received by all, literate and illiterate, because it was presented in a pleasant way. The second stage involved the writing of the constitution and freedom of press; such freedom gives sanction to writing freely against religion, religious people, and the ulama. In the third stage, the constitutionalists began to practice whatever oppression they could." He further argued that "the most important problem of all is the drafting of a constitution. This matter involves three innovations, all of which are against Islam and are forbidden: (1) writing a law contrary to Islamic law; (2) forcing subjects to obey a law which is not presented by the shari'a; and (3) punishing subjects for their failure to obey the written law."[28]

Na'ini's text was a response to this critique. He argued:

There remains no room to doubt the necessity of changing a despotic regime into a constitutional one. This is true, because the former consists of three sets of usurpations and oppressions: (1) it is a usurpation of the authority of God and injustice to Him; (2) it is a usurpation of the Imam's authority and an oppression of the Imam; and (3) it is also an oppression of the people. In contrast, a constitutional system only oppresses the Imam, since his authority is usurped. Thus, a constitutional regime reduces three sets of oppression to merely one; consequently it is necessary to adopt it.[29]

Na'ini also attacked the clergy's attempt to make the constitutional government religiously unlawful; stating in rebuttal that both Shi'i and Sunni theology actually recognized the legitimacy of a parliamentary state:

It is permissible in the *Sunni* tradition because the system of election of parliamentary representatives corresponds to the doctrine concerning the authority of the "people of loosening and binding" [*ahl-e hall va 'aqd*]. As for the regime's legitimacy among the Shi'a, during the Greater Occultation, the mujtahids are

28. Hairi, *Shi'ism*, p. 199.
29. Ibid., pp. 193–94.

responsible for the Muslims' affairs. If a number of mujtahids or their envoys give their approval to parliamentary decision, the constitutional system would also become lawful according to the Shi'a.[30]

Thus Na'ini was calling upon the Shi'i mujtahids to issue a fatva making the constitution and the parliamentary system religiously lawful. Against Nuri's accusation that a constitution was an antireligious innovation, he replied that "legislation would be an innovation [bid'a] and consequently against Islam only if one stipulates a non-Islamic clause as a provision of the shari'a and then puts it into effect. But if one does not associate the non-Islamic provision with the shari'a, then there would be no innovation."[31] Finally, Na'ini tried to seal his argument with a further invocation of Islamic tradition: "since the interference of the people, that is to say, their participation in the elections, prevents the tyrant from exercising oppression, the people's right to, and their responsibility for, state affairs are established under the principle of *nahy az munkar,* which is an obligatory duty of every individual and can be realized through the institution of popular elections."[32]

With the military victory of the constitutionalists in July 1909 and the election of a second parliament, these debates receded into obscurity. The subsequent decade in Iran was marked by weak, incompetent governments as well as by disillusionment with the utopian promise of constitutionalism. The proconstitutionalist clergy, in particular, were doubly disillusioned since the changes that did occur were at the expense of their traditional functions. It began to seem that, after all, the "secret" of European civilization was not actually the panacea for the problems of Iran. This evolving climate of social disintegration and political demoralization paved the way for the emergence of Reza Khan's power and the establishment in 1921 of a centralized military-based state.[33]

Reza Shah's Reforms and the Conflict with the Clergy

Reza Shah's rule (1921–41) was built on a foundation of massive repression and limited reform. He brutally crushed several local popular uprisings, eliminated political opposition (from communists to liberal demo-

---

30. Ibid., pp. 296–97.
31. Ibid., p. 199.
32. Ibid., p. 206.
33. It is often said that Reza Khan was a British stooge and that his 1921 coup was designed and aided by the British. It is true that General Ironside, impressed by Reza Khan's military performance in suppressing local risings, laid the groundwork for the 1921 coup. (See Richard Ullman, *Anglo-Soviet Relations, 1917–1921,* vol. 3 [Princeton, 1966], pp. 354–69, 383–89.) However, the political disillusionment following the constitutional regime allowed Reza Khan to win support from many former leaders of the constitutional revolution.

crats to protesting clergy), and launched a series of administrative and economic reforms. Ironically, many of these—the establishment of a modern educational system; the creation of a regular conscript army; the founding of a secular judicial system; and so on—were reforms that the constitutionalists had long fought for. Hence, many former constitutionalists came to give disgruntled support to Reza Shah. On the other hand, those who remained in opposition to his dictatorial rule tended only to quibble with details of his reforms. Constitutionalist opposition was, therefore, partially disarmed by the shah's theft of part of its program. (A similar situation arose in the early sixties in relation to the National Front's attitude to the reforms of Mohammad Reza Shah.)

The clergy's dissatisfaction with Reza Shah, however, was more substantive, since practically every area of the regime's innovation in administration and state policy intruded upon the prerogatives of the ulama: Modern schools and universities destroyed the ancient monopoly of the clergy and devalued the *madrasa* system. Top state bureaucrats were now recruited, not from the madrasa, but from the university or those sent abroad on government scholarships. From 1926 on, the jurisdiction of religious courts was reduced and finally abolished. The establishment of a Ministry of Endowments curtailed the role of the clergy in administering *vaqf* properties, while the tax system, which imposed new levies on consumer goods like tea and sugar, forced the clergy in many areas to sanction counting state tax payments as part of khums and zakat. Even in the arena of social services, the construction of new hospitals, baths, libraries, orphanages, and so on, represented an encroachment upon a sphere of traditional clerical hegemony. Finally, in 1936 the state directly attacked certain traditional practices—ordering the compulsory unveiling of women in public, and banning certain rituals like the cutting of one's forehead during *'ashura* ceremonies.[34]

Except for unusual figures like Sayyed Hasan Modarres, however, the clerical response to this expansion of state authority was largely an unhappy silence. The clergy was chastened not only by the regime's repressiveness, but also by its awareness that there was support for many of these reforms. The first systematic formulation of a position of the clerical opposition was delayed until 1944, three years after the abdication of Reza Shah. Ruhollah Khomeini's book, *The Discovery of Secrets* (*Kashf al-Asrar*), was a reply to the writings of Ahmad Kasravi[35] and his followers, who had condemned the clerical opposition to Reza Shah as a reactionary mixture of fanaticism, superstition, and corruption. Kho-

34. See Fischer, *Iran*, pp. 95–120.
35. Kasravi was one of the most important and prolific historians of Iran. Although not an atheist, he opposed all existing religions and organized a circle of followers in search of the "true religion."

meini utilized a variety of polemical devices to refute these charges and clarify the reasons for clerical resistance to the regime. Kasravi was assassinated in 1946 by the *Fedayan-e Islam,* and the debate was not continued; Khomeini's book remained relatively unknown until its republication in 1979. Its retrospective significance comes from the insights it provides into the political evolution of Khomeini's thinking. The first half of the book is devoted to theological exegesis, but the second half presents the first programmatic assertion of the clergy's political role advanced since the days of the constitutional movement. It also contains many of the political ideas that Khomeini would elaborate almost thirty years later (1971) in his *Velayat-e Faqih* (alternatively titled *Islamic Government*). A synopsis of the passages of *Kashf al-Asrar* that deal with governmental reform will aid in establishing the coordinates of modern Shi'i political ideology in its Khomeinite version.

The first principle of Islamic government, according to Khomeini, is that the only acceptable legislator is God. "No one but God has the right to govern over anyone or to legislate, and Reason suggests that God himself must form a government for people and must legislate. The laws are but the laws of Islam" (p. 184).[36] Furthermore:

This law that legislates everything, from the most general problems of all countries to the specifics of a man's family, from the social life of all of humanity to the personal life of a man living alone in a cave, and from before man's conception in the womb to after his placement in the tomb—this law is nothing but God's religion: Islam. We will later provide incontrovertible proof that Islamic law relating to government, taxation, legal and criminal codes—on everything concerning the administration of a country from the formation of an army to the formation of ministries—lacks nothing. It is you who are ignorant of this, and all our misfortunes stem from the fact that a country which, in fact, possesses such laws, has extended a begging hand to alien countries and has implemented their forged laws, conceived from the poisonous minds of selfish men.

Khomeini's second principle is that a true Muslim should only "obey God, His Prophet, and those in authority among you" (*Qur'an* IV:62):

Who are these people of authority and what kind of people should they be? Some say that they are kings and rulers, and that god has ordered people to obey and follow their kings and sultans. Thus they would say that God has enjoined obedience to Mustafa Kemal Pasha as president of Turkey or to Reza Khan as shah of Iran. Further, the Sunni would consider all the caliphs of Islam, including Mu'awiya Ibn abi Sufyan, Yazid Ibn Mu'awiya, and other Umayyad and Abbasid

---

36. All references are to the 1979 Persian edition of *Kashf al-Asrar.* The book is a response to a book by a follower of Kasravi.

rulers, as divinely sanctioned authorities. . . . Now we ask our God-given reason
for judgment: God sent the Prophet of Islam with thousands of heavenly laws and
established His government on the belief in the uniqueness of God and Justice.
. . . Would this same God order men to obey Ataturk who has disestablished state
religion, persecuted believers, oppressed the people, sanctioned moral corruption, and, in general, opposed the religion of God? Moreover, would he order us
to obey [Reza Khan] Pahlavi who, as we all know, did all that he could to uproot
Islam? . . . We must conclude that people of authority cannot be kings and rulers.
And a glance at the record of the caliphs, even according to the *hadith* and the
Sunni histories, would support the same conclusion. (pp. 109–10)

After reiterating the orthodox Shi'i doctrine that the imams were the
legitimate authorities from Muhammad to 874, Khomeini argues that in
the contemporary world the most legitimate authority should be that of
the *mujtahids,* the *faqihs,* those most knowledgeable in the laws of Islam.
In his later 1971 book he specifically calls upon the faqihs to assume
directly the leadership of government, but in 1944 he was not yet prepared
to go so far:

When we say government [*Hokumat* and *Velayat*] in our time belongs to the
faqihs we do not mean to say that the shah, the ministers, the soldiers, and the
dustmen should all be faqihs. But we do propose the following: According to the
same procedure by which a constituent assembly is formed, and that this
assembly then chooses a new ruler . . . we can form such an assembly, but
composed of pious mujtahids who are wise in divine law, just, free of temptation
and ambition, and desiring nothing but the welfare of the people and the
implementation of God's laws. These religious men would then elect a just sultan
who would not disobey divine law nor practice oppression nor transgress against
people's property, life and honor. . . . Similarly for the majles, why should it not
be composed of pious faqihs or be placed under their supervision? [p. 185]. . . .[37]
Clearly, even the mujtahids do not have the right to allow *anyone* to rule. Even
the Prophet and the Imams were not allowed by God to do this. They can only
confer authority upon someone who does not violate God's laws—these being
founded on reason and justice—and who accepts the formal law of the country to
be the divine laws of heaven, and not European laws or worse. (p. 189)

Khomeini also discusses at length the clergy's view of the "harmful"
changes wrought by Reza Shah's reforms and administrative initiatives.
His critique comprises five salient elements:

37. The constituent assembly and majles described in this 1944 work are strikingly similar
to the Assembly of Experts convened in the summer of 1979 and the current Islamic
assembly. When Khomeini first announced his scheme for the Assembly of Experts many of
his bourgeois-nationalist allies felt betrayed, while much of the left was disillusioned. But, as
a study of his early writings clearly shows, Khomeini had not disguised his schemes; the
main fault was with the wishful thinking and ignorance of his nationalist and left-wing
collaborators.

1. He is obsessed with the pervasive moral corruption and cultural decadence that he sees resulting from these policies:

The clergy insist that this shameful unveiling [of women], this "Movement of Bayonets,"[38] has wracked both spiritual and material damage upon our country in gross violation of the laws of God and His Prophet. The clergy insist that this melon-shaped (men's) hat, a foreign leftover, is a disgrace to the nation of Islam, forbidden by God and damaging to our independence. The clergy insist that these coeducational schools, mixing young girls and lustful young boys, destroy chastity and manliness. . . . They insist that these shops selling wines and these factories making alcoholic drinks erode the minds of our youth, debasing reason, health, chastity, and courage amongst the people—by God's decree the drinking and selling of wine are forbidden, and these places should be shut down. They also insist that music creates a mood of fornication and lust, undermining chastity, manliness, and courage—it is forbidden by religious law and should not be taught in schools lest it promote vice. (pp. 213–14)

2. Khomeini condemns the principle of universal conscription introduced by Reza Shah on the grounds that it coerces youth, exposes it to corruption and prostitution, and ultimately only trains it in the arts of thuggery and robbery. Instead he proposes the adoption of an Islamic approach to national defense, which in peacetime would be based on a volunteer army inspired by religious motivation that would be deepened by Islamic education. In wartime, compulsory service would be founded on the universal obligation of *jihad*, which Islam imposes upon every able-bodied Muslim man (pp. 242–45). Again, the key to the mobilization of the nation would be religious propaganda, and he proposes the establishment of a special ministry for this specific purpose. It would seek not only to inspire each citizen, but also to train him to proselytize others (pp. 246–48).

3. Khomeini surveys the various traditional taxes levied in Islam (pp. 255–58) and proposes a new tax system based on traditional religious principles. In particular, he condemns import taxes as damaging to commercial interests, although he accepts the idea of limited tariffs on foreign goods, provided they do not unjustly penalize domestic merchants and traders (pp. 266–67).

4. Not surprisingly, he opposes the existing Ministry of Justice and its judicial procedures. In his opinion, the restoration of judges trained according to Islamic law would simplify trial procedures and eliminate costly lawyers' fees and parasitic judicial personnel (pp. 296–301). Moreover, he claims that the full implementation of the Islamic penal code would eliminate injustice, theft, and corruption within a year. "If you want to eradicate theft from the world, you must cut the hands off thieves, otherwise your prison sentences will only help thieves and perpetuate

38. Soldiers were ordered to tear apart women's veils on the street with their bayonets.

theft. Human life can only be made secure through the guarantee of punishment, and only the death penalty ensures society's survival, since prison sentences do not solve any problem. If adulterous men and women were promptly given a hundred lashes each, venereal disease would disappear in this country" (pp. 274–75).

5. Khomeini even expressed his deep skepticism about the utility of "modern medicine and European surgery," glorifying traditional methods and practices instead (pp. 279–81). Furthermore, he ridiculed the Ministry of Culture and the national media, which he saw as transmitting and teaching only moral corruption (pp. 282–83).

In conclusion, Khomeini emphasizes that it is because of the very completeness and integrity of Islam as a legal, cultural, and political order that the European powers, conspiring to defeat and colonize the Muslim countries, aim above all to uproot its institutions and to substitute alien laws and customs.

The appearance of Khomeini's book, despite its obscurity at the time, marked a certain watershed in the development of Shi'i political consciousness. Whereas the clergy had for decades been reacting instinctively and in piecemeal fashion to the transformation of Iranian society, Khomeini recognized that the accumulation of changes was resulting in a new social and political structure. He was the first amongst clergy of his rank systematically to try to understand the implications of the conflicts between an emerging bourgeois state and the old Islamic institutional order. Yet his ideas had little immediate impact, and he remained an isolated figure even amongst the clergy. The majority of the Shi'i hierarchy continued to keep aloof from national politics, while in the turbulent period following World War II nationalist politics were dominated by mainly secular forces of the Tudeh Party and the National Front.

Post-1953 Developments and a New Politicization of the Clergy

The CIA-backed coup of 19 August 1953 which overthrew Mosaddeq also sparked a crisis in the ranks of Iranian nationalism. In the subsequent recomposition of the nationalist movement, clerical elements for the first time began to assume an active political and ideological leadership in the struggle against the Pahlavi dynasty. Important figures from the National Front, like Bazargan and Taleqani, broke away and founded the Freedom Movement, "as a bridge between the universities and the theological circles . . . since the entry of religious leaders into the struggle was the need of the time and desire of the people."[39] In 1955 Taleqani arranged for

39. From an early pamphlet issued by the Freedom Movement to explain its aims, recently quoted by Bazargan in one of his election pamphlets to bolster his claim that leaders like himself had dragged the clergy from their mosques into politics, which they were now ungratefully forcing him out of.

the republication of Na'ini's book—out of print since 1909—with his own
introduction, which emphasized the responsibility of the clergy in politics. Meanwhile, in Tehran and Qom sections of the clergy were beginning
to discuss how to organize themselves. In Tehran regular lectures on the
clergy's role in politics and the need for reforms of the hierarchy created
great excitement, with many of the prominent clerical figures in today's
regime contributing to them. The proceedings were regularly published in
a journal, *Goftar-e Mah* (*Lecture of the Month*). S. Akhavi has summarized the main themes of these lectures as follows:

(1) the need for an independent financial organization for the clergy; (2) the
necessity of a *shura-yi fatva*—i.e., a permanent committee of *mujtahids,* the
members of which were to be drawn from the country at large, to issue collective
authoritative opinions in matters of law; (3) the idea that no *Shi'i* society is
possible without the delegation of the *Imam's* authority; (4) an interpretation of
Islam as a total way of life, therefore incorporating social, economic and political
issues into the religious ones; (5) the need to replace the central importance of
fiq[h] in the *madrasah* curricula with *akhlaq* (ethics), *aqa'id* (ideology), and
falsafah (philosophy); (6) the need for a new concept of leadership of youth based
on a correct understanding of responsibility; (7) the development of *ijtihad* as a
powerful instrument for the adaptation of Islam to changing circumstances; (8) a
revival of the nearly defunct principle of *al-amr bi-ma'ruf wa al-nahy'an al-
munkar* as a means of expressing a collective and public will; (9) specialization
among *mujtahids* and making *taqlid* (emulation of a *mujtahid*) contingent upon it;
(10) the need for mutuality and communal spirit to overcome the individuality and
mistrust that pervades Iranian culture.[40]

While these Tehran lectures were taking place, Khomeini was holding
regular weekly meetings in Qom with other clerical leaders to discuss
their attitude toward governmental policies. This was the period of the
American "Point Four" programs, as United States advisers pushed the
newly reinstalled shah to make fiscal and social reforms that would put
the shattered Iranian economy on a more solid capitalist foundation. In
the early 1960s the land-reform program, together with increased infrastructural investment and expanded credit for local capitalists, accelerated capital accumulation in Iran while undermining traditional sectors.
The influx of American advisers reinforced the antiforeign elements in
Khomeini's outlook; while the fact that some of the entrepreneurs who
profited from the new government policies were either Jewish or Baha'i
increased his fears for the future of Islam. With the death in 1961 of
Ayatollah Borujerdi, the chief Shi'i mujtahid, the last obstacle was
removed for Khomeini's surfacing as leader of the clerical opposition.

40. Shahrough Akhavi, *Religion and Politics in Contemporary Iran* (Albany, 1980), pp.
119–20.

Although Borujerdi had opposed the clergy's involvement in politics, he had nonetheless helped establish much of the organizational apparatus indispensible to Khomeini's rise. As Algar has noted, "one important achievement that is to his [Borujerdi's] credit is the reorganization of what is called *Hauza-yi Ilmiya,* the teaching institute in Qom. He established a network for the dissemination of religious knowledge throughout Iran as well as the collection of *zakat* and *khums.*"[41] This gave invaluable financial stability and independence to the clerical hierarchy as well as an organizational structure that proved vital during the 1977–79 mass mobilizations.

From autumn 1962 on, Khomeini's manifestoes and agitations propelled him into increasing confrontation with the central government, leading to the famous 5 June 1963 demonstration, which the army ruthlessly crushed. To this day, there is much confusion, both inside and outside Iran, over the issues involved in this confrontation and their significance for future events. It is important, therefore, to try to give a detailed account of what exactly happened and why.

One common misconception has been that Khomeini's opposition to the shah was an outgrowth of resistance to agrarian reforms which were seen to threaten vaqf lands as well as landowner kinsmen of the clergy. Although several ayatollahs opposed land reform, in relation to Khomeini, this oft-repeated claim has little or no factual basis. Aside from pilot land-distribution schemes initiated in the early fifties, a weak land-reform bill was passed in spring 1960, then amended so as to create a new and much stronger bill and implemented from January 1962 onward. The first demonstrations and petitions of Khomeini and his followers, on the other hand, only began in October 1962, and were directed, not against the agrarian reform (already in progress for over nine months), but against the new local election bill that the Cabinet had passed on 7 October 1962. (The Cabinet had assumed charge of the legislative process following the dissolution of Parliament by royal decree the preceding year.) Never was agrarian reform as such disputed by Khomeini. Once, when the original bill was being discussed in Parliament in February 1960, Ayatollah Borujerdi had written a letter to Ja'far Behbehani, his nephew and a member of Parliament, complaining that the bill was ill-advised and contrary to the shari'a[42] and this opposition weakened the bill. Several ulama agitated against the 1962 reform, but Khomeini did not come out against the land-distribution programs.

The clergy reacted with great sharpness against proposals concerning women's rights and suffrage. There were many statements by religious leaders, including Khomeini, that equal rights for women were a violation

41. Algar, "Iran and Shi'ism," p. 12.
42. Akhavi, *Religion,* p. 91.

of the shari'a. The local election bill that sparked the first open protests in October 1962 was seen as so objectionable because it would give the vote to women, as well as replacing the Qur'an in the swearing-in ceremony with "my holy book" (i.e., would recognize the holy books of other religions). To oppose this bill Khomeini called a meeting of the top clergy in Qom. The meeting resolved to send a telegram to the shah demanding the annulment of the bill, and to dispatch envoys and messages to the clergy throughout the country, warning them about "the dangers that the bill entails for Islam and for the people of Iran."[43]

It is indicative of the outlook of much of the clergy that the election bill more than the land reform should have been the catalyst for the emergence of organized opposition to the shah. The shah's program included the total suppression of all opposition, the massive strengthening of the repressive apparatus (army, police, and SAVAK), and the implementation of structural changes—like land reform—that would facilitate capitalist growth. From the clerical viewpoint, this was the final stage in the undermining of traditional Islamic society that had been initiated in the mid-nineteenth century by reformist ministers like Amir Kabir, continued by the constitutionalist movement, and quickened by the proforeign, anticlerical policies of Reza Shah and his son. By the early sixties, however, the clergy had come to accept certain reforms, provided they were compatible with Islam, rejected foreign influence, and were supervised by the clergy. The principal reason that the local election issue more than agrarian reform became the storm center of clerical protest was because it could be much more clearly and unambiguously linked to a defense of Islam on a populist basis without overtones of the class interests of the Shi'i hierarchy. Moreover, as the early manifestoes of Khomeini's group stressed, female suffrage encompassed a broad array of traditionalist moral and social concerns ("women's participation in social affairs is prohibited and must be prevented, since such participation involves many forbidden [haram] and corrupting interactions"). The linkage between the controversy over the election law and the defense of Islam per se was explained by the oppositionists at Qom. For example, in one of his telegrams to the prime minister, Khomeini vividly sketched out his familiar motifs of foreign conspiracy and internal decadence:

It is incumbent upon me, according to my religious duties, to warn the Iranian people and the Muslims of the world that Islam and the Qur'an are in danger; that the independence of the country and its economy are about to be taken over by

43. A full account of these events appears in Sayyed Hamid Ruhani, *Barrasi va tahlili az nahzat-e Imam Khomeini* [An Analysis of the Movement of Imam Khomeini] (Qom, 1977). This 960-page book contains an invaluable complete compilation of Khomeini's statements and lectures from this period; otherwise its primary distinction is its revolting anti-Jewish, anti-Baha'i bigotry.

Zionists, who in Iran appear as the party of Baha'is, and if this deadly silence of
Muslims continues, they will soon take over the entire economy of the country
and drive it to complete bankruptcy. Iranian television is a Jewish spy base, the
government sees this and approves of it.[44]

Confronted with massive and unexpected protest against the local
election bill, the government was forced to back down and annul the
legislation. Significantly, Khomeini did not yet see himself as engaged in
all-out opposition to the regime; rather he still hoped to persuade the shah
and his advisers to adopt Islamic policies. A famous speech of Khomeini's immediately after the defeat of the election bill provides insight
into the self-confident hopes and aims of the clergy at this early stage in
the development of the movement.

The independence of all the Islamic countries is owing to these people [the
clergy]. It is they who have so far defended Islamic sovereignty; it has also been
these invaluable men who have always calmed the rebellious masses, but only
insofar as national independence has not been endangered. Otherwise, Islam
makes insurrection and rebellion the imperative duties of the clergy; this is why
the recent movement of the clergy was a religious and Qur'anic insurgency—
indeed, it was according to their holiest obligations as Muslims that they engaged
in this. . . . Moreover, had a word been issued, a public explosion would have
occurred. Who quenched this fire? Why don't they [the government] understand
this? Why are they trying, by every means, to alienate and break the support of
the clergy? . . . Why do they not instead rely on the clergy? . . . If people see that
the government protects the interests and welfare of Islam and Muslims, and that
it serves the nation, then they will support the government . . . But, alas, the
government cannot comprehend these facts, it refuses to understand that without
the clergy the country has no backbone. . . . I advise the shah not to lose this
force! . . . To give such advice is incumbent [*wajib*] . . it is the duty of the ulama
and the clergy to give advice and to show the way to everyone, from the shah
down to the most minor officials.[45]

A second round of conflict between the government and the clergy
arose over the 26 January 1963 referendum. This put to vote a six-point
program that included land reform, woman suffrage, nationalization of
forests and pastures, and a workers' profit-sharing scheme. The referendum was interpreted by the clergy as a rejection of its demand for greater
influence in the government and a further attempt to curb its social
influence and political role. Moreover, the referendum was part of a
strategy to create popular support for the regime and divide the clergy's
mass base. In light of these threats to its social survival, the clergy

44. Ibid., pp. 177–78.
45. Ibid., pp. 197–205.

abandoned hope of influencing the regime and went over to frontal opposition, starting with a call for a boycott of the referendum. It must be emphasized, however, that none of the specific planks in the referendum was the sole cause of clerical opposition; rather the clergy opposed the *whole project* that the government was launching. Moreover, as Khomeini's statement on this occasion makes clear, the clergy was beginning to project its own global alternative "Islamic" program.

Khomeini first rules out a referendum as unconstitutional, but goes on to say, "for the time being, because of certain considerations, we will ignore the fact that a referendum or a national approval is worthless as far as Islam is concerned." He also protests the holding of a referendum under an atmosphere of intimidation, repression, and fear; pointing out that people do not understand the consequence of their vote and that:

people who are responsible to the law and to the nation have fooled His Highness into doing this job for them. . . . If these people want to do something for the good of the people, why do they not turn to the program of Islam and Islamic experts, so that all classes will enjoy a comfortable life, and so that all will be happy in this and the other world? Why are they instituting cooperative funds that are robbing the fruits of the peasants' labor? With the establishment of these cooperatives, the Iranian home market will be lost, and both merchants and farmers ruined while other classes will consequently suffer a similar fate. . . . The clergy registers the danger for the Qur'an and our religion. It seems that this compulsory referendum aims to lay the basis for the removal of the clauses [in the constitution] linked to religion. The Islamic ulama had previously felt the same danger to Islam, Qur'an, and country when the government took measures to change the local elections. Now it seems that the enemies of Islam are trying to achieve the same thing through fooling a bunch of naive people.

This time, however, the government was determined to refuse concessions to the clergy and went ahead with its referendum. Continuing agitation from Qom resulted in repeated clashes between the army and the city's religious students (*tollab*), culminating in Khomeini's famous public denunciation of the shah in his 'ashura speech of 3 June 1963. His subsequent arrest in the early morning of 5 June sparked riots and demonstrations in Qom and Tehran that were crushed by the army. The Tehran demonstration, in particular, was significant, because not only did clerical followers come into the streets and the bazaar close down in protest, but for the first time students at Tehran University also joined in. The students were led by The Student Committee of the National Front, the only remaining active wing of the almost moribund National Front. Previously, this committee had refused to endorse the clerical opposition to woman suffrage and had instead advanced the slogan, "Reforms, yes! Dictatorship, no!" But with the virtual disintegration of its parent body

(which now found much of its reform program co-opted by the dictatorship), the student National Front turned toward Khomeini as the viable
symbol of opposition. Although the student role in the 5 June 1963
demonstration was limited, it was historically significant as the first
rapprochement between the nationalist movement on the campuses and
the anti-shah clergy. With socialism and secular nationalism in disarray,
Islam, unscathed by the disaster of 1953, came forward to fill a political
vacuum, offering itself as *the* radical alternative to the shah's tyranny.

The socioeconomic transformations in the next fifteen years provided
the material force—discontented and dispossessed millions who identified
Islam as their salvation—to make this alternative a potent reality. The
development of Iran as an underdeveloped capitalist, semi-industrial
society magnified traditional inequalities and created new ones. Millions
were uprooted from the land by the development of agricultural capitalism, while urban employment failed to keep pace. Construction booms
were fitful and uncertain; the industrial labor market grew slowly or not at
all. Moreover, the economic troubles of 1975–77 brought 30 percent
inflation and a million unemployed. The result was the burgeoning of giant
slums around the cities and the creation of a huge class of urban paupers.
Tehran alone expanded from one million people to five million in fifteen
years, and the majority of its new population were uprooted immigrants
who filled the endless slums of the city's south. Traditionally fatalist,
deprived of coherent social organization, the displaced poor were mes-
merized by clerical agitation around the themes of Islamic justice and the
voluntary equalization of wealth. If only the rich would follow Qur'anic
teaching and give proper alms, poverty would go away; if the rich
refused, however, it became the sacred duty of the poor to restore a moral
order congruent with Islam. Idealizing a minimal reliance upon posses-
sions, the clergy attacked the rich for their sumptuary habits and moral
decadence. As the clergy became increasingly involved in local neighborhood organization and the initiation of "Islamic cooperative shops," it
seemed more and more drawn toward an image of a generalized but
righteous poverty as a desirable future.

The clergy's attacks on the right—particularly the non-Muslim bourgeoisie around the Peacock Throne—also struck a responsive chord in the
mass of traditional urban petty bourgeoisie. The mass production of
consumer goods and the growing centralization of distribution had ruined
broad strata of this class. As the plight of the traditional petty bourgeoisie
worsened, they became more willing to participate in the popular fury
against big capital and its foreign associates. The petty bourgeoisie was
especially bitter at the failure of the shah's government to provide any
protection against the onslaught of mass-produced goods or foreign
competitors. This bitterness was intensified in a violent direction by the

government's response to the economic crisis of the mid-seventies: in order to clear room for the further expansion of big capital within the internal market, the regime abetted the wholesale elimination of small producers.[46]

These desperate layers of the urban petty bourgeoisie and urban poor provided the strongest mass support for the Islamic movement, which began to proselytize them in the late sixties and early seventies. As the clergy deepened and expanded its hegemony within the popular sectors, Khomeini sharpened and refined his political ideology. No longer was a ruler nominated by the clergy a sufficient guarantee of Islamic justice; now he asserted that the clergy itself had to assume power. "If the rulers are to follow Islam, they must follow the faqihs and must ask the faqihs about the laws and decrees. Under such circumstances, it is clear that the faqihs are really ruling. Therefore the act of government must formally belong to the faqihs and not to those who, owing to their ignorance of the laws, must follow the faqihs."[47] Developing this conception in his *Velayat-e Faqih,* he outlines a "program of struggle for the establishment of an Islamic government." As a necessary first stage he proposes a period of propaganda and education amongst the masses, concentrated not so much on traditional theological themes as upon the political, economic, and legal doctrines of Islam, "in order to create a social current, so that the conscious, pious and dutiful masses would gradually organize themselves in an Islamic movement, would rise up and form an Islamic government" (pp. 174–75). He also suggests that the clergy use traditional Muslim gatherings, like Friday prayers or the annual hajj, as means of conducting mass political education (pp. 179–80). Furthermore, he advocates the employment of public ceremonies, such as 'ashura, as political protests through which the masses could be gradually steeled into a fighting force to destroy the regime (p. 182). Thus, at one and the same time, Khomeini's book is both a statement of program and a manual for activists.

The prominence given in this discussion to Khomeini's writings and leadership should not, of course, be allowed to overshadow some consideration of Ali Shariati's contribution to the growth of Islamic militancy. Although Khomeini's narrow focus on the question of state power proved decisive in the struggle against the shah, Shariati's numerous lectures and writings contributed in a unique way to the ideological renaissance of Islam among an entire generation of Iranian youth. We cannot properly evaluate Shariati's role here, but Algar's observation seems quite accu-

46. For a fuller discussion of these points see M. Ja'far and A. Tabari, "Iran: Islam and the Struggle for Socialism," in *Khamsin,* no. 8 (1981):83–104.

47. First published in 1971, *Velayat-e Faqih* (or *Hokumat-e Islami*) is a transcript of a series of lectures given by Khomeini. All quotations are from the Persian third edition.

rate (although I do not share his positive estimation): "There is a certain stimulating quality in his [Shari'ati's] writings, a mind at work, which is a rare thing in the Muslim world. . . . Whatever one may think of this or . that statement or doctrine of Dr. Shari'ati, his achievement that cannot be denied is that he led back a large part of the alienated middle-class generation to an identification with Islam. . . . People were ready to participate in the Revolution under the leadership of Imam Khomeini to a large degree because of the influence upon them of Dr. Shari'ati."[48]

It is important to emphasize that the recent Iranian experience represents an *unprecedented and unique* experiment in Shi'ism's long history: It is the first time that the clergy have directly operated the state without a secular structure either superimposed on it (as during the Safavid period) or parallel with it (as during the Qajar epoch). Many of the problems faced by the clergy in the period since February 1979 stem from the novelty of this experiment: Muslim clergy learning to rule a twentieth-century capitalist society. Despite the repeated assurances of most liberals and leftists that it is an impossible project, I see no *a priori* reasons why it cannot last within certain limits. Also, even its alleged ultimate unfeasibility—a case that has yet to be proven—does not automatically imply the emergence of a crisis favorable either to the revolutionary left or to any form of democracy; on the contrary, it is possible to imagine alternative outcomes including a disintegration of society in its modern class structure and a profound social retrogression. Quite possibly, the clerical stratum will partially adapt itself to the exigencies of capitalism and international politics, modifications and concessions will be made, and the remaining problems attributed to "internal counterrevolution and imperialist conspiracy."

This historical survey of the clergy's political role indicates how the left's alliance with the Islamic opposition against the shah, as well as the support of some major leftist groups (Tudeh, Fedayan Majority) for the Khomeini regime, have been shortsighted and politically disastrous. It should be clear that throughout the late nineteenth century and the twentieth century, the basis of most clerical opposition to the state was a reactionary resistance to even minor social reforms. Even its struggle against the odious Pahlavi military dictators was based, not on any intention to create a socially more progressive or politically more tolerant regime, but on intransigent opposition to any change that would diminish or undermine its traditional prerogatives and powers. The clergy's attitude toward an authentic socialist government would, if anything, be even more antagonistic and violent than its hatred of the Pahlavi shahs. Socialists must grasp this elementary lesson and its implications if they are to have any hope of transforming Muslim societies.

48. Algar, "Iran and Shi'ism," pp. 47, 49.

CHAPTER FIVE

The Revolutionary Character of the Ulama: Wishful Thinking or Reality?

WILLEM M. FLOOR

In several works it is asserted that opposition to tyranny is a fundamental and pervasive characteristic of Shi'i Islam.[1] But I believe the revolutionary character ascribed to the Shi'i ulama in Iran has been greatly exaggerated, and that the ulama's perception of the socioeconomic and political structure of Iranian society often did not basically differ from that of the secular power elite. I will analyze here the causes of the ulama's opposition to the state during the early 1960s. It was in large part his analysis of these events that made Hamid Algar partially amend his earlier conclusion regarding the ulama in Qajar Iran, namely, "that they failed to perceive the nature of what was being demanded and its implication for Iran and themselves."[2]

The ulama's position and role in Iranian society arose partly from Iran's being a preindustrial state. Such societies are dominated by a small power elite, which controls the important societal functions. The holders of such functions, whether these are political, economic, or religious, are mainly drawn from important families. The power of such families could continue beyond the life of a dynasty,[3] although some families rise and fall quickly.

Within the religious stratum the holders of the most important functions were also drawn predominantly from high-status families. One of their functions in society was to legitimize the rule of the political elite.

1. Cf. Hamid Algar, "The Oppositional Role of the Ulama in Twentieth-Century Iran," in *Scholars, Saints, and Sufis,* ed. Nikki R. Keddie (Berkeley and Los Angeles, 1972), p. 231.

2. Algar, *Religion and State in Iran, 1785–1906: The Role of the Ulama in the Qajar Period* (Berkeley and Los Angeles, 1969), p. 259.

3. See W. M. Floor, "The Office of Kalantar in Qajar Persia," *Journal of the Economic and Social History of the Orient (JESHO)* 14 (1971):252–68; Abol-Fazl Qa'emi, *Oligarshi ya khandanha-ye hokumatgar-e Iran,* i, *Khandan-e firuz farmanfarma'iyan* (Tehran, 1351/1972), ii, *Khandan-e isfandeyari* (Tehran, 1354/1975).

Because of that function they were able to influence, if not wield, political power. Although persons of lower-class origin might advance within the religious organization and even reach the highest functions, this was rare. Even when a lower-class person entered the ranks of the elite, this did not change the basic class cleavage.[4]

Because of the legitimization of power through religion, its values and norms were of great importance for the political structure of preindustrial Iran. The religious system provided most of the formal legal structure. This meant that religious leaders, with their broad legal, social, and educational functions, influenced the limits of power of the ruling class. (Judicial functions were dominated and education monopolized by the religious class.)

Opposition to the state in nineteenth-century Iran was characterized by two objectives, one anti-imperialist and the other anti-Qajar. The anti-imperialist opposition resulted from the encroachment of foreign, non-Muslim states upon Iranian, Muslim territory. This opposition was aimed against "infidel," foreign political and economic penetration of Iran. Iran's government increasingly came under the influence of infidel foreign powers, Russia and Great Britain. Here the ulama acted as upholders of traditional values, promoting the territorial integrity of the *Dar al-Islam* against the *Dar al-Harb*.[5]

The second objective, the antityrannical opposition of the ulama, is less traditional. There is reference to such an opposition as a minority movement in the late Safavid period.[6] I believe that the antigovernmental opposition by the ulama in Qajar Iran was caused by two factors. First, this opposition was usually local, aimed at acquiring more political influence or total political control on the local scene. For such purposes the ulama had private armies.[7] Although Iran formally had a central government, its real power normally did not extend much beyond the capital city. Local elite families often administered their regions as they saw fit, providing they acknowledged the shah as their legitimate ruler. This acknowledgment was backed by the regular flow of taxes and presents to the capital.[8]

Second, a new aspect to ulama opposition arose in the nineteenth century, when the state initiated a policy that encroached upon the

4. See e.g. Michael M. J. Fischer, *Iran: From Religious Dispute to Revolution*, (Cambridge, Mass., 1980).
5. For an analysis of this conflict in the nineteenth century see Algar, *Religion and State*.
6. Ibid., pp. 28ff.
7. Ibid., pp. 108ff. See also W. M. Floor, "The Political Role of the Lutis in Iran," in *Modern Iran: The Dialectics of Continuity and Change*, ed. Michael E. Bonine and Nikki R. Keddie (Albany, 1981).
8. See note 3.

ulama's position, both socioeconomically and politically. The state increasingly tried to restrict the role of religious courts and to cut down state pensions to the ulama, while beginnings of secularization of knowledge as a result of contacts with Europe threatened the ulama's monopoly on education.[9] If the Shi'i ulama appeared to espouse a popular cause, there was more often a parallelism of interests than the ulama's advocating a cause for the same reasons as the other groups involved.[10]

The outlook of most ulama regarding the political and socioeconomic structure of Iranian society did not differ essentially from that of the secular elite. The working conditions of those peasants who worked land that was either the private property of religious leaders or *vaqf* property administered by the ulama, were no better (and were often worse) than those of the peasants working on the land of landlords or the state.[11]

More could be said about the role of the religious class in Iran as defenders of the existing order, but this would require a separate study.[12] For our purposes, the broad outline sketched above suffices. It is not surprising that Algar, in his book on the ulama in nineteenth-century Iran, concluded that "any wish to reshape definitively the norms of political life and the bases of the state was foreign to the ulama in Qajar Iran."[13]

The role of the ulama in twentieth-century Iran made Algar partially change his mind regarding to the conclusion of his book on their role in the nineteenth century. Taking Ayatollah Khomeini's role as pivotal for his argument, Algar says that Khomeini's "hostility began to be openly expressed in 1963" and that "the real targets of Khumayni's criticism of the regime in 1963 appear to have been the following: autocratic rule and violation of the constitution; the proposal to grant capitulary rights to American advisors and military personnel in Iran and their dependents; the contracting of a $200 million loan from the United States for the purchase of military equipment; and the maintenance of diplomatic, commercial, and other relations with Israel, a state hostile to Muslims and Islam."[14] He denies that religious agitation was directed against the government's plans for land reform and women's franchise.[15] Hereunder I

---

9. Algar, *Religion and State.*

10. Ibid.

11. A. K. S. Lambton, *Landlord and Peasant in Persia* (London, 1953).

12. Algar, *Religion and State,* pp. 14ff., briefly touches on this matter, as does Nikki R. Keddie, "The Roots of the Ulama's Power in Modern Iran," Keddie, ed., *Scholars, Saints, and Sufis,* pp. 211–29.

13. Algar, *Religion and State,* p. 260.

14. Algar, "Oppositional Role," p. 246.

15. Ibid.

will present an alternative explanation and note the conservative issues for which most of the ulama agitated.

From 1953 until 1962 only a few problems marred the otherwise good relationship between the government and most of the ulama. This relationship was largely due to the quietism favored by Ayatollah Borujerdi, the last sole *marja'e taqlid* (source of imitation) of the Shi'is.[16] According to Mohammad Reza Shah, he "over a long period . . . was in frequent contact with . . . Burujerdi. . . . it had been to this religious leader that he had turned for counsel during the years of Mosaddeq, when the monarchy itself was feeling winds of change. Burujerdi, the arch-priest of religio-national tradition, supported him."[17] This also held for the less quiet religious leader, Ayatollah Kashani, a fierce nationalist and political leader who broke with Mosaddeq and implicitly supported the shah. Kashani challenged the government, however, when in 1954 Iran normalized its relations with the United Kingdom. He, together with other political leaders (such as Dr. Baqa'i of the Iranian Toilers party) protested against this policy and tried to foment trouble for the government. Dr. Baqa'i, unlike Kashani, used this occasion to attack the autocratic nature of the government.[18]

In 1955 the ulama caused demonstrations against the Baha'i community in Iran. The ensuing riots led the government to protect some Baha'i religious centers by military force.[19] The last religiously oriented outburst took place in that same year when the Fedayan-e Islam, an extremist

16. Ibid., p. 244.

17. E. A. Bayne, *Persian Kingship in Transition* (New York, 1968), p. 48.

18. Algar, "Oppositional Role," p. 242, and especially Baqa'i's collection of speeches and letters, recently published, *Doktor Mozaffar Baqa'i Kermani dar pishgah-e tarikh* (Kerman, 1358/1979). As Kashani had good relations with the shah and General Zahedi in those days, one is surprised by the sympathetic treatment of Kashani in Iran today. The story being officially aired in Iran is that Mosaddeq's fall was due to the fact that he had opposed the religious leaders and had grown apart from Kashani. This treatment has as yet not been accorded to Dr. Baqa'i, who stood with Kashani. This historical turnabout is, among other things, based on a letter from Kashani to Mosaddeq dated one day before the 1953 coup, in which the former offers his services to Mosaddeq and warns him about an imminent American-engineered coup (see *Ettela'at*, Tir 18, 1359 and Yann Richard's chapter in this volume). This letter's authenticity is doubted by some. A few months earlier *Ettela'at* published a letter by Kashani begging the shah not to leave Iran. Kashani had very good relations with the shah, and the involvement of some ulama in the Zahedi coup is indicated by the fact that prior to the coup Zahedi found refuge in the house of Ayatollah Bani Sadr. Falsafi, the famous preacher who in 1963 made antigovernment speeches, was also known for his earlier cordial relationship with the court and Zahedi. A picture showing both Falsafi and Zahedi was recently published in the magazine (now suspended) *Bamshad* 2, 23–30 Tir 1358, pp. 48–49. The accompanying article also contains interesting information on Falsafi's role as a loyal servant of the shah.

19. Shahrough Akhavi, *Religion and Politics in Contemporary Iran* (Albany, 1980), pp. 76ff.

fundamentalist religious group, attempted to assassinate the then prime minister Hosain Ala.[20]

From 1955 until 1961 no major differences were manifested between the ulama and the government, although many have noted the growing despotic and totalitarian trend of the shah's government during that period.[21] This did not mean that the ulama agreed with the government's policy during that time. Borujerdi, for example, "although he privately made no effort to conceal his disapproval of some of the regime's policies, he also made it clear that he was in no way prepared to promote disorder. Some of the discontented looked towards Qum for a sign. All that they saw was an adroitly non-committal attitude, adopted with considerable urbanity."[22]

Borujerdi's quietism, the restrictions put on the activities of Kashani, and the government's patronage of Ayatollah Behbehani[23] and his group in Tehran proved helpful in silencing those ulama who may have wished to speak out against the government.[24] Particularly important was Borujerdi's unique position as sole marja'-e taqlid, whom all should follow.

When, however, the cabinet of Manuchehr Eqbal introduced, with the shah's blessing, a land-reform bill to the majles in 1960, relations with the ulama become very strained. In fact, "His [Borujerdi's] opposition to the Shah's program brought about the end of an effective dialogue between the regime and the clergy."[25] When it became clear that the government wanted to introduce the land-reform bill, landlords appealed to Borujerdi and other religious leaders to speak out against this policy, which they said was both unconstitutional and in violation of the shari'a. Borujerdi acceded, and wrote the following letter to Ayatollah Behbehani in February 1960:[26]

In the name of God, the Compassionate, the Merciful
To His Eminence Hojjat al-Islam Behbehani,
I beg to inform Your Eminence that when some time ago rumors were heard

20. P. Avery, *Modern Iran* (London, 1965), p. 461.

21. See R. W. Cottam, *Nationalism in Iran* (Pittsburgh, 1965), p. 288.

22. Avery, *Modern Iran*, p. 481.

23. Ayatollah Mohammad Mosavi Behbehani, the son of Abdollah Behbehani who was one of the leaders of the constitutional movement.

24. It was probably with the Behbehani group in mind that Avery, *Modern Iran*, p. 481, wrote: "Meanwhile in Tehran the divines were feasted on festive days. . . . These feasts were paid for by the government. The robed and turbaned figures who sat down to the good victuals did not look like the fomenters of a revolt." On the Behbehani group see: Algar, "Oppositional Role," p. 224; and Akhavi, *Religion and Politics*, p. 103.

25. Bayne, *Persian Kingship*, p. 48.

26. *Echo Reports*, a weekly publication of the "Echo of Iran," Tehran, 17 February 1962, no. 6 (334), p. 4.

concerning the restriction of ownership (of land) by way of advice and discharge of my duty, I verbally pointed out to His Excellency the Prime Minister the incompatibility of this with the laws of the sacred religion of Islam. The answers I received were not convincing, and at this moment I am receiving numerous letters from various persons and bodies in many towns asking this humble person's views. Since it is improper to hide the divine laws, I have no choice but to answer the people's questions. Although every time I have pointed out something to the authorities it was evident to them that I had been motivated solely by the desire to preserve the religious laws and the interests of the State, I am surprised that in this matter there is every evidence of haste in approving the Bill without deliberation and study and in the absence of His Imperial Majesty. I entreat Your Eminence to inform the two Houses of Parliament in any manner you consider appropriate to refrain from approving (the Bill). I pray to God Almighty for the betterment of the affairs of the Muslims. [23 February 1960]

The same day he received this letter, Ayatollah Behbehani wrote to Sardar Fakher Hekmat, chairman of the majles, saying, "the Land Reform Bill has disturbed public opinion and made all Muslims uneasy. . . . Because the said Bill contains articles which are opposed to the teaching and basis of the sacred religion and the constitution it is surprising . . . that even its debate has been allowed . . . the said Bill is not legal even if it is approved."[27]

In his letter Ayatollah Behbehani referred to two articles of the constitution. Article two stated that no law may be approved by the majles which is contrary to the religion and teaching of Islam. Article fifteen stated: "No owner may be dispossessed of his property except for a legitimate reason."

Both letters had the desired effect on the majority of the majles deputies, who were against the bill anyway. Backed by the highest religious authority, the deputies worked for the amendment of the bill. In this they were successful, as all passages considered offensive by the ulama were deleted, and the resulting law had so many loopholes and exceptions as to be useless as a reform.[28]

Besides this setback, Eqbal's position had already become insecure because of his inability to balance the budget or the balance of payments, and American support for his government was also considered insufficient. What finally clinched his resignation was the rigged elections he organized, which aroused widespread opposition.

On 27 August 1960 Eqbal resigned and was succeeded by Sharif-Emami as prime minister. The shah expressed his dissatisfaction over the elections and urged the new deputies to resign, which was in violation of the

27. Ibid.
28. A. K. S. Lambton, *The Persian Land Reform 1962–1966* (Oxford, 1969), pp. 56ff.

constitution. Sharif-Emami had to organize new elections, and he also had to cope with the effects of an economic depression that had hit Iran. Many merchants went bankrupt, while the purchasing power of the poor was further reduced below its already very low level.[29] New elections were held early in 1961, when nationalist political parties like the National Front and the Iranian Toilers Party were very active. Dr. Baqa'i, with his Guardians of Freedom, worked to expose the rigging of the elections.[30]

The students' strike of January 1961, organized by the National Front, was a sign of the growing restiveness among politically articulate strata of the population. A strike and demonstration by the underpaid teachers, starting on 2 May 1961, led to Sharif-Emami's fall. A teacher was killed by the police, and the strike leaders were arrested.[31]

Under pressure from the United States, the shah appointed Ali Amini, a man of independent means and mind, as premier. Because he had American support and wanted to implement a reform policy, he was acceptable to the shah, who needed United States aid in view of Iran's difficult economic position. Amini agreed to accept the function of prime minister on two conditions: that the shah dissolve the majles and that he grant Amini special powers. The shah agreed to both, although special powers were granted only six months after Amini came to power.

On 6 May 1961 Amini presented his cabinet, which included, among others: Darakhshesh, the leader of the teachers' strike, as minister of education; a former Tudeh Party member, Alamuti, as minister of justice; and Hasan Arsanjani, who as minister of agriculture was to become the personification of land reform during the next two years.[32]

Amini soon ran into trouble with the ulama and the political opposition, especially the National Front. Although the two groups had different reasons, their opposition mainly centered on the demand for free elections. To counter opposition from the ulama, mainly the Behbehani group, Amini worked to improve his relations with rival religious leaders. Borujerdi had died on 30 March 1961, and no single candidate proved strong enough to qualify as his successor as sole marja'-e taqlid. This was not for want of candidates, as many did their best to obtain that position. The most important were Ayatollahs Milani (Mashhad), Khansari (Tehran), Shariatmadari (Qom), and Hakim (Najaf). The shah, by sending a telegram of condolence to Ayatollah Hakim on the occasion of Borujerdi's death, tried to influence the selection of marja'-e taqlid in favor of Hakim. The latter was an Iraqi citizen, residing in Najaf, which would

29. Avery, *Modern Iran*, p. 491; *Iran Almanac 1963* (Tehran, n.d.), pp. 276ff., gives data on the disastrous economic situation of Iran.

30. Dr. Baqa'i, *Dar pishgah-e tarikh; Iran Almanac 1963*, p. 92.

31. *Iran Almanac 1963*, p. 384.

32. Avery, *Modern Iran*, p. 493.

diminish the influence of Qom as a religious center. The shah's support was of no avail, however.[33] Amini, on the occasion of the fortieth day after Borujerdi's death, went to visit the latter's relatives in Qom in order to solicit their support.

On 10 August 1961 Ayatollah Behbehani asked the shah to order new elections. Amini, not to be outdone, visited Behbehani's rival and political opponent Ayatollah Kashani in the hospital. Newspaper photos showed him kissing Kashani's hand. Thus, Amini made it clear that he might seek religious support elsewhere. A few days later Amini visited Imam Reza's shrine in Mashhad, had talks with religious leaders there, and had himself publicized sweeping the courtyard of the shrine.

Although Amini failed to attract the support of the more important religious leaders, he nevertheless silenced part of the religious establishment. Amini underscored his Indian summer with the ulama by appointing for the first time in Iranian constitutional history a deputy minister for religious affairs. He also intimated that restrictions on religious mourning ceremonies would be alleviated and that the sale of alcoholic beverages would be restricted. All this left a good impression on religious circles.[34]

Amini's attempts to improve relations with the political opposition were less successful. Although he had made a deal with the National Front before he became prime minister, contacts soon cooled. In exchange for National Front support, Amini had promised free elections, in which the Front might participate, as well as granting the National Front freedom of action. The National Front never became a regular party but continued to be a combination of several oppositional groups. During the elections for the twentieth majles (1960) it had split; a group under Mehdi Bazargan worked for a boycott of the elections. The majority, however, hoped that by having its leader Allahyar Saleh elected it might expose the misdeeds of the government.

The rapprochement with Amini came to an end when a political demonstration on 21 July 1961 was suppressed by troops, National Front leaders having been arrested on the eve. When these were released, the National Front tried less demonstrative methods by holding a press conference. Troops, however, stopped journalists from reaching Allahyar Saleh, who then issued a communiqué on 20 August 1961.[35]

The National Front, among other things, stated, "The excuse offered by Dr. Amini for the postponement of elections is made even worse by his

33. *Echo Reports*, "Prime Minister Ali Amini and the Clergy," Tehran, 17 August 1962, no. 28 (308).

34. Ibid.

35. *Echo Reports*, "The National Front after 30th Tir 1340," Tehran, 7 September 1961, no. 31.

statement that the majles will stand in his way of reforms and an anticorruption campaign. In his message on Constitution Day—the constitution suppressed by Dr. Amini himself—Dr. Amini claimed that he has been trying to create a favorable atmosphere to start elections on the basis of equality and justice. . . . It is self-evident that a truly representative majles, elected on the basis of equality and justice, will never stand in the way of reforms and anticorruption campaigns. It would, however, stand in the way of dictatorship and the violation of laws by the government. It is this latter reason that has forced Dr. Amini to suppress the constitution and to refuse to carry out its provision." The statement added, "Dr. Amini's government has sent delegations to foreign countries to seek loans in the absence of the majles, although article 25 of the constitution emphasizes that all loans both from internal and external sources are subject to the approval of the majles. . . . In view of our constitution, the National Front warns all internal and foreign sources that any loan given to the government of Iran in the absence of the majles shall not be binding on the Iranian people and shall be considered null and void."[36]

The statement also demanded free elections. The National Front did not remain acquiescent as it had in previous years and, via better organization and more cohesion about its political line, the National Front acted more effectively and with more unity. This resulted in a pamphlet on 27 October 1961 outlining the political objectives of the Front, which had three main aims:[37]

1. to guarantee people's rights in accordance with the Constitution and the UN declaration of Human Rights;
2. to establish a legitimate government elected by a free and popular vote;
3. to adopt an independent foreign policy based on nonalignment.

Amini now accused the National Front of cooperating with the reactionary opposition, including right-wingers such as the SAVAK chief Taimur Bakhtiar, and Sardar Fakher Hekmat, the former chairman of the majles.

On 14 November 1961 Amini announced that the shah had granted him unprecedented executive powers. The next day the National Front announced its opposition to these new powers. Amini then ordered the arrest of the leaders of both right and left oppositional groups. The shah justified the grant of extensive powers by saying they were necessary in order to introduce reforms and amend the election laws.

Opposition to Amini nevertheless grew. He announced the so-called amendment of the land-reform law on 7 January 1962. Since Arsanjani,

---

36. From a clandestinely printed and circulated pamphlet in my possession.
37. Ibid.

minister of agriculture, knew that the opposition would attack the amendment, he stated on 18 January 1962 that the amended law was not against the constitution or religious law: "True, Borujerdi had declared himself to be against the 1960 bill, but the majles had approved it. If the fatva had been a proper one, then all deputies who had voted for it were acting unlawfully as well, since the fatva was binding for them. . . . All we are doing is to enforce it, which under the constitution I am required to do, but we have amended that law. . . . Because it could not be enforced [otherwise]."[38]

Sardar Fakher Hekmat protested Arsanjani's statement in an open letter on 19 January 1962, accusing Arsanjani of distorting the truth. He said that the Eqbal government had presented a bill which was contrary to Islamic law; Borujerdi therefore had spoken out against it. Hekmat had informed the shah of Borujerdi's objections and the shah then ordered Hekmat to see that the bill be amended so that it would be compatible with religious law and the constitution. The bill then was amended by the Agricultural Committee of the majles so that it was in agreement with the religious law. The new text then was approved by Borujerdi.[39]

Meanwhile the political situation worsened, when on 22 January several National Front leaders and some right-wing leaders were arrested. Students of Tehran University who had been on strike since 17 January out of sympathy with their colleagues of the Higher Teachers College protested. The students clashed with the military, which resulted in many wounded and damage to University property.[40]

Ayatollah Behbehani meanwhile deliberated what to do. As Tehran University remained closed and his nephew was under arrest, on 9 February 1962 he invited selected important persons to his house to discuss the political situation.[41] He proposed that he would send the shah a text that they all approved, in which he said that the shah should investigate what deeds had been committed by the authorities "on the pretext of maintaining order," and that the shah should make known his disapproval of these deeds. The text added that "all these atrocities . . . arise from the delay in the opening of the majles and from the lack of freedom for the people, which is unprecedented . . . and which is the subject of strong protests from the entire population. . . . I consider it my

38. See *Echo Reports,* 17 February 1962, p. 5.
39. Ibid.
40. Zonis, *Political Elite,* pp. 72–73.
41. These persons were: Hasan Taqizadeh (ex-president of the senate), Dr. Matin Daftari (former prime minister), Sardar Fakher Hekmat (former speaker of the majles), Abdol Rahman Faramarzi (editor of the *Keyhan* newspaper), Allahyar Saleh (leader of the National Front), Mohammad Soruri (prominent lawyer), Shaikh Baha' ad-Din Nuri (prominent religious leader).

duty to request Your Majesty to instruct the government immediately to begin the process of parliamentary elections. It is certain that honest representatives of the people freely elected without interference from any side will endorse all proper aims, God willing."[42]

The shah, however, told Behbehani that he did not like the tone of this telegram, and that unless it was changed he would not accept it. Behbehani refused to back down, and the telegram was sent back. On 23 February 1962 Arsanjani again attacked the religious circles who opposed land reform as the agitation against the amended law continued.[43] On 18 July 1962 Amini resigned as a result of the growing opposition to his government as well as his inability to balance his budget, for which he blamed the United States government, which had withdrawn its aid to Iran.[44]

On 19 July 1962 Asadollah Alam, a close friend of the shah, was appointed prime minister, and promised early elections to pacify the opposition. He promised to implement the six-point imperial decree issued to the preceding cabinet, which included land reform and a provincial and local council election bill.

The agitation against land reform did not abate. Alam was forced to visit Behbehani and other religious leaders to try to win them over and to assure them that the land-reform bill was not incompatible with Islamic law and the constitution. However, the religious leaders were not convinced and continued their opposition. They had believed that with the fall of Amini the idea would be shelved and were surprised to see Arsanjani staying on as minister of agriculture. The most prominent among the ulama opposing land reform were Ayatollahs Behbehani, Golpaigani, and Khansari (Tehran), Hakim (Najaf), Shaikh Baha ad-Din (Shiraz), and Mar'ashi-Najafi (Mashhad).[45]

42. *Echo Reports*, 17 February 1962, pp. 6–7.

43. *Iran Almanac 1963*, p. 42.

44. Avery, *Modern Iran*, p. 495.

45. *Iran Almanac 1963*, p. 433; *Echo Reports*, "Landlords, Tribal Khans and Clergymen versus the Government," Tehran, 24 November 1962, no. 360, p. 4; according to another Iranian work, B. Jazani, *An Introduction to the Contemporary History of Iran* (London, n.d.), p. 117, "the clergy, almost without exception, opposed the whole land reform project." Jazani, like Akhavi, *Religion and Politics*, p. 92, rightly rejects a simple economic explanation of the ulama's opposition to land reform. For Akhavi "it was simply the first issue over which their general dissatisfaction over the course of events was publicly expressed," while Jazani stressed the fact that the reform measures were "detrimental to the position of the clergy in society" and that therefore, despite inner contradictions, they had to stand against the reforms. "From the very start of land reform, the farm lands distributed were declared by the clergy to be Qabsi (usurped); but, faced with the choice of land and religious decrees, the peasant went for the former. This was the first blow to the position of the clergy" (p. 117). For a view stressing the temporal priority of clerical opposition to a new elections bill, see Azar Tabari in this volume.

Another issue intensifying opposition to the government was woman suffrage. The position of women had already given rise to debate, as modernists had been advocating a more liberal attitude to women's role in society and allowing them the same rights as men. The religious leaders believed that the rights allowed to women in the constitution and Islamic law were completely satisfactory. Giving them equal rights to men would lead to corruption and chaos and to disruption of the very basis of family life in Iran. By doing so the government would act against Islam.[46]

Hence, when on 8 September 1962 the Alam government published the text of a bill on provincial and local council elections which allowed women to vote, the ulama vociferously spoke out against this innovation. There were two other reasons why the bill was opposed by the ulama: it did not clearly specify that voters had to be Muslim, and further, the term Holy Book instead of Holy Qur'an was employed in order to allow non-Muslims to vote.[47]

It was with this bill that Ayatollah Khomeini made his first appearance on the national political scene. Khomeini, like his colleagues, was against woman suffrage and he whipped up public opposition to the bill. His supporters spread rumors that women would be called up for military service and that male civil servants would be replaced by women.[48] The

46. See on this issue, Akhavi, *Religion and Politics,* p. 95; Jazani remarks, "when the regime put forward the secondary aspects of the reform, the enfranchisement of women provided the clergy with the necessary excuse to rouse the masses to move and oppose the regime," *Introduction,* pp. 117–18.

47. *Iran Almanac 1963,* p. 433; for a detailed analysis of this whole issue as seen through the eyes of a member of the religious opposition see: Ali Davvani, *Nahzat-e do maheh-ye ruhaniyan-e Iran* (Qom, 1341). From the copious material presented by Davvani (most of the telegrams exchanged between the ulama and the government as well as the pamphlets and fatvas issued by the ulama on this issue) it is clear that the religious leaders opposed the bill on three grounds: (a) The absence of a qualification for an elector or a candidate for election to be a Muslim; (b) the absence of the obligation to take oath on the Qur'an; and (c) woman suffrage. The case presented by Davvani and the religious leaders appears to be open to criticism. Art. 7 (section 3) of the Electoral Law (1909) states that candidates for election should be Muslims "unless they represent the Christian, Zoroastrian, or Jewish communities, in which case they must be sound in their respective beliefs." Religion as a qualification for voters was not mentioned (art. 4). The Fundamental Law of 1906 (art. 11) requires that members of the majles take oath on the Qur'an, but this did not apply to non-Muslim members of the majles. Although the election laws (of 1906 and 1909) excluded women from voting and from being elected it is not stated anywhere that the election laws, which were explicitly only applicable to the election of the majles and the senate, had to be applied to provincial and local councils. The fact that women vote in the Islamic Republic of Iran raises doubts about the anti-Islamic nature of the government's proposal for women's franchise.

48. *Echo Reports,* "The Case of Mr. Khomeini," 18 November 1964, no. 457, p. 2; Khomeini himself also contributed to the credibility of these rumors. He said that eighteen-year-old girls had been taken by force to the barracks, which in his eyes were but whorehouses; see Sayyed Hamid Ruhani, *Barrasi va tahlili az nahzat-i Imam Khomaini,* 4th ed. (Qom, 1358/1979), pp. 316, 319–24.

ulama, now really aroused, put enormous pressure on the government. Several fatvas and opinions were issued by the ulama against land reform and woman suffrage.

Ayatollah Khansari declared:

The purpose of this gathering . . . is to respond to cables and letters from Tehran and other parts of the country requesting that the attention of the government be drawn to the protection of the laws and the sacred teachings of Islam. It is therefore a source of regret that persons who by virtue of religion . . . hold office in this land should pass decrees changing the teachings of Islam and undermining it under the guise of land reforms, or go against the religion by allowing women to participate in social affairs. I hereby declare my views on:

1. The dispossession of people. It is a capital sin to dispossess people of their property through forcible seizure or decrees; the dire consequences of such action will not be confined to the individual, but will affect the general public. I further proclaim that no prayers or ablutions held on such lands will be acceptable.

2. Women's interference in social matters. Since this will involve women in corruption and is against the will of God it is prohibited by Islam and must be stopped.[49]

Khomeini's views on women's voting we know from cables that he sent to the shah and Prime Minister Alam. To the latter he said:

Pursuant to my previous cable I beg to inform you that you pay no heed to the advice of the ulama and that you think that you are able to act against the Holy Qoran, the Constitution, and the general feeling of the population. The ulama advised you that your illegal bill is contrary to Islamic Law, the Constitution, and the laws of the Majles. The ulama made it public that women's franchise and the abrogation of the condition to be a Muslim to be allowed to elect or to be elected is contrary to Islam and the Constitution. If you think that you can replace the Holy Qoran by the Zoroastrians' Avesta, the Bible and by some misguided books, you are mistaken. If you think that you may weaken the Constitution, which is the security of the Country's sovereignty and independence, with your illegal bill, then you are wrong.[50]

As a result of this wide protest, Alam wrote a letter to Behbehani assuring him that the government would not press the issue of woman suffrage and would shelve the local council election bill until after majles elections, which happened on 27 November 1962. On 16 December the government announced the withdrawal of voting rights for women.[51]

49. *Echo Reports*, 24 November 1962, no. 360, "Landlords, Tribal Khans and Clergymen versus the Government," p. 6.

50. Ibid., p. 7; the abridged translation of Khomeini's cable is from the text published in Davvani, *Nahzat*.

51. *Iran Almanac 1963*, pp. 48, 410; according to Ahmad Ashraf, "Iran: Imperialism,

Where land reform was concerned, the government tried to reassure the majority. During a meeting with smallholders, Arsanjani assured his audience they had nothing to worry about. Land reform was aimed at breaking the power of the big landlords only. He also issued a statement ordering peasants to pay the landlord's share on pain of punishment. This government action may have been in response to Ayatollah Milani's complaint to the shah that petty landowners would be hurt by land reform.[52] These steps by the government were generally considered a defeat for it.

Surprisingly, Alam's policy toward the National Front was more liberal than Amini's. The Front was shaken by the setbacks suffered under Amini and was rather inactive during the last months of Amini's tenure of office. Alam, in order to win the nationalists to his cause, released all the

Class and Modernization from Above," Ph.D. dissertation, New School for Social Research, New York, 1971, the following written protest messages were sent to the shah in November 1962: telegrams from Ayatollahs Shariatmadari and Golpaigani; a declaration of 132 ulama; a declaration of 26 ulama of Tehran; a declaration of religious associations of Mashhad and a letter of Ayatollah Milani; and a declaration of 10 ulama of Qom. For a more detailed view of the activities by the religious circles see Davvani, *Nahzat*.

52. *Iran Almanac 1963*, pp. 388ff.; I do not wish to convey the impression that there were no differences among the ulama. Akhavi, *Religion and Politics*, p. 93, warns that "the clergy did not react as a monolithic force." It is, however, difficult to distinguish factions among the ulama. Akhavi, ibid., pp. 100ff., identifies four different groupings, but these differ completely from a similar analytical exercise made by Ashraf, "Iran: Imperialism," pp. 220–26, suggesting the existence of two groupings, one speaking as landowners, the other speaking for the bazaaris. In the first faction Ashraf lists Ayatollahs Borujerdi, Behbehani, Khansari, Tonakabuni, and Amoli. In the second, more progressive group, he lists the Ayatollahs Khomeini, Milani, and Shariatmadari. The latter two were classed by Akhavi among the conservatives! On 2 February 1963 Milani wrote to Alam that land reform would be detrimental to petty landowners; see Fischer, *Iran*, p. 179. A third classification of the ulama is given by Dr. Baqa'i in a pamphlet. He distinguishes three groups. The first and largest is apolitical and sticks to religious matters. The second and smallest group is the real political leaders who fight both for Islam and the people. Baqa'i states that very few fall in this category and, in recent times he knew only two who qualified, Kashani and Khomeini. The third, small group consists of leaders who use religion for their own parochial ends. Baqa'i, without naming them, says that there are three in this category, *Dar pishgah-e tarikh*, pp. 397–98. So far the only ayatollahs known to me who clearly did not oppose land reform were Shariatmadari, Ruhani (see Cottam, *Nationalism*, p. 308, n. 13), and Taleqani (see Akhavi, *Religion and Politics*, p. 93). Khomeini's position is less clear. I have not found any statement in which he opposed land reform, although he did oppose the shah's reform policy. This probably is the reason why E. A. Doroshenko, *Shi'itskoe dukhovenstvo v sovremennom Irane* (Moscow, 1975), p. 109, states that Khomeini was against land reform. One of his biographers, Ruhani, *Barrasi*, p. 170, n. 1, states that he does not know of any religious leader who opposed land reform. He mentions the fact that Arsanjani sent a telegram to Shariatmadari, Golpaigani, and Najafi in Esfand 1340 to congratulate them with *'id-i fitr* and to thank them for their support of land reform. In view of the conflicting evidence, this point needs more research.

National Front leaders who had been in jail since February 1962. If he expected a positive reaction from the nationalists, he must have been disappointed, since none came. Rather, students linked with the National Front staged demonstrations against Alam when he visited Tabriz in September 1962.

This did not change Alam's position with regard to the Front, and he even allowed foreign journalists to interview Dr. Mosaddeq. The National Front meanwhile reorganized and prepared for a national congress. It demanded free elections as required by the constitution. Alam then unexpectedly visited Allahyar Saleh, the unofficial leader of the National Front. Alam expressed his wish that the National Front would support his government and advise it how to deal with current economic difficulties. He even offered the Front a few places in his cabinet.

The National Front was willing to cooperate with Alam on three conditions:

1. that the constitution be observed and respected, and that its principles guaranteeing a limited constitutional monarchy be sincerely adhered to;
2. that elections be held immediately and in accordance with the existing law;
3. that corruption be fought and reforms carried out, on the basis of legal liberties.

Alam did not wish to discuss the shah's powers, because he considered such a discussion neither realistic nor practical. The National Front leaders stressed, however, that the shah should reign instead of rule; otherwise he was acting in flagrant violation of the constitution. Continuing to rule without a majles was dictatorial and despotic, and would only estrange the people from the shah and the monarchy.[53]

In view of basic differences, the two sides could not continue discussions. The National Front issued a statement on 28 November 1962 in which it outlined its position with regard to the talks and the government in very strong critical words. Interestingly, the statement also contained a mild and indirect criticism of the views aired by religious leaders, such as those referred to above. The Front stated, "Despotic excesses have reached an extent that has forced the usually tolerant clerical class, which constitutes one of the moral foundations of the country, to show signs of deep unrest, thus causing widespread public anxiety. The National Front hopes that malicious people do not publish material in their name which might be considered as reactionary in the present day world, or might be interpreted as opposition to the benefit of the people."[54] This part of the

---

53. Zonis, *Political Elite*, pp. 73ff.; Cottam, *Nationalism*, pp. 305–06.
54. From a clandestinely printed and circulated pamphlet.

statement refers to clerical positions with regard to land reform and woman suffrage, both of which were advocated by the Front.

Since Alam had failed to obtain the support of the National Front and had backed down on the question of woman suffrage, the religious opposition believed that they might block the government's program. Ayatollah Behbehani wrote Alam a letter in which he said: "We have been and still are against land reform. We do not wish to discuss it, because land reform has reached a stage from where its reversal is impossible, but we cannot remain silent about vaqf property." Alam then paid a visit to Behbehani and later confirmed the contents of their talks by a letter in which he stated that the distribution of religious endowments (vaqf) was not against Islamic law or contrary to the will of the endower. The government at the same time accused some religious leaders of misappropriation of the vaqf property administered by them.[55]

Because of the continuing opposition of religious leaders as well as the nationalist middle class, the shah decided to outmaneuver them by calling for a national referendum to demonstrate that the Iranian people favored the reforms. The National Front, other political parties, and religious leaders ordered their followers to boycott the referendum. On 23 January 1963 the police broke up a meeting in Tehran of some religious leaders, landlords, and bazaaris who allegedly were discussing what steps might be taken against the referendum. Alam accused the landlords of plotting against the government, and at the same time referred to "two religious leaders" (Ayatollahs Khomeini and Qomi) who had ordered the boycott of the referendum. The shah on that same day declared in Qom during a land-distribution ceremony that the ulama were "black reactionaries."[56]

On the eve of the referendum, 25 January 1963, Khomeini and other religious leaders were taken into custody, from which they were soon released. The success of the referendum did not bring political disturbances to a halt, however. Students of Tehran University staged a demonstration on 2 February 1963 against the government.

On 27 February 1963 the shah announced that the government would grant women the right to vote. This statement resulted in agitation by the religious leaders, who ordered their followers to close the bazaars in all important towns, and organized demonstrations. During the unrest that followed in several cities clashes occurred between the police and demonstrators. Many posters denouncing the right of women to vote were placed on buildings in Qom. The unrest finally led to an attack by government forces on 23 March 1963 on the Faiziyeh theological school in

55. *Iran Almanac 1963*, pp. 433, 394–95.

56. Ibid., p. 433; *Echo Reports*, "Religious Demonstrations and Clashes," 8 June 1963, no. 386, p. 4.

Qom. Many students had gathered there to commemorate the death of Imam Ja'far. During the sermon delivered by Hajji Ansari, opposing women's franchise, government agents tried to create disturbances by protesting his views. Many were wounded in the shooting which followed.

The government thereafter continued to attack the ulama. During a speech in Mashhad on 1 April 1963, the shah called them "a hindrance to the progress of the country." The newspapers followed suit and depicted the ulama as reactionaries who unnecessarily brought the people of Iran into conflict with Islam. They advised the ulama to stay out of politics, which was outside the pale of religion.[57]

The ulama replied by printing and secretly distributing pamphlets attacking the government and the shah. The most active among the ulama appealed to their colleagues to use the occasion of Moharram (the month of mourning) to air their views on government policies. These antigovernment activities started in late May. The government expected trouble and did not allow religious processions in some areas. It did not, however, forbid them altogether, in order not to provoke the religious opposition during an inflammable period. In their pamphlets the ulama stressed the government's interference with freedom of religion. Ayatollahs like Shariatmadari and Mar'ashi Najafi criticized the government for attacking the Faiziyeh theological school, for preventing people from attending mosque services, and for lacking respect for religion and its representatives, the ulama. I have not found writings suggesting the overthrow of the shah's regime or demanding structural socioeconomic and political changes. As noted, the National Front advised the ulama to show moderation regarding the proposed reform program. The National Front took the line: "Land reform, yes! The shah's dictatorship, no!" but this line was not adopted by the ulama, who preferred to act on their own for their own objectives.[58] An important letter by Ayatollah Milani (below) mentions corruption and suppression of the people, but these were not his main reasons for opposing the shah's regime.

There was unrest in several major cities. On 3 June 1963 a policeman was killed in Mashhad when he tried to assist two plainclothesmen in arresting a man who was reading aloud a letter from Ayatollah Milani to Ayatollah Khomeini that was posted on a wall near the Gauhar Shah Mosque. When the police tried to remove the letter, the crowd attacked them and a policeman was killed. This incident was the immediate cause of the so-called Moharram riots in all major cities.

57. *Iran Almanac 1963*, pp. 433–34.
58. Based on clandestinely printed and circulated pamphlets in my possession. Naturally, the religious opposition accused the National Front of noncooperation and even of opposing the religious leaders; see Ruhani, *Barrasi*.

The letter in question was very inflammatory, and had been distributed clandestinely in many towns. It stated:

I have no news and I am worried about the fate of the Qom theological students who were injured during the March demonstrations and who have been thrown out of hospitals on the orders of the security organization. . . . As stated, the future looks dark and grim. The ruling body . . . may even increase the number of injured persons to such a number that they will fill and overflow the hospitals. You are aware: that at present our religious and national interests are threatened and violated by the corrupt ruling body. . . . It would be strange for a Muslim to allow himself to remain silent under these circumstances. We have tolerated the Gengiz-type attack on the sacred grounds of the Qom theological school, we have tolerated jailing, torture, and persecution of our national and religious men. We have tolerated the attack on our universities and other seats of learning of the people. We have condoned the suppression of every individual and public right and freedom, we ignored graft, corruption, decadence, and betrayal. . . . But how can we tolerate the disgrace of having our Islamic country turned into a base for Israel and Zionism? It is my, and Your Grace's duty, to resist! . . . In view of the heavy censorship of all publications . . . all honorable preachers much use the occasion of the Moharram mourning days to enlighten the Muslims on the subject. . . . The people must be told that the ruling body no longer insists that a judge must be a Muslim as it makes any debauched person or communist a judge. The people must be told of how the path has been opened in Iran for agents and spies of Israel.[59]

That same day Ayatollah Khomeini delivered in Qom a violent speech against the shah and his government. He began by asking why it was that Yazid had acted so brutally and inhumanly against Imam Husain, and replied that this was because Yazid had opposed the rights of the prophet's family. He then continued to ask why it is that the tyrannical government of Iran opposed the ulama, why it had ordered the attack on the Faiziyeh school; what had the innocent sayyed who was killed during that attack done to the government? Khomeini told his audience that this was because the government opposed the foundations of Islam and its ulama, because it did not want this moral foundation to exist. He then substituted "Israel" for "government" and harped on this subject. Khomeini told his audience that Israel was against the Qur'an, against Islam, and did not want science to hold its own in Iran, and therefore it had ordered the attack on the Faiziyeh school: "Israel wants to take our economy in its clutches. Israel wants to destroy our trade and agriculture. Israel wants to destroy that which stands between them and domination. This buffer is formed by the ulama who have to be broken; this buffer is the Faiziyeh school and other theological schools, which have to be destroyed; the theological students may be the future buffer and they

59. *Echo Reports,* "Tehran Riot Trials," 26 August 1963, no. 397, pp. 1–2.

therefore have to be killed. In this way Israel gets what it wants, and in this way the government of Iran threatens us with contempt to achieve its base wishes."

Khomeini then spoke about harassment by government agents who yelled at the ulama and students that they were parasites. He asked his audience who were the real parasites: men like Hajj Shaikh Abdol Karim, whose family when he died did not even have money to buy their supper, or Borujerdi, who on his death was 60,000 tomans in debt? No, the real parasites were those who were filling foreign banks with their ill-gotten gains and who build big palaces. It was up to the nation to decide who were the real parasites.

Khomeini then reminded his audience that those old enough to remember knew that the people were glad when in 1941 the Allies attacked Iran, because Reza Shah left. "I do not want you to go like your father; my advice to you is heed the ulama, listen to them, they want the welfare of the country, do not listen to Israel, you do not need Israel." He finally asked his audience whether Islam was not in danger, because the SAVAK told the ulama not to discuss three subjects: not to say bad things about the shah, not to attack Israel, and not to say that Islam was in danger.[60]

Similar attacks were delivered by other religious leaders and preachers in other cities and towns of Iran. The next day, 4 June 1963 or the tenth of Moharram, the anniversary of the martyrdom of Imam Husain, Khomeini was arrested by the security organization shortly before dawn, as was his colleague Ayatollah Qomi. The excuse for this arrest was their alleged part in planning for disturbances that day. Whatever the truth of this, disturbances started that same day. On hearing the news of the two ayatollahs' arrest, the mourning processions changed into antigovernment demonstrations. There followed some days of clashes between demonstrators and troops and police. The latter had received orders to shoot to kill on 5 June. Many people lost their lives during these clashes, and many more were wounded, but disturbances continued until 8 June. Martial law was proclaimed in Tehran and Shiraz, which saw the worst rioting.

The government accused the religious leaders of having misused their influence and of having received financial support from an unnamed foreign government. Alam accused the religious leaders of being reactionary and of opposing land reform and woman suffrage.

During the trial that followed the Moharram riots, those accused of organizing the demonstrations were sentenced to death. No reference was made to the alleged role of the ulama in organizing the disturbances or of money received from a foreign power. "Following an understanding that

60. Anonymous, *Zendeginameh-ye Imam Khomeini*, vol. 2 (Qom, n.d.), pp. 38–43 (this book contains many of Khomeini's speeches and was published by the Faiziyeh theological school).

has been reached between the security authorities and Their Eminences Ayatollahs Khomeini, Qomi, and Mahallati that they will not interfere in political matters, and since this understanding has given the assurance that the gentlemen will not act against the security or interests of the state, these gentlemen have been moved to private houses."[61]

Soon after Khomeini's release and transfer to a villa in Tehran, a clandestine pamphlet attributed to Khomeini denied such an understanding with SAVAK. Khomeini did not acknowledge an understanding with a state that he considered un-Islamic. Khomeini stayed for two months in the Tehran villa and then was given more freedom. However, he was arrested again in his house on the eve of the elections in October 1963, after he had ordered their boycott. He remained under house arrest in Tehran until May 1964, when the new prime minister, Mansur, ordered his release. This appears to have been made possible by a new understanding with the SAVAK that he would stay out of politics.

However, Khomeini did not honor the understanding, if it existed. He continued his antigovernment activities, and acquired a more progressive public image by allowing his followers to listen to the radio, to see television, to deposit money in government banks, and by reconsidering his opposition to woman suffrage. Khomeini further appealed to the opposition forces to form a united front against government controls in economic life and to establish freedom of trade and business.[62]

Another opportunity for attacks on government policy was provided by the bill for diplomatic immunity and privileges for United States military personnel and the bill seeking a $200 million United States loan for the purchase of military equipment. The bills were approved by the majles on 13 and 25 October 1964.[63] The next day, Khomeini strongly attacked the

61. See note 59; Algar, "Oppositional Role," pp. 247–49; *Zendeginameh-ye Imam Khomeini*, pp. 50–80, 90.

62. See note 48; at that time he was described in this source as follows: "He is now considered one of the most famous and influential of Shi'a ulama of Qom, judging by the large number of aspirants learning theology from him and the amount of donations he receives from his followers. It is reported that his followers in Iran and Pakistan contribute about one million rials a month to him to spend for religious purposes as he sees fit. Most of the contributions go towards the upkeep of his religious school. Each theological student receives a loaf of bread for himself and each member of his family plus a monthly cash allowance."

63. Both bills had already been presented to the majles at the end of 1963, but the discussion on the diplomatic status of United States personnel was postponed till the very end, and then it was only discussed in a closed session of the majles and the senate. For a detailed discussion of this issue see Dr. Baqa'i's pamphlet "Hast ya nist?" 1 Aban 1343, which was republished in *Kapitulasiyun, gonahi ke Hoveida be an e'teraf kard*, Kerman 1358/1979. It is of interest that Baqa'i's pamphlet, published three days prior to Khomeini's speech, did not provoke a reaction either from the public or from the government (see also note 64).

government in a speech and stated that the approval of the bills had been tantamount to treason. Moreover, Khomeini tried to arouse his audience to oppose the government. An abbreviated version of this speech was printed and circulated clandestinely (see the appendix to this chapter). The government then accused him of having broken his understanding with the government. On 4 November 1964 SAVAK issued a statement: "Since, according to reliable information and sufficient evidence, Mr. Khomeini's attitude and provocations have been considered contrary to the interest of the state, and to the security, independence, and territorial integrity of the state, he has been exiled from Iran effective 4 November 1964."

Khomeini was sent by special aircraft to Turkey. The authorities at first declined to give any information as to his whereabouts. An attempt by some of his followers to close down the bazaar one week later failed to get significant support, which indicated how effective SAVAK had become. It also indicated that the opposition was licking its wounds and did not have the same appeal as in 1963.[64]

Conclusions

We have seen that the ulama formed part of Iran's traditional power elite. The religious system served in part to preserve the existing order by appeals to tradition and absolute values. Modernization and foreign (non-Muslim) penetration encroached upon the influence of the religious class in Iranian society. The ulama's opposition to Western encroachments and governments that promoted them was largely aimed against change and at a return to traditional values and order. In some cases the ulama also gave voice to popular grievances, particularly those of the bazaar classes, to whom they were tied. This opposition did not change during the twentieth century. By 1953 the ulama largely supported the shah against Mosaddeq, who promised fundamental changes in Iranian society. In the 1950s the ulama only opposed the government on issues relating to foreign policy. Between state and ulama good relations existed, which only became problematic when the government wanted to introduce land reform. Then the ulama began to agitate against the government. Their recorded words were not aimed primarily against the growing dictatorial nature of the regime, as were those of the political opposition. In 1962 agitation by the ulama increased when the government wanted to give women the vote. When the government attacked the ulama directly and used physical force

---

64. See note 48; Zonis, *Political Elite,* pp. 45–46; for a translation of this important speech see appendix to this chapter. Algar wrongly assumed that this speech was given in 1963, Algar, "Oppositional Role," pp. 246–47; for the Persian version of this speech see Ruhani, *Barrasi.*

against them, the latter directly challenged the government. However, even then the ulama continued to be restricted in their aims. The ulama's failure to combine their efforts with those of the political opposition also suggests that their position was not aimed at radical change. Although it is too early to say, I have the impression that the essence of the 1977–79 events did not basically differ from those of 1962–64. The main difference now appears to be that all opposition forces worked together until power changed hands, because of a parallelism of interests. Apparently the lesson of 1963 was not lost upon them.

In conclusion, I reiterate that the oppositional role of the ulama was limited in its objectives. The ulama did not demand or agitate for a structural change of society, which was characterized by exploitation and oppression of the majority of the population. The ulama were reformers of a nonsecular type rather than social revolutionaries.

Although most of the ulama have been socially conservative, they nevertheless were effective in the overthrow of the shah's regime in 1979. This was possible largely because of cooperation with the political opposition, who aimed at destroying the established regime. The ulama's failure to form a united front with the political opposition in 1963 was in part the result of both sides' perceiving their incompatibility, which was not perceived in 1978–79.

Appendix: Khomeini's Statement of 27 October 1964

Do the Iranian people know what has been going on in the majles over the past few days? Do you know of the crime that has been committed without the knowledge of the people and in a clandestine way? Do you know that the majles, acting on behest of the government, has signed away the proof of the slavery of the Iranian nation? It has given the United States proof of savagery of the Iranian people. The government has obliterated all our Islamic and national pride; it gave the lie to all the boasts and claims of the government leaders in the past few years; it relegated Iran to the level of the lowest and most backward of the countries of the world. It insulted the Iranian army, its officers and noncommissioned officers; it held in contempt the Iranian judiciary. Acting on the proposal of the present government, the majles approved, within a few hours of secret talks without the knowledge of the Iranian people, the most disgraceful decree passed by its predecessor, thus placing the Iranian people under American bondage.

Now, all American military and nonmilitary advisers, with their families and domestic servants, are free to commit any crime or act of treason they wish without the Iranian police so much as to arrest them. Why? Because America is the land of the dollar and because the Iranian government needs dollars! According to this shameful vote (of the majles) if an American adviser or if a domestic servant of the American advisers henceforth insults a respected leader of the nation, or an honorable citizen, or even a senior government official; if they commit any act of treason, the police will not have the right to arrest them, nor will an Iranian court have the right to try them. But on the other hand if disrespect is shown to even a dog owned by the Americans, then the police must take action and the court must try the case.

Today, when colonial territories are bravely freeing the bonds that have chained them, the so-called progressive majles and those who boast of a civilization of two thousand and five hundred years and of equality with the most advanced countries, vote for the most shameful and offending decrees of ill-reputed governments, and defend the decrees of such governments. I am informed by certain sources that similar legislation was proposed to the governments of Pakistan, Indonesia, Turkey, and West Germany, but none of them would tolerate such an enslaving proposal. It is only the Iranian government that plays with the honorable and Islamic reputation of its people in this way.

The ulama and religious leaders maintain that the bayonet must not interfere with matters of destiny of the country; that the members of Parliament must truly represent the people; that the government must have a broad and popular base; that the suppression of the press should end and that it should no longer be supervised by various (police) agencies; that the people should not be deprived of their freedom. They have demanded all this so that the people would not be subjected to such indignities. The members of Parliament are opposed to such documents of our slavery, and yet none of them raised a voice against the bills, except for two or three deputies who mildly expressed their concern and resumed their seats in silence. Why? Because these deputies have no claim on public support, because they are puppets and therefore dare not oppose. They can be ousted with a single hint, they can be sent to jail.

Do the Iranian people know that the armed forces officers no longer have to take an oath by the Holy Qur'an, that the new phrase is "By the Book in which I Believe"? This is the very danger to which I have repeatedly referred—a danger for the Holy Qur'an, a threat to our beloved Islam, a threat to the Islamic country and to our independence. I wonder what harm has the oppressive establishment suffered in the hands of the Qur'an that it should in this way reject it and Islam with such persistence. Had the government embraced the Qur'an and Islam, no foreigner would have dared to demand our proof of slavery, the trampling upon our national and Islamic heritage. The separation of the government from the people and the lack of popular backing for the government inevitably lead to such calamities. I therefore proclaim that this disgraceful vote of the majles is contrary to Islam and the Qur'an and, therefore, illegal. I further proclaim that the vote was contrary to the wish of the Islamic nation of Iran, that the members of Parliament are not the true representatives of the Iranian people, but representatives of the bayonet and therefore their votes are worthless for the nation, Islam, and the Qur'an. If the aliens decide to abuse this vote, it will be the end of the Iranian nation. The world should know that all the problems besetting Iran and other Islamic nations are the doings of the aliens of the United States. The Muslim nations hate aliens in general and Americans in particular because they attribute all their misfortunes to the improper interference of these foreign governments.

It is the aliens who plunder our rich underground resources; it is the British who have been cheaply taking, for years, our black gold. It was the aliens who occupied our country and who, without any cause or provocation, attacked us from three directions; who killed our soldiers. Until yesteryear the Islamic nations were enslaved by the British and their lackeys, today they are in the clutches of America and its agents. It is America which supports Israel and its sympathizers. It is America which gives strength to Israel to make refugees of the Arabs. It is America which directly or indirectly imposes "deputies" on the Iranian people. It is America which considers Islam and the Holy Qur'an harmful to itself and which tries to remove them. It is America that considers the clergymen as thorns in the flesh of colonialism and feels it necessary to jail, torture, and insult them. It is America that brings pressure to bear on the Iranian government and majles to approve such a disgraceful decree, which insults all our Islamic and national pride. It is America which treats the Islamic nation as worse than savages.

It is up to the Iranian people to break this chain. It is up to the Iranian army not to allow such disgraceful happenings in Iran. It is up to them to demand in every possible way that their superiors tear up this proof of our colonization, to overthrow this government, to oust from the majles all those deputies who voted for this shameful bill. It is up to the Iranian people to demand of their religious leaders to break their silence and to take action in this regard. It is up to the ulama to ask all Islamic bodies not to condone this matter by their silence. It is up to the teachers in theological schools to demand action from the ulama. It is up to the theological students to demand of their teachers not to ignore the matter. It is up to the Muslim people to demand of their preachers to inform all those who may not be aware of the issue. It is up to our preachers to use their strong logic and arguments and to protest against this disgraceful act, to awaken the Iranian people. It is up to university professors to inform the youths of what has been going on behind the scene. It is up to the university students to object strongly to this shameful act and to inform the outside world of the opposition of the people by their orderly demonstration of this opposition. It is up to the students in foreign countries not to remain silent over a vital affair which affects the prestige and integrity of the religion and nation. It is up to the leaders of Islamic governments to let the world hear our shouts of protest, and to broadcast the complaints of this unfortunate nation from their free facilities. It is up to the ulama and preachers in other Islamic nations to let out a flood of protests capable of washing away the stigma on the face of the Islamic brethren in Iran. It is up to all the Iranian people to overcome their minor and ephemeral differences and to work for their independence and freedom from slavery. It is up to the honorable statesmen to inform us of what goes on behind the scenes in the majles. It is up to the political parties to agree on common action in this matter.

The aim of the ulama and preachers, no matter where they are, is the same—to uphold the principles of Islam and the Qur'an, and to support the Muslims. There are no differences among the ulama, the guardians of Islam, in this regard. Even if there may be some differences on other matters, they are trivial and should not preclude the possibility of unanimity of view. Government agencies are mistaken in their belief that their poisonous utterances can divert us from our sacred objective, or if they think that they can achieve their ends through ignorant fanatics. I, a humble servant of the great ulama and of the Iranian nation, am willing to bow to other ulama in time of national emergency, and even to the most humble of the people, in order to uphold the great principles of Islam. Therefore, it is incumbent upon the fanatical youths and novice students of theology to withhold their tongue and pen and to refrain from anything that might lead to discord. The ulama and religious leaders are thinking of general reforms in order to put an end to chaos and disorder, if the government lets us think and gives us an opportunity to embark upon internal purges and reforms. But it is this type of problem raised by the government that deprives us of the opportunity to attend to all-embracing reforms and purges. The danger that is felt to be threatening Islam and the Holy Qur'an does not leave us time to think of other matters. This issue is so important that it has overshadowed our own particular problems.

Do the Islamic people of Iran know that at this very moment many ulama, preachers, theological students, and many other innocent Muslims are in jail; that they have been in detention for a long time contrary to all laws and without trial? There is absolutely no recourse for them against such medieval practices. All this came in the wake of the massacre of 4 and 5 June of last year, which left a deep wound in the heart of the nation. Instead of thinking of ways of improving the economy, to prevent the bankruptcy of the traders, to think of bread and water for the destitute during the winter months ahead, of finding employment for the unemployed youth, the ruling clique is bent upon destructive measures referred to above and upon such measures contributing to moral corruption as the employment of women teachers for boys' high schools and men teachers for girls' high schools, upon insisting on employing women in government offices to spread corruption.

Today, the Iranian economy is controlled by America and Israel. The Iranian market has been taken out of the hands of the Iranians and Muslims. The dust of bankruptcy and poverty has settled on the faces of the businessmen and farmers. The gentlemen's reforms have created black markets for America and Israel. There is no redress for the Iranian people. I am deeply concerned about the condition of the poor next winter, as I expect many to die, God forbid, from cold and starvation. The people should think of the poor and take action now in order to prevent the atrocities of last winter. The ulama should appeal for public contributions for this purpose. [The End.]

RECENT RELIGIO-POLITICAL LEADERS

CHAPTER SIX

Ayatollah Kashani: Precursor of the Islamic Republic?

YANN RICHARD
Translated by Nikki R. Keddie

The Iranian revolution startled Western observers, although some might have been fascinated by the breadth of the popular movement and its search for a moral in public affairs, or enthusiastic over its antidictatorial and anti-imperialist aspect. Westerners could hardly understand the disdain of the triumphant Iranian revolution for the values of the Western political tradition: democracy, the rights of man, the liberation of the individual, of women, or of mores.

For its part, the Islamic revolution has continued to evolve according to its own logic; limits on freedom of speech, armed repression in Kurdistan and among the Turkomans, and directed referenda are among the more negative aspects of a new political philosophy, which has also allowed the achievement of a certain national unity and laid some bases for a policy of independence and for a more just social system. This philosophy is crowned by the principle of *velayat-e faqih* (the power of the "jurist-theologian"), expressed in section 8 of the new constitution. Its first systematic formulation was in a course of Ayatollah Khomeini at Najaf on "Islamic government," which was published in the 1970s; it passed unnoticed at the time, outside of some Shi'i religious circles.

Unable to deny their surprise at events as strange as the "Islamic revolution," Iranologists have set to work to try to explain it: socioeconomic, geopolitical, strategic, cultural, and other causes are being discussed. Several studies have shed light on problems that had been masked

The research for this paper was done during a stay at the Institut Français d'Iranologie in Tehran. I wish to thank for their help the *Ayat-e ezam*s Abol Fazl and Reza Zanjani; also Mozaffar Baqa'i Kermani, Mehdi Bazargan, and Hosain Makki, who witnessed some of the events discussed; and Mohammad Hasan Faqfuri (Faghfoory), Mahmud Kashani, and Mohsen Mirza'i, who helped me a great deal in my research.

101

by the superficial glitter of the shah's success. The extraordinary social and ideological machinery of Iranian Shi'ism has been described, especially in the basic works of S. Akhavi and M. Fischer.[1] There are, on the other hand, a few Western specialists on Shi'ism who give exegetical lessons trying to prove that the ulama have no right to succeed to the imamate, though in practice these lessons came too late.

Here we will deal not so much with theory as with history. Recourse to modern Iranian history may give us some lines of explanation of the political forms chosen by Iranian revolutionaries. The ideological statements of the Islamic Republic's cadres make reference to past experiences. To mention some model figures who served as beacons to Khomeini's partisans: Mirza Shirazi and his opposition to Naser ad-Din Shah in the Tobacco Protest of 1891; Shaikh Fazlollah Nuri, who opposed the "pro-Western and anti-Islamic" constitutional Revolution of 1906, was executed in 1909; Sayyed Hasan Modarres, a religious opponent of Reza Shah, exiled and killed in 1936; Dr. Mosaddeq and his struggle against imperialism.

This brief enumeration gives an idea of a political tradition whose culmination we see today. Ending it with Mosaddeq involves a paradox, since this great fighter for oil nationalization is decried by today's majority party in the Islamic republic. The almost total recent absence of the National Front from the political scene was, until the spring of 1981, balanced by the position of President Bani Sadr, who appeared in some respects like a new Mosaddeq. The political struggle between Bani Sadr and Ayatollah Mohammad Beheshti, who led the Islamic Republican Party until his death in June 1981, seemed to continue, with a different balance of forces, the struggle between the two major leaders of the early 1950s: Mosaddeq and Ayatollah Kashani.

New Views on Kashani

Ayatollah Kashani's importance for today's IRP, especially because of Kashani's ideological struggle against the Mosaddeqists, is clear from a reading of the Iranian press and from certain important publications discussed below. The current polemical position may be summarized as follows: Mosaddeq, overthrown by the coup d'état of 28 Mordad 1332/19 August 1953, kept, for the nationalist opponents of the shah's regime, a martyr's halo. His legend was kept alive by the intellectual and bourgeois opposition, whereas Kashani, who aided in the fall of this nationalist rival, thus losing his political prestige, had until recently no defender

1. S. Akhavi, *Religion and Politics in Contemporary Iran* (Albany: State University of New York Press, 1980); and M. Fischer, *Iran: From Religious Dispute to Revolution* (Cambridge: Harvard University Press, 1980).

except ulama for whom the last twenty-five years of the monarchy were disastrous in every way, and who had little chance to give coherent expression to their viewpoint. Previously it was said that Kashani betrayed Mosaddeq and helped General Zahedi in his coup d'état out of fear of the communists, but now one hears praises of Kashani, who is credited with achieving the nationalization of oil and with mobilizing the masses on 30 Tir 1331/21 July 1952 to overturn the government of Qavam as-Saltaneh and bring back Mosaddeq.

Many radio and television broadcasts, sermons, and press articles have contributed to this rehabilitation.[2] As for recent studies that tend to present Kashani as the true hero of the nationalist movement of 1950–53, some give a new and interesting view of that period, although the bias based on the ideology of the Islamic revolution is clear.[3] As Mahmud Kashani, Ayatollah Kashani's son, shows, the study of the thirtieth of Tir uprising and its consequences teaches people errors that should not be repeated. In 1952 it was Kashani who led the people and gained victory. Mosaddeq acted as if he owed Kashani nothing, which produced a split in the popular movement and led to the failure of 1953.

According to Mahmud Kashani, just as Mosaddeq showed no gratitude to Kashani for having restored him to power on 30 Tir, and then was defeated, so those who, after the victory of the Islamic revolution, tried to spread the slogan, "Islam without the clergy," are counterrevolutionaries who are trying to divert the revolution in order to take power. "They," Imam Khomeini warns, "want your efforts and your blood, but do not want either Islam or you yourselves."[4]

These revisions are accompanied by a systematic campaign of denigration against Mosaddeq, which has both internal political reasons in the government and more basic reasons. These involve a fundamental rejection of Western ideological influences in the Islamic world such as humanism, the rights of man, and progress. Mosaddeq is rejected because he stood across the path of a Kashani and represented that class of Iranians who devoted great efforts to Westernization and parliamentary democracy. He represented the secular line of the constitutional revolution which fundamentalist ulama of today, pointing to Shaikh Fazlollah

---

2. E.g., a television broadcast of 15 March 1979; and the incendiary preaching of Falsafi at Qom's Madraseh-ye Faiziyeh in front of Khomeini, on the fortieth day after the death of Ayatollah Motahhari; and interview of Mahmud Kashani (the ayatollah's son) in *Payam-e enqelab*, no. 12, 7 Mordad 1359/1980.

3. The most impressive is Mahmud Kashani, *Qiyam-e mellat-e mosalman-e Iran: 30 Tir 1331* (Tehran, 1359/1980). On the Shi'i rising of 1920 see Mohammad Sadeqi Tehrani, *Negahi be tarikh-e enqelab-e eslami-ye 1920-e Eraq va naqsheha-ye ekhtelaf bain-e Mosaddeq va Kashani* (Tehran, 1358/1979). On this literature, see *Abstracta Iranica,* III-V, supplement to *Studia Iranica* (Leiden: E. J. Brill, 1980–82).

4. Kashani, *Qiyam-e mellat,* pp. 127 and 118ff.

Nuri, reject. The label that today's Iranian leaders paste on Mosaddeq they found in a book published in 1967, where, to please SAVAK, is "proved" Mosaddeq's adherence to Freemasonry. In fact it deals with an oath of adherence to a semiclandestine political organization that had few points in common with real Masonic lodges, the Society of Humanity (*Jam'eh-ye adamiyat*). Mosaddeq was a member for about a year, in 1907–08.[5]

It is true that Mosaddeq favored secularizing institutions, and that he preferred, as he frankly told Kashani, that the ulama not intervene directly in political affairs. He sometimes referred to the thought of the founders of the Iranian masonic tradition, although this was far from being his only source of inspiration.[6] But the opposition between Mosaddeq and Kashani was not so simple as one might imagine: if the cultural backgrounds of the two were very divergent, one leaning toward humanism, the other toward theology, their points of convergence were not negligible. Kashani did not reproach Mosaddeq for his masonic sympathies—which he did not know about—but for his lack of respect for the constitution and for the principles of the rights of man. He attacked Mosaddeq, for example, for a famous "public security" (*amniyat-e ejtema'i*) law, which permitted the arrest of people for their intentions (which later served the shah to justify arbitrary arrests). In other words, it was not over the secularization of politics that their conflict arose, but over the particular application of this secularization.

The recent attacks against Mosaddeq, which have clear current political aims, have not remained unanswered. Among the ulama, some have continued to show open homage to Mosaddeq, as did the late Ayatollah Mahmud Taleqani on 20 February 1979. Many in diverse groups, notably the "Islamic left," have defended the memory of the anti-imperialist prime minister overthrown with the help of the CIA.[7]

Our task is not here to judge whether Mosaddeq or Kashani was responsible for the failure of the nationalist movement. Passions are too strong, the documents are sometimes mutilated, or hidden out of fear, and not all witnesses have said their last word. Historians still stumble when

5. See Esma'il Ra'in, *Faramushkhaneh va faramasunri dar Iran*, new ed., vol. 1 (Tehran, 1357/1978–79), p. 640; and the restatement by the National Front, *Asnad sokhan miguyad: Aya Mosaddeq "faramasun" bud?* (Tehran, 1359/1980).

6. See Hosain Makki, *Doktor Mosaddeq va notqha-ye tarikhi-ye u dar daureh-ye panjom va sheshom-e taqniniyeh*, new ed. (Tehran, 1358/1979), p. 230.

7. See Jebheh-ye demokratik-e melli, ed., *Chahardah-e esfand-e 57: Yadnameh-ye Doktor Mosaddeq* (Tehran, 1358/1979); Ali Asghar Hajj Sayyed Javadi, "Be tarikh dorugh nagu'id," *Jombesh* 31, 27 Esfand 1357/1978–79; "Ekhtelaf-e Mosaddeq-Kashani bar sar-e Islam bud?" *Ettela'at*, 23 Khordad 1358 (1979–80).

trying to extract this important period from propaganda debates, and the most assured affirmations must be put in the conditional mood.[8]

A Biographical Sketch

By examining certain critical periods in which Ayatollah Kashani played an important role, one may understand better what, in the recent rehabilitations, is in the domain of ideological projection and what makes historical sense. Sayyed Abol Qasem Kashani was born in Tehran about 1882, in a family of Shi'i ulama, at a time when there was a ferment of new ideas. When he was sixteen, his father, Ayatollah Sayyed Mostafa Kashani, took him on pilgrimage to Mecca, and they went to live in Najaf, Iraq, where his son profited from courses from the great masters: Akhund Molla Mohammad Kazem Khorasani, to whom he was very close during the constitutional revolution, and Hajj Mirza Hosain Khalili Tehrani. At the age of twenty-five Kashani was considered by his teachers as a mujtahid, which was exceptional for one so young. A few years later, when World War I broke out, the ulama became involved in the conflict and defended the Ottoman cause against the British. A first choice was then made in the life of Kashani: instead of devoting himself to teaching, by responding to the invitation to preside over the *Madraseh-ye Elmiyeh* of Najaf,[9] he chose political and military struggle against British penetration.

Later, Kashani was to have founded at Najaf the *Madraseh-ye Alavi,* where not only Islamic knowledge was to be taught, but also exact sciences and military techniques. This project, which aroused the indignation of the ulama, could only be undertaken thanks to the support of the *marja'-e taqlid* (source of imitation), Ayatollah Mohammad Taqi Shirazi (d. 1920). Instead of staying at Najaf and accepting the invitation of Ayatollah Shirazi to write a "practical treatise" (*Resaleh-ye Amaliyeh*), which could have made him, despite his youth, a candidate for eventual succession to the *marja',* Kashani made the decisive choice to leave theological studies in order to continue the fight against colonialism, and he went to Kazemain in order to be freer to act.

It was there that his father died "as a result of the war," in 1918 or 1919. Some hostile journalists attributed his struggle against the English to his desire to avenge his father, but this was not the main reason for his anti-imperialist struggle, which continued throughout his life. His activities are

8. There is, however, an interesting thesis by Mohammäd Hasan Faghfoory, "The Role of the Ulama in Twentieth Century Iran, with particular Reference to Ayatullah Haj Sayyid Abul-Qasim Kashani," Ph.D. dissertation, University of Wisconsin, Madison, 1978.

9. Ibid., p. 119.

better explained by his belief in independence than by a desire for vengeance.

Kashani was one of the leaders of the revolt of the Iraqi tribes against the British mandate, from June to October 1920. The very active participation of the Shi'i ulama in this revolt, even though nearly all were foreigners (Iranians), may be in part explained by the anti-British feelings provoked by the Anglo-Persian Treaty of 1919. Ahmad Shah, who was then in London, refused to sign this treaty, and on his way home, he met Kashani, who prepared him a warm welcome at Kazemain. But the point of departure of the Iraqi revolt was the *fatva* pronounced by Ayatollah Shirazi in response to the Treaty of San Remo (April 1920), which set up British mandates over Iraq and Palestine, and French ones over Syria and Lebanon. The fatva said: "It is not licit for a Muslim to choose a non-Muslim to govern Muslims." Kashani struggled against colonialism within a group named the Iraqi Muslim Arab Society.

The revolt led the British to change their policy and put Faisal on the Iraqi throne in order to seem to make concessions to the revolt. A recent book by Sadeqi Tehrani shows that the ulama led operations in the name of Islam, in contact with former Ottoman bureaucrats, and that the differences between Shi'is and Sunnis were unimportant in the face of foreign occupation. It is possible that such unity was the most enlightened tendency in the movement, and it was perhaps the one supported by Kashani. However, there were probably more distinctions made by the Shi'i ulama than appears at first, and it is likely that the Shi'is saw in this revolt the occasion to "obtain power and preponderance after so many years passed under Sunni domination."[10]

After the failure of the revolt the leaders were pursued, and Kashani, condemned to death in absentia, fled to Iran. He reached Tehran on 19 February 1921, three days before the coup d'état of Reza Khan, which made Sayyed Zia ad-Din prime minister. Ahmad Shah sent the royal carriage to meet Kashani at the shrine of Shah Abdol Azim, but Kashani proudly refused to use it.

Then came an obscure period in Kashani's life; his biographers take up his story again in the 1940s. Kashani, used up by the failure of the Iraq revolt, no doubt began, as facts suggest, to make an alliance with the future Reza Shah.[11] One may be surprised that a man who had partici-

10. Elie Kedourie, "Réflexions sur l'histoire du royaume d'Irak," *Orient*, 11 (1959): 61. See also Ali Davani, *Nahzat-e do maheh-ye ruhaniun-e Iran* (Qom, 1341/1962), p. 39. For the thesis of a unified struggle of Shi'is and Sunnis, see Sadeqi Tehrani, *Negahi be enqelab-e eslami*, pp. 33 ff.

11. See Abdollah Amir-Tahmaseb, *Tarikh-e shahanshahi-ye a'lahazrat Reza Shah-e kabir*, 2nd ed. (Tehran, 2535 imperial/1976), pp. 428, 475, 485, 548, 566, 593, 604, 613. See also Faghfoory, "Ulama," pp. 58ff., 137–38; A. H. Hairi, *Shi'ism and Constitutionalism in Iran* (Leiden, 1977), pp. 138ff.

pated in the anti-British revolt in Iraq did not reflect more on the results of a movement that was, in its origins, protected by the British. But such an alliance is understandable in the light of the great efforts of the future sovereign at this time to give pledges of good will to the religious classes; he made a pilgrimage to Najaf and participated barefoot in the mourning celebrations of Moharram. If we cannot prove that Kashani had friendly relations with Reza Shah, we do know that he was elected to the constituent assembly that, in December 1925, deposed the Qajar dynasty and entrusted the Iranian monarchy to the Pahlavis. To be elected, the support of Reza Khan was more important than that of the people (neither Mosaddeq nor Modarres nor the activist writer Malek ash-Sho'ara Bahar, who had shown their opposition to the monarchist desires of Reza Khan in the fifth majles, was elected). Kashani participated actively in the debates, even proposing an amendment, and voted for the Pahlavi monarchy.

The political evolution of Reza Shah must have displeased Kashani. It is said that he opposed the Russian-educated minister of court, Taimurtash. Invited to a royal *salam* ceremony, Kashani is said to have refused to stand up upon the entry of Reza Shah into the audience chamber, and he was never reinvited. At the time of the Irano-British oil agreement of 1933, Kashani is said to have protested. But no trace remains of this opposition, whereas Modarres was pursued, arrested, and probably killed, and others are known to have resisted various authoritarian reforms of the new ruler (such as conscription, unveiling women, and state control over pious foundations [*vaqf*]).[12]

A letter from Kashani to Hajj Mirza Mehdi Zanjani (who was also in the constituent assembly of 1925), dated 10 February 1928, proves the political preoccupations of Kashani: "You certainly know that the only remedy [to current difficulties] is to reform the national assembly. . . . The ignorance of the people and the lack of attention of the ulama to this fundamental and vital point [i.e., elections], profits corrupt, greedy, impious individuals, fascinated by what is foreign." This letter, where Kashani demands of his interlocutor the greatest vigilance in the choice of candidates from Zanjan for the majles, shows that he had not abandoned his critical sense or his political activity at this time.[13]

A point in common between Kashani and Reza Shah in his last period was the confidence they had in the Germans, who were a counterbalancing influence against the British. Kashani clearly had Germanophile sentiments ever since World War I. The Nazi secret services, which enjoyed great liberty in Iran, survived the fall of Reza Shah (September

12. See Faghfoory, "Ulama," pp. 138ff.; Akhavi, *Religion*, pp. 23–59.
13. In the private collection of Mohsen Mirza'i.

1941) and the invasion of Iran by the Allies. In January 1942 they organized a network called the Iranian Nationalist Movement, led by Mayer and Schulze-Holthus, which included General Fazlollah Zahedi and Ayatollah Kashani, with probable contact with the Japanese embassy.[14] Zahedi was exiled to Palestine, and Kashani hid for several months in Tehran, but was finally denounced to the British police in 1943. Taken prisoner, Kashani was held in the town of Arak, then sent to Rasht to be interrogated by the Soviets, and finally kept at Hajjiabad near Kermanshah.[15] Freed in 1945, he returned to Qom in triumph. The ulama went out long distances to meet him and rolled out carpets where he passed. "His Excellency Ayatollah Borujerdi," wrote a witness, "sent out a bus with his most brilliant colleagues; Ayatollahs Sadr and Khansari sent automobiles full of ulama; Ayatollah Najafi Mar'ashi himself went out five leagues, and the entire theological university, including myself, went out one league . . . with most of the inhabitants of Qom, merchants and notables."[16]

After having regained his Tehran home, Kashani apparently continued to support popular movements. In the summer of 1946, when he went to Mashhad on pilgrimage, tumults broke out upon his passage in the towns of Semnan and Shahrud. On 17 July 1946 he was arrested at Sabzavar on the order of Prime Minister Qavam as-Saltaneh. The latter wanted to apply a severe law limiting freedom of the press, against which Kashani protested. A demonstration took place in the Soltani mosque in Tehran to demand Kashani's release. But it was in vain: he remained confined to the village of Behjatabad near Qazvin.[17]

The next year Kashani was freed. At that time a group of deputies was constituted around Kashani's reputed son-in-law, Shams Qanatabadi, who called themselves the *Mojahedin-e Islam*; all were politically close to Kashani. Another organization, this one secret, had been created in 1943 around Sayyed Mojtaba Mirlauhi, known as Navvab-e Safavi, the *Fedayan-e Islam*. Their ideology included a return to strict Islamic ways and the use of violence and assassination against those seen as obstacles to

14. See JAMI (Jebheh-ye Azadi-ye Mardom-e Iran), *Gozashteh cheraq-e rah-e ayandeh ast* (n.p., 1976), p. 69; Faghfoory, "Ulama," p. 207, which cites the English translation of Berthold Schulze-Holthus, *Frührot in Iran*, trans. *Daybreak in Iran* (London, 1954); 1980 German edition, *Aufstand in Iran* (Munich).

15. See Nurollah Larudi, *Asiran, fajaye'-ye ommal-e tabahkar-e Englis dar Iran* (Tehran, 1332), p. 181.

16. See Mohammad Sharif Razi, *Ganjineh-ye daneshmandan*, Vol. 1 (Tehran, 1352/1973), p. 269.

17. See Faghfoory, "Ulama," pp. 210ff. Hassan Arfa, *Under Five Shahs* (London, 1964), p. 361, gives a relatively sympathetic portrait of Kashani and notes that he began to support Qavam's government when Qavam undertook to cede oil fields to a Soviet-Iranian company, which was a way to break the British monopoly.

the realization of Islamic ideals. Their first public act was to attack the writer Ahmad Kasravi, who had written critically of Shi'ism and other religions, in 1945, and to kill him in 1946. After a speech in which Kashani, in May 1948, called for volunteers against Zionist terrorists in Palestine, the Fedayan-e Islam supported him strongly, especially in their organ *Parcham-e Islam* (the Flag of Islam). This support meant that when the attempted assassin of the shah in February 1949 was found to be carrying a press card from *Parcham-e Islam,* it was a pretext to exile Kashani, who was arrested at night and driven under very difficult conditions to the Qasr-e Shirin frontier. From there he went to Beirut.[18]

There was certainly a more serious reason for the exile. As Hosain Makki said to the majles on 25 July 1949, Kashani was exiled because he had published a declaration in favor of the nationalization of oil. This is confirmed by a message from Beirut the same year from Kashani, where he spoke of the injustice of giving oil free to foreigners at a time when it was needed to end poverty in Iran.[19]

The Lebanese exile lasted until spring 1950. Political agitation was growing in Tehran: nationalist forces succeeded in bringing about a return of the elections to the sixteenth majles, which had been falsified, and nationalists entered the majles in increased numbers. Kashani having been elected, the pleas of Hosain Makki and Ha'erizadeh in the majles succeeded in bringing his return to Tehran. Some say that the American embassy also intervened with the shah for his return, because of their worries about the activities of the Tudeh Party and their belief that it was better to have a popular movement dominated by religious leaders than an uncontrollable wave of communism.[20]

Kashani's arrival in Tehran in June 1950 was a triumph. The crowd massed from the eve of his arrival on the road to Mehrabad Airport. Many of the ulama formed a committee of welcome;[21] Falsafi could not pronounce his prepared speech because of the crowd's impatience. Kashani was, notably, welcomed by Mosaddeq and Makki. His vehicle was sometimes carried by a delirious crowd. The end of the route was the slowest, in the narrow streets close to Kashani's home north of the

18. See D. N. Wilber, *Contemporary Iran* (London, 1963), p. 92; and Kashani, *Qiyam-e mellat,* pp. 120ff.

19. See Hosain Makki, *Naft va notq-e Makki,* 2nd ed. (Tehran, 1357/1978–79), p. 395; and *Ruhaniyat va nahzat-e melli,* document 4.

20. Mohammad Hasaneyn Heykal, *Iran, kuh-e ateshfeshan,* Persian trans. (Qom, n.d.) (the Arabic original is Cairo, 1951), p. 73; Faghfoory, "Ulama," p. 110, notes the same American policy but without clarifying the period. It was probably after the presidential elections of November 1952, won by Eisenhower, that the Americans decided on the role they would play in the Irano-British conflict.

21. Some ulama refused to greet him; for example, Ayatollah Abol Fazl Zanjani, who disapproved of the Fedayan-e Islam (interview, 26 November 1980).

bazaar, which had been richly decorated with arcs of triumph and carpets. In the evening Dr. Mozaffar Baqa'i Kermani read a message of thanks that Kashani was too tired to read himself: "My dear brothers, as nothing in this world occurs without material causes, don't limit yourselves to praying, but unite, devote yourselves to social problems and self-sacrifice in order not to leave the field free to traitors who, by their passions, their brigandage, and their ambitions will let all the values of this nation be annihilated."[22]

The important period that followed is better known. Ayatollah Kashani, collaborating with the National Front, put all his strength into the service of the nationalization of oil. In a declaration of 21 December 1950 he denounced the exploitation of Iran by the Anglo-Iranian Oil Company. In this struggle he carried along some ulama, trying to make a veritable anticolonialist crusade. However, the means employed by groups who called themselves followers of Kashani sometimes exceeded parliamentary political traditions. When Khalil Tahmasebi, a member of the Fedayan-e Islam, assassinated Prime Minister Razmara on 7 March 1951, he owed his spectacular acquittal to the declarations of Kashani, who took responsibility for this "execution," and congratulated its "heroic" perpetrator. It is true that General Razmara was inclined toward dictatorial methods, and that he was at the time the hope of the Westerners, as well as being very antireligious.

The harmonious relations between the Fedayan and Kashani were soon to end. Kashani had now to support the policies of Mosaddeq's government, which was the hope of the nationalist forces. Nationalization of oil was voted by the majles, and Mosaddeq became prime minister on 30 April 1951. Kashani could then convince the oil workers in Khuzistan to stop the strike they had begun on Tudeh Party instigation.

Iran was soon plunged into a long electoral period, from November 1951 to March 1952. The result of the elections was an unprecedented success for the National Front and for the clericals. Kashani's supporters were strong, and he could henceforth exercise pressure on the government. Mosaddeq, who needed a docile Parliament to conduct his delicate negotiations with the British, wanted to take over all executive power. He asked for full powers, but the deputies refused. He then turned to the shah to ask for what the latter considered to be the domain of the sovereign: the Ministry of War. The shah's refusal gave Mosaddeq an excuse to resign on 17 July 1952. As was noted in *Le Monde* that day, Mosaddeq really resigned over his not having obtained full powers. He retired to his home, where he refused to accept any visitors.

Qavam as-Saltaneh was named prime minister but was overthrown

22. *Ruhaniyat,* document 6.

after two days as a result of two bloody demonstrations, on 30 Tir 1331/21 July 1952. Recent studies, especially by Mahmud Kashani, insist correctly on the preponderant role of Ayatollah Kashani in this movement. It was he who gathered journalists, refused any compromise with Qavam's emissaries, issued a fiery communiqué promising to go himself into the street dressed in a shroud to obtain the return of Mosaddeq. Kashani wrote: "Foreigners, by the intermediary [of Qavam] are preparing to strike at the bases of religion, of liberty, and of the country's independence, and to put the Islamic nation back into captivity. The plot to separate religion and politics that was for centuries propagated by the British, which tries to stop the Islamic nation from taking control of its destiny and from fulfilling its religious and social duties, is today the directing line of this ambitious man [Qavam]."[23] Qavam ordered the arrest of Kashani at his home on 29 Tir, but it was not achieved, owing to the crowd of people around his house after the BBC's revelation of the order for his arrest.

Strengthened by mass support, Mosaddeq returned to power, this time getting the Ministry of War (now baptized the Ministry of National Defense). His sole real part in this victory was the verdict of the Hague Tribunal, published on 30 Tir, which supported Iran against Great Britain. But Mosaddeq did not want to share credit for the thirtieth of Tir with the clericals who were its principal artisans, and he thus revealed a political contradiction within the nationalist movement that was gradually to ruin it.

Some days later Kashani let Mosaddeq know that he had expected to be consulted about ministerial nominations,[24] and that if things did not change he would be forced to leave both Tehran and Iran, in order no longer to be on the political scene (that is, in order not to seem to authorize a policy that was foreign to him). Mosaddeq's answer, on 28 July 1952, was a challenge. He wrote, "If you want reforms to occur, you are begged to abstain from intervention in political affairs for a time, as no change will be possible if the one invested with responsibility has not absolute freedom of action. If you agree with this manner of acting, I have the honor to be your servant; and if not, why does your excellency speak of leaving Tehran?" This all-or-nothing policy may be understood as follows: Mosaddeq knew that Ayatollah Kashani, who was isolated among the clerics, had not aroused the people on the basis of purely religious slogans, but on the basis of an anti-imperialist policy, the program of the National Front. Did not the crowd cry "Mosaddeq or

23. In Kashani, *Qiyam-e mellat*, p. 35.
24. According to Mahmud Kashani, *Qiyam-e mellat*, p. 113, by letter; but it seems that only Mosaddeq's answer has been preserved.

death"? The old leader knew, in retiring to his home, that he would arouse a strong public reaction, and Kashani was its detonator. One may compare Mosaddeq's attitude to that of Reza Khan in 1923, who left Tehran but was recalled by a great popular movement,[25] or to that of Abdul Nasser after Egypt's 1967 defeat. It is a well-known Eastern political trick. That the thirtieth-of-Tir movement was Mosaddeq's is indicated by the fact that the popular mobilization did not decrease once Kashani was out of power; and when the two great leaders were in opposition, the winter of 1952–53, and Kashani, by his ambiguous attitude, appeared to support the monarchist demonstrations organized by Ayatollah Behbahani, Mosaddeq continued to have a large following, especially in traditionally religious milieux like the bazaar.[26] The direct participation of a cleric in power was at that time unthinkable, and public opinion was mistrustful when people saw Ayatollah Kashani, whose extraordinary combativeness they admired, mix too closely in governmental affairs.

A consolation was offered to Kashani; the majles chose him as president on 7 August 1952, accepting that he, permanently excused for his absence, would be represented by the vice-president. The next day the deputies gave full powers for six months to Mosaddeq.

A dispute soon arose; at the end of summer 1952, Ayatollah Kashani took the initiative for a great Islamic congress that he proposed to gather in Tehran. Its goal was to create permanent mutual-aid institutions to struggle against the colonial powers. On his own authority he made contact with the embassies of Islamic countries and on the occasion of the *Hajj,* discussed the project with the top Saudi, Syrian, and Jordanian authorities. The message sent to the Muslim nations of the world noted the disunity that weakened the Islamic world and favored the submission and corruption of peoples by the colonial powers. The congress would take on the task of examining all the problems of the dominated peoples, including the non-Muslims. A fund for mutual assistance would be created to aid the least-favored countries to develop and defend themselves. Kashani hoped to use the anti-British sentiments of Muslim peoples to uphold the Iranian cause.[27]

Such an initiative was certainly premature in the eyes of Mosaddeq: how could Iran invite such a gathering before solving its own problems?

25. See Abdollah Mostaufi, *Sharh-e zendegani-ye man,* 2nd ed. (Tehran, 1343/1964), Vol. 3, p. 602; L.-P. Ellwell Sutton, "Reza Shah the Great," in G. Lenczowski, ed., *Iran under the Pahlavis* (Stanford: Hoover Institution, 1978), p. 22.

26. See R. W. Cottam, *Nationalism in Iran* (Pittsburgh: Pittsburgh University Press, 1964), p. 279; interview with Ayatollah Abol Fazl Zanjani, 26 November 1980.

27. Persian text in Kashani, *Qiyam-e mellat,* pp. 166ff.; see also Faghfoory, "Ulama," p. 249.

Kashani was told that the finances of the Ministry of Foreign Affairs were insufficient for it. Dr. Hosain Fatemi, minister of foreign affairs, was upset to see Kashani making contacts with other countries without consulting him. Following an interview of Fatemi with Ayatollah Abol Fazl Zanjani in fall 1952, the latter asked Kashani to go himself to Lebanon, in order to leave Mosaddeq elbow room, and to retain the right to return if the situation demanded.[28]

Kashani stayed in Tehran, but the failure of his project was not entirely due to the obstacles put before it by Mosaddeq's government. In fact, his call received only a weak echo outside Iran and was soon forgotten.

The main theme of opposition between the two men was given by the weaknesses in Mosaddeq's policy, which made him demand a six-month prolongation of full powers. Attempts at reconciliation, notably in January 1953, had only ephemeral results, even though certain members of the National Front, who broke with Mosaddeq, tried to maintain contacts in both camps. The growth of the Tudeh Party increasingly worried the clericals, who feared that Mosaddeq might become the victim of his tolerant relations with the Communists. The most virulent deputy in his criticism of the government was Dr. Mozaffar Baqa'i, who perhaps wished to become prime minister, and who kept the best relations with Kashani until the end.

The coup d'état that overthrew Mosaddeq had two rehearsals; the first took place from 28 February to 1 March 1953. Mosaddeq, who had in the fall achieved the exile to California of Princess Ashraf and the queen mother, learned around 20 February that the shah and Queen Sorayya were preparing to leave Iran. The minister of court, Hosain Ala, at that time contacted Kashani to indicate the danger represented by the shah's absence, despite Mosaddeq's encouraging him to leave. Kashani sent an envoy to the queen to "make the shah reverse this decision."[29] On 28 February, at the very moment when Mosaddeq had gone to say goodbye to the shah and queen, the partisans of Kashani and especially of Tehran's leading ayatollah, Behbahani, demonstrated before the palace to convince the shah not to leave and to cry, "The shah or death." The uprising then moved against Mosaddeq's house, near the palace, where the door was broken down by thugs led by the notorious Sha'ban Ja'fari, called Bimokh, "the brainless." Mosaddeq took refuge in Parliament and was

28. Interview with Ayatollah Abol Fazl Zanjani, 26 November 1980.
29. See Princess Sorayya's *Ma vie*, trans. M.-L. Ponty (Paris, 1963), p. 113. A Persian translation after the Islamic revolution (*Hala, khodam harf mizanam*, trans. M. Ameri [Tehran, 1358/1979], p. 68) replaces Kashani's name with "the opponents of Mosaddeq." See also *Khandaniha*, nos. 47 and 48, 12 and 16 Esfand 1331/1953; *Taqrirat-e Mosaddeq dar zendan: yaddasht shodeh tavassot-e Jalil Bozorgmehr*, ed. I. Afshar (Tehran, 1359/1980), pp. 126ff.; and Cottam, *Nationalism*, p. 280, who gives the wrong date of 27 February.

booed by the crowd, but saved his life. He had lost esteem while the shah gained in popularity. This was certainly a test for those who hesitated to undertake a coup d'état: it appeared possible to sustain a reversal of power, thanks to the opposition of the clerics to Mosaddeq, reinforced by the monarchist sentiment of the mob.

The second attempt was made in August 1953. Various blunders by Mosaddeq, who seemed thirsty for power, gave rise to discontent. Communist agitation had become a daily occurrence. Talk of a coup d'état was rife. It is not certain that Kashani had contact with General Zahedi before the coup, but Kashani, who had fallen in prestige, especially after being ousted from the presidency of the majles, was divided between his desire to impose himself on Mosaddeq by making him follow a less demagogic policy on the one hand, and a strong desire to bar the way to communism at any price on the other.

The Americans were, for many, potential saviors at the beginning of the 1950s. In the fall of 1952 Mosaddeq and Kashani had turned to the American ambassador, Loy Henderson, for aid. When President Eisenhower refused, in a letter of 29 June 1953, the aid that Mosaddeq had again requested a month before, he put the Iranian government in a weak position before public opinion.[30]

The second coup attempt failed, on 16 August 1953. The shah had named Zahedi prime minister in place of Mosaddeq, but Colonel Nasiri was arrested before he could give Mosaddeq his letter of dismissal. A great movement of antiroyalist anger took hold of the crowd, which overturned statues of the shah and his father. The sudden flood of communist activity, which went as far as an attempt to destroy the tomb of Reza Shah, frightened the conservatives, and especially the clericals. The atmosphere was ripe for a coup d'état; everyone spoke of it and knew that something was being prepared. It was in this charged climate that Kashani is said to have sent the following letter, dated 27 Mordad/18 August, to Mosaddeq:

Although it has become difficult for me to make myself heard, my religious and national duty as a servant of Islam outweighs my personal feelings. Despite the vexations and the noisy propaganda that you are making [about me], you know better than anyone that my concern is to preserve your government, in which you yourself seem to have lost interest. From the experience of Qavam's taking power and from your recent obstinacy, I have become certain that you wish, as on the thirtieth of Tir, to abandon the nation and leave as a hero. You did not listen to what I said when I insisted that the referendum[31] not take place, and you insulted

30. See Cottam, *Nationalism*, pp. 224, 282.
31. The referendum took place 3–15 August, and authorized Mosaddeq to decide on new legislative elections without the shah's consent. It was a success despite the boycott sanctioned by Kashani's and Baqa'i's partisans. See Cottam, *Nationalism*, pp. 282–83.

me. You had my house stoned; you put my friends and my children in prison;[32] you dissolved the majles from fear that it might overthrow you; and now you have left neither Parliament nor a base for the nation. I succeeded with much difficulty in controling Zahedi in the majles, and you adroitly made him leave;[33] he is now on the point of making a coup d'état. If you truly do not aim, as on the thirtieth of Tir, to retire in order to leave the memory of a hero . . . this letter that I am writing will remain in the history of the Iranian nation to prove that, despite all the reproaches I could make against you, I warned you about the certitude of a coup d'état from Zahedi. Am I mistaken in thinking, as I told you during our last meeting at Dezashib[34] and as I also reproached Henderson, that America helped us to take oil from the British in order to be able now, by appearing generous toward our nation and the world, to tear from us those riches by means of your own hands? With my letter, no excuse will be acceptable tomorrow. If I am really mistaken in thinking as I do, I will send to you, if you wish, [my son] Sayyed Mostafa and Naser Khan Qashqa'i for negotiations.

Mosaddeq's answer was brief: "Your letter reached me from the hands of Mr. Hasan Salemi. I am supported by the confidence of the Iranian nation. Greetings."[35]

This correspondence merits examination. First, its authenticity has been questioned by someone close to Ayatollah Kashani. The ayatollah, he says, favored the coup d'état and the document was later forged to whitewash Kashani. Such doubts are reinforced by the convoluted style of the letter and by the delay in its publication—as far as we know, for the first time in 1979. Finally, Kashani was not a man to justify his stands by diplomatic maneuvers. However, and with the reservations imposed by a document of which only a photographic facsimile is available, those who know best affirm the authenticity of the letters, of which the originals are now in the Federal Republic of Germany.[36]

32. Following the killing of the police chief Afshar-Tus, in which Dr. Baqa'i and General Zahedi were implicated, several persons close to Kashani were jailed, including one of his sons. See Cottam, *Nationalism*, p. 282.

33. Zahedi was hit by the public security law; he was implicated in the failed coup d'état of February 1953, and again in the killing of Afshar-Tus on 20 April 1953. Protected by Kashani, he took refuge in the majles with Baqa'i. Then he had to flee, and found different hiding places (some say with Ayatollah Bani Sadr, and then with Mostafa Moqaddam) whence he had contact with the shah. See Sorayya, *Ma vie*, p. 120; Wilber, *Contemporary Iran*, p. 97; Cottam, *Nationalism*, p. 282; JAMI, *Gozashteh*, pp. 598–99.

34. On 27 January 1953, H. Makki tried to reconcile Kashani and Mosaddeq, in the course of a meeting that took place at Dezashib, close to Shemiran, but their relations worsened.

35. This correspondence was reproduced for the first time in the revue *Gozaresh-e ruz*, 1 Khordad 1358/1979–80, by Mohammad Ali Yusefzadeh; then in *Goftari-ye kutah dar bareh-ye vaqaye'-e 28 Mordad 32*, 2nd ed. (Tehran, 1358/1979–80), by the Islamic Republican Party, and in many other recent publications.

36. See *Ruhaniyat va nahzat-e melli*, p. 23, n. 51. Dr. Salemi, the grandson of Kashani, holds the letter and Kashani's correspondence. No one in Iran has apparently seen the

This correspondence may prove, as those who now publish it claim, that Kashani did everything to keep Mosaddeq from delivering Iran to the Americans and to Zahedi. One could also say that Kashani, who probably knew General Zahedi since 1941 and had dealings with him in the period before the coup d'état, was trying to separate himself from the general, knowing that the failure of 16 August would not stop his activities, but also that his success was not sure. Kashani desired the overthrow of Mosaddeq, but he doubtless would have preferred a more elegant solution than that of Zahedi. Whatever the explanation might be, the relations between Zahedi and Kashani were not immediately bad; one of the first gestures of the new prime minister was to visit Kashani. Zahedi promised him that he would liberalize the regime, and that he would continue the work of the National Front, in particular the nationalization of oil. But he kept his word only on one point; he freed the clerics who had been majles deputies.[37]

The coup d'état, of which the real origin, in the absence of the shah, may not have been clear to everyone, included elements close to Ayatollah Kashani, whom he could doubtless have restrained if he had opposed their project. To cite two names: Ayatollah Sayyed Mohammad Behbahani, who gave his name to the famous "Behbahani dollars," had monarchist demonstrators recruited in the lower quarters of Tehran. As a religious personage Behbahani gained a great deal from the coup d'état, and his name progressively supplanted that of Kashani in the press.[38] It is inconceivable that Behbahani could have undertaken this action if Kashani had really been opposed to it. Another intimate of Kashani, General Nader Batmanqelich, became chief of the general staff after the coup; he claims never to have acted, either before or after the coup, without referring to Kashani.[39]

There is also agreement, especially among the current defenders of Kashani, that Mosaddeq's inertia, of which the response to the letter of the ayatollah is an example, poses serious questions. Mosaddeq was also warned by the Tudeh Party of the imminence of the coup d'état. After the arrest of Colonel Nasiri, on 26 Mordad, Mosaddeq could have taken

---

original of Kashani's letter; some suggest that it was destroyed when Mosaddeq's house was pillaged, with Salemi keeping only a photograph that he is said to have taken before he brought the letter to Mosaddeq. This does not seem in accord with the facts. Others, like H. Makki, say that Kashani himself wrote two copies to be able to keep one. In any case, according to Makki, it cannot be a falsification, even by Mohammad Kashani, another of Kashani's sons, who is said by some enemies of Kashani to be capable of imitating very well his handwriting.

37. See *Ruhaniyat,* "jim-1," pp. 25ff.
38. See Akhavi, *Religion and Politics,* p. 74; Faghfoory, "Ulama," p. 286.
39. See *Enqelab-e eslami,* no. 416, 13 Azar 1359/1980.

effective measures to neutralize Zahedi. The passivity of the old nationalist leader at the decisive hour makes his current detractors say that the
events of 28 Mordad were not a coup but a plot.[40] It is known that Loy
Henderson, who returned precipitously to Iran after the failure of the 25
Mordad coup, visited Mossaddeq to tell him that his government would
henceforth recognize only Zahedi as prime minister. Henderson waved
before the old nationalist aristocrat the specter of a communist plot
controlled by the Soviet ambassador, Lavrentiev. Mosaddeq refrained
from calling out the masses who remained faithful to him, especially the
Tudeh, whose activity had suddenly become too visible.[41] One may thus,
with the necessary precautions, say that neither Kashani nor Mosaddeq
really did what he could have to stop the coup d'état. One of them desired
the change, the other feared an evolution that he could no longer master.
Both would lose face politically.

As for Kashani, his political ideal remained the same, and he soon came
to express publicly his bitterness in the face of the annihilation of the
achievements of the national movement. Unhappily, those who continued
to struggle, notably around Ayatollah Reza Zanjani in the Resistance
Movement (*Nahzat-e moqavamat*), did not accept the collaboration of
Kashani, whom they distrusted and who always wanted to have the
leading role. Kashani's continued resentment toward Mosaddeq cut him
off from many of his former sympathizers in the National Front, who after
the coup idealized the role their leader had had. Besides, the difficulties of
the new dictatorship made any direct opposition impossible. Censorship
hindered Kashani from making his opposition heard, and he was even
imprisoned.

His first public protest after the coup d'état took place in fall 1953,
when it was announced that diplomatic relations between Iran and Great
Britain would be restored. "That day will be a day of mourning," he
declared to journalists, "as England would not recognize our right [to oil]
and provoked an economic blockade. The Americans now insist on
threatening the government with ending their aid."[42]

Later, on 5 January 1954, Kashani wrote to Zahedi to warn him against
tampering with the elections to the eighteenth majles. "If the elections are

40. Interview with Mahmud Kashani (who was too young at the time, and reports what he
heard from witnesses), 24 August 1980. A book by the Mojahedin-e Enqelab-e Eslami,
Negareshi kutah bar nahzat (Tehran, 1979), p. 48, says: "In fact, if one sets aside sympathy
for Mosaddeq, and forgets his past, there is no proof that demonstrates that he was opposed
to the coup d'état of 28 Mordad."

41. See JAMI, *Gozashteh*, p. 613; Jean Larteguy, *Visa pour l'Iran* (Paris, 1962), pp. 195–
96.

42. See the text of the press conference of 11 December 1953, spread secretely in Iran, in
Ruhaniyat, document 59.

manipulated, no decision taken by this assembly will have any validity in the eyes of the nation, and it will have the same fate as the oil agreement imposed on us in 1933." A communiqué passed out a month later spoke in the same terms as this letter to Zahedi, and finished thus: "there is no doubt but that the publication of this text will bring upon me attacks and accusations in a press which is subsidized by the government and from abroad. I accept all this suffering because I decided from the first day of struggle to risk all difficulties, and all pains, to defend the honor, the integrity, and the religion of the nation."[43]

A few days later Kashani, having failed to make himself understood in the climate of dictatorship that reigned in Iran, sent to Beirut a letter to Dag Hammarskjöld, the new secretary-general of the United Nations, in which he complained of the terrible conditions of political life in Iran:

There is no more liberty except for traitors and foreign agents. . . . As long as this illegality lasts, it is clear that no signed treaty or law will have validity for the Iranian nation. . . . The aim of this letter is to make known that . . . the Zahedi government is trampling on the principles of Iran's constitution, the articles adopted by the United Nations and the Universal Declaration of Human Rights . . . and all its decisions are therefore illegal. . . . This could have disastrous consequences for peace in this part of the world.[44]

The anger of Kashani burst forth again when he learned about the treaty concluded between Iran and the international consortium to use the petroleum resources of Iran, in October 1954. As is known, this treaty annulled the gains of nationalization and delivered the exploitation of Iran's oil to international companies (including 40 percent to British Petroleum). In a declaration issued in Iran, Kashani expressed his astonishment at the collaboration of the United States with Great Britain to recommence the exploitation of Iran's riches. "For the hundreds of millions of dollars that the American colonialist capitalists will gain from oil, the oppressed nation will lose all hope of liberty and will have a negative opinion about all the claims of the Western world." American aid to Iran, which profited only a few people, did not reach a hundredth of what the United States took from Iran. The West, and especially America, which claimed to fight the influence of communism in the world, should see that their "conduct as colonialist oppressors in Iran, in Egypt, in Morocco, in Palestine, and in other weak countries stricken by 'injustice' accelerates the advance of communism and the possibility of a new world conflict. The Iranian nation will not allow its economic destiny to

43. Text in *Ruhaniyat,* documents 60 and 61.
44. Text in *Ruhaniyat,* document 62.

be decided outside the country, especially not in London." In closing, Kashani said:

As long as blood flows in the veins of the nation, the foreigner cannot install in this country his brigand's display case, and the agents of colonialism, with the disastrous propaganda they deploy against me for their shameful enterprises in Iran and in the world, cannot turn me from the continuation of the tireless combat that I have undertaken against their injustice. I have always risked my worthless life, and I will risk it until my last breath for the glory and independence of my nation. With the fire that was lit in my heart by the radiance of the sacrifice of my ancestor Hosain ibn Ali, I prefer death with honor to life with shame. . . . Let us defend the legitimate rights of the nation, even if we must sacrifice our lives for them.[45]

Although government censorship did not allow a wide diffusion of these messages, and all public demonstrations of support for Kashani had become impossible, he continued to denounce what he considered contrary to Iran's interests. Unable to keep this bothersome man from speaking, the government decided to arrest him and to accuse him, at the same time as the Fedayan-e Islam leaders Navvab-e Safavi and Tahmasebi, of complicity in the killing of Razmara. The ulama least favorable to Kashani then intervened: Ayatollah Abol Fazl Zanjani asked Iran's top ayatollah, Borujerdi, to intervene with the shah.[46] Kashani was freed. The last trace of his political activity is a letter he wrote to the United Nations on the problems of Algeria and Tunisia, on 12 February 1958.[47] One may, however, say that from the time of his leaving prison in January 1956, Ayatollah Kashani was a man politically finished. Shortly before his death in March 1962, the shah visited him; Kashani could no longer talk, but is said to have turned away his head so as not to see the shah. According to other sources, however, a final dialogue occurred between the two men; the ayatollah, unexpectedly visited, proved to the shah that he had no rigid prejudices.

Kashani and the Islamic Republic: The State of the Problem

The question posed today is, Did or did not Kashani open the way to what later became the Islamic Republic? The answer must be divided into

---

45. Text in *Ruhaniyat,* document 63.
46. In his letter, Zanjani referred to the sad fate of "Mr. Kashani," who was said to have been put into the striped uniform of prisoners. Borujerdi, in a letter dated 25 January 1956, answered that he had done what was necessary for "Hojjat al-Islam Kashani" (from the collection of Ayatollah Zanjani).
47. Documents cited in Faghfoory, "Ulama," p. 160, n. 1.

several parts. First, Kashani was not a marja'-e taqlid.[48] Some say that if he had written his "practical treatise" Kashani could have become a spiritual leader. The importance of this problem appears more clearly in the analyses made today by the Khomeinists of the failures of the past; if a national movement is not directed by the spiritual head of the community, they say, the movement will never end in true victory.[49] This group argues that to be accepted as marja' one needed the maximum possibility of attracting all Shi'is unanimously. A political mujtahid like Kashani exposed himself to propaganda encouraged by the British for the separation of religion and politics, meaning that he might play the game of colonialism by provoking a schism in the community. It was, they say, in order not to run this risk that Kashani renounced writing a treatise.[50] (In fact, he wrote no book.)

This choice had major consequences for the relations of Kashani with the theologians of Qom, dominated until 1962 and even after by "quietist" tendencies. In particular, Ayatollah Borujerdi was firmly hostile to the direct participation of turbanned clerics in political struggles. In February 1950, when Kashani was in exile in Beirut, a meeting of ulama presided over by Borujerdi at Qom decided that one who intervened in political affairs should quit the religious habit.[51] This was at the beginning of the oil-nationalization crisis, and Kashani, who returned to Iran some months later, nonetheless found partisans among the clerics. But his relations with Borujerdi were never good thereafter. Both had studied at Najaf but, Kashani's defenders say, the level of Kashani there was higher; he followed three cycles of courses with the master of the time, Akhund Khorasani, and Borujerdi only one. To the negative attitude of Borujerdi on the political engagement of clerics (he threatened once to exile himself to Najaf in order not to have to warn those who engaged noisily in politics) Kashani answered with hostility, as in an affair concerning Qom vaqfs in autumn 1952, or when he refused Borujerdi's ritual hospitality during his stays in Qom.[52]

Second, Kashani was not a professor. During quiet political periods he did educate theological students at home. But this was not an essential activity for him. He was not cited among the professors of Qom or of

---

48. A *marja'-e taqlid* is a great ayatollah "taken as a model" by his disciples because of his high theological achievements. The Shi'i believer utilizes the "Practical Treatise" of his *marja'* as a guide for religious observance in daily life.

49. See Sadeqi Tehrani, *Negahi kutah be tarikh-e enqelab*, pp. 33ff.; confirmed in an interview with Mahmud Kashani, 24 August 1980.

50. Ibid.

51. See Akhavi, *Religion and Politics*, pp. 63–64 and n. 6. (Akhavi gives a wrong date.)

52. Ibid., pp. 67 and 70–71.

Tehran, and none of his courses merited publication (contrary, for example, to those of Khomeini).

Third, in politics, Kashani had no very solid principles. The struggle against colonialism, which was in a way his raison d'être, did not stop him from committing errors that a more serious analysis of situations would have spared him. We may cite, for example: his temporary alliance with Reza Shah; his alliance with the Fedayan-e Islam, a terrorist group whose methods were the contrary of any parliamentarist policy (this alliance was short, and Kashani preferred later the alliance with Mosaddeq and political struggle, and he himself became the target of the Fedayan before making a new alliance with them against Mosaddeq);[53] his alliance with the shah at the time of the abortive coup d'état of 28 February 1952; his acceptance of the presidency of the majles, although he never went there to express his ideas himself—he opposed the giving of full powers to Mosaddeq, but did not utilize (because he was a cleric?) the only tribune that would have allowed him to oppose them effectively; and his readiness on his return from Mecca in fall 1952, to propose the replacement of the Mosaddeq government by a government of Ha'erizadeh or Zahedi![54]

Fourth, Kashani was unjust toward Mosaddeq. His aggressiveness toward him, even after the coup d'état, was excessive. He declared to a Palestinian journalist on 1 September, 1953:

We are satisfied . . . truly satisfied! The situation is good and the danger has been definitively dispelled . . . for this man, Mosaddeq, had deviated from the road. . . . He merited his fate . . . he did nothing for his country . . . Mosaddeq revolted against the shah and forgot what the shah represents, the influence he has on the people. The shah wanted to dismiss Mosaddeq four months earlier, but I opposed this. Later we were against him in this struggle, and we won out over him! . . . Mosaddeq betrayed both me and his country because he wished to monopolize the three powers.

Later, to the question "What punishment do you think he deserves?" Kashani answered, "That which he deserves according to the holy law of Islam is the punishment that is given the one who has betrayed the mission confided by his country in war, the sentence for a traitor, which is death!"[55]

Fifth, the ideological bases of Kashani's political engagement were scarcely worked out. It is clear that he did not act out of pure ambition, even though this reproach is the leitmotif of all his detractors: his central

---

53. See Faghfoory, "Ulama," pp. 188–203: "Kashani and the Fadayan-e Islam."

54. He told this at the time to Ayatollah Reza Zanjani (personal interview 9 December 1980).

55. Naser ad-Din al-Nashashebi, *Madha jara fi'l sharq al-ausat?* (Beirut, 1961), pp. 46ff.

ideal was to free the people colonized or dominated by great powers in order that the riches of their countries could serve to improve the life of their poor populations. (The Anglo-Iranian Oil Company [AIOC] was the best example of domination for economic motives.) Islam was used as an indisputable reference; it was the source of values, which colonialism tried to destroy by introducing divisions in society and trying to separate religion from politics. But Islam, a political religion, was not for Kashani an aim that suppressed all else: sometimes Kashani invoked the Iranian constitution of 1906–07, based on democratic principles, or the Universal Declaration of Human Rights, the United Nations Charter, and so forth.

Sixth, one does not find in Kashani discussions on capitalism and communism, both of which he in fact rejects: the former because it is (as in the case of the AIOC) the exploiter of poor nations. As to the latter, one is surprised to see Kashani at times accepting compromise with the Communists, and sending two mollas as delegates of Iran to a Communist-led congress in Vienna in fall 1952 (against the advice of Mosaddeq), this despite a profound antipathy for the Marxist materialist philosophy.[56]

Seventh, the political action of Kashani had no very clear class content. Himself from a family of modest ulama, he was never a great financial operator, contrary to certain ulama of his time. He defended the rights of the oppressed, to whom he was close, and whose natural aspirations for justice he addressed, but his struggle did not have a very strong social dimension. With regard to the theologians, who on the whole received him badly, Kashani did not construct political theories reserving for them special rights, and did not attract them especially toward being deputies. He himself never undertook an electoral campaign, and was elected without presenting himself as a candidate. His closest political collaborators, Baqa'i Kermani, Ha'erizadeh, and Makki, were Westernized secularists.

Eighth, Kashani had no sort of fanaticism. The testimony of those who met him and could, because of their political and cultural divergences, have had a negative judgment on his conduct, is unanimous in recognizing his intelligence with regard to problems of the contemporary world and his openness of spirit, including his positions on certain traditional mores, such as the education of girls. But he was not a reformer.[57]

Ninth, Kashani had a remarkable sense of public relations. In this sense, the accusation that he had collaborated with the Germans, an accusation raised by the British, is plausible. In no situation did he fail to find a party disposed to listen to him. Similarly, his contacts with the

56. See Faghfoory, "Ulama," p. 156; Arfa, *Under Five Shahs*, p. 361; interview with Ayatollah Reza Zanjani, 8 December 1980.
57. See Arfa, *Under Five Shahs*, pp. 361 and 389ff.

foreign press, which was rather hostile to him in principle, were in general excellent, and he gave a large number of interviews, which allowed him to defend his thought and define his anticolonialism. He had himself photographed, for example, at an exhibit of textiles made in Iran, designed to combat the importation of European textiles.

Tenth, Kashani felt the international dimension of colonialism, and extended Iran's struggle not only to all Islamic nations but also to other oppressed peoples of Asia or Africa. He felt from the beginning the importance of the Palestinian question. He wrote before his arrest in World War II to Rashid Ali al-Gilani, the Iraqi religious chief, and to the grand mufti of Jerusalem who had taken refuge in Iraq, Hajj Amin al-Husaini, a letter in which he said: "We have all a common goal. We are preparing our next blow, and I hope that everything will go as foreseen. We hope that our common struggle will help the Muslims to free themselves of the yoke of the enemy and lead them to freedom and independence."[58]

Eleventh, Kashani enjoyed triumphs, at least on two occasions: upon his liberation from captivity in 1945 and on his return to Beirut in 1950. These two manifestations, whose precedents must be sought in the epoch of the constitutional revolution (when the ulama returned from Qom in August 1906), showed the great potential power Kashani held. It is a paradox of Iranian history that his four arrests (in 1943, 1946, 1949, and 1955) could take place without provoking more demonstrations.

Twelfth, this political glory is, in smaller degree, really comparable only to that which Ayatollah Khomeini knew later. The comparison, which some make today to rehabilitate Kashani, is not without foundation. The two men knew each other well; it is said that Kashani was the artisan, around 1930, of the marriage of Ruhollah Khomeini, then a young molla, with the daughter of the famous Ayatollah Saqafi, who taught in Tehran. After the war, the frequenters of Kashani's home often saw there "Aqa Ruhollah." Khomeini is said to have been at Kashani's when the house was attacked with stones and bricks by Mosaddeqist counterdemonstrators on 31 July 1953. Khomeini's intransigent character may have pushed Kashani, a subtle politician, to say that Aqa Ruhollah was not made for politics.[59] It is surprising that the most complete biography of Khomeini, which speaks at length of his relations with Ayatollah Borujerdi, says not a word of those he had with Kashani.[60]

It is too soon to assess the work of Kashani, against whom many unjust

58. *Taraqqi*, 45, 20 Farvardin 1330/1951, p. 3, cited in Faghfoory, "Ulama," p. 208.
59. Testimony of H. Makki and M. Baqa'i to me in the summer of 1980. Kashani's judgment on Khomeini was reported to me by Reza Saqafi. On the attack on Kashani's house, see *Ruhaniyat*, document 54; Faghfoory, "Ulama," p. 269, n. 2.
60. See (Ruhani), *Barrasi va tahlili*, pp. 97ff.

accusations have been made, and who is now the object of an excessive cult. We must wait until a collected edition of his declarations and interviews is available in order to evaluate the thought of this bold political leader, who broke the wall barring political affairs to the ulama. Amid many failures, his life at least illustrates well a belief that he held close to his heart, and which he made his guide: Islam forbids all separation between politics and religion. Amid a generally reactionary clergy he was an example of a religious leader open to the struggles of his time.

CHAPTER SEVEN

Shariati's Social Thought

SHAHROUGH AKHAVI

Preliminary Observations

This essay deals with the social thought of Dr. Ali Shariati (d. 1977). It must rest upon an analysis of his numerous lectures and writings on the sociology of Islam. Shariati seldom directed his attention to social theory as such, although his works abound with themes that are recognizable elements of social theory—even if they are not fully worked through. Nevertheless, his broad concern with the problematic of social justice and his insistence on applying sociological analysis to the critique of contemporary Islam permits one to distill the essence of his theory. The difficult style and eclectic nature of much of his thinking complicate the task of the analyst. However, the originality of certain of his contributions, together with the significant impact his thought has had upon Iranian intellectuals in search of a political culture and ideology of development make the task worthwhile.

Before analyzing his social thought, it will be helpful to provide a brief biographical sketch of his life. A few things can be said with assurance about Shariati before his arrest in 1957 for participating in the activities of the National Front, the political coalition led by the nationalist prime minister, Mohammad Mosaddeq (d. 1967), and subsequently by his associates. Shariati was born in 1933 in a village near the northeastern city of Mashhad. The household was a religious one, and his father was himself a respected reformist member of the clergy and acknowledged as a teacher of the religious sciences in his own right. The young Shariati early became acquainted with the discourse of the official clergy of Iran as a consequence. He studied the introductory and intermediate cycles of religious education in his father's courses. He also apparently was educated in the Mashhad secondary-school system and attended the Mashhad teacher's college. By the time of the coup d'état of 1953 he was a twenty-year-old nationalist, already active in reformist causes. During the next four years Shariati continued his political activities, while also

125

teaching school and then studying in the Mashhad Faculty of Letters. In 1957 the regime arrested both father and son, and it remains unclear when they were released.

In 1960 Shariati went to France for his doctoral studies. The period of his stay in Paris has been the subject of a good deal of rumor, especially in regard to the eminent thinkers with whom he is said to have been on terms of personal acquaintance and/or friendship. These individuals allegedly included Jean-Paul Sartre, Louis Massignon, Jacques Berque, Georges Gurevich, and others at the University of Paris. It seems that the degree to which he personally knew these luminaries or studied under their close supervision has been exaggerated by those contributing to the legend that has inevitably grown around him. His doctoral degree was not in sociology but in medieval Iranian philology under Professor G. Lazard—a fact uncovered by Yann Richard, who found Shariati's dissertation in Paris.

The consensus is that Shariati was radicalized on third-world issues as a student participating in the political extracurricular activities of Iranian students in Paris. More specifically, his contributions to the Algerian nationalist newspaper, al-Mujahid, played no small role in his emergence as a protest leader. According to some who knew him in Paris, he also played a leading part in the organization of the Iranian student opposition in Europe. His inclination toward sociology was likely stimulated more by his political commitments than his formal course work.

Upon concluding his dissertation, Shariati returned to Iran, only to be arrested at the Turkish frontier. He was released six months afterward and permitted to teach in the secondary-school system in his home region. This eventuated in an appointment at Mashhad University, something that could not have occurred without some kind of patronage. While teaching there, he introduced a course on the sociology of Islam, which was as novel as it was popular. His success in attracting students generated envy among his colleagues and superiors, as well as the regime's concern. Hence, his appointment was terminated, although once again it is uncertain when these developments occurred. He must have been in close contact with like-minded individuals in Tehran during this period, and the termination of his appointment at Mashhad University no doubt spurred him to settle in the capital.

Some time around 1965 he came in touch in Tehran with a number of men whose activities within the Monthly Religious Society had abruptly been halted by the government in March 1963. These individuals had been seriously inquiring into the condition and structure of the Iranian religious institution during the immediately preceding three and a half years, and it seemed as though Shariati's new approach and the substantive and methodological concerns of the group had much in common. When a philanthropist who hoped the work of the Monthly Religious Society would continue donated the necessary land, the institution known as the Husainiyeh Ershad was born. While Shariati's colleagues were leading forces in the Husainiyyeh Ershad in their own right, Shariati himself gradually became *primus inter pares,* and in time his name became virtually synonymous with the institution. In 1973 the regime arrested him and closed the Husainiyeh Ershad. For about two years he remained in prison and in 1975 was released into internal exile in Khurasan province. After a desultory period of inactivity, he was allowed to leave the country. In 1977 he made his way to England, where he mysteriously died. The discovery of his body on 19 June 1977 was met with the widespread belief that he had been murdered by the shah's secret intelligence organization, SAVAK.

Shariati and his associates presented innumerable lectures on Islamic themes. These raised old issues in a new light. The discussions of theoretical tenets of the faith that had long been at the center of clerical discourse were now presented from the perspective of social action and organization, as opposed to routine ethical pietism. Although he was not consistent in abiding by the method, typical of much of his writing was the effort to be comparative. The tone of his works is optimistic and affirmative, but it always reflects an edge of didacticism and, one must say, apologia.

Shariati's topics and themes were hardly new, but the method by which he—as an Iranian—analyzed them was unprecedented. Suffice it to say that Shariati's influence upon large numbers of Iranian youth in the 1960s and 1970s has been of fundamental importance to their view of the world. This will more than likely continue to be the case, whatever line the contemporary clergy adopts with respect to his thought. It is to the content of such thought that we now turn. If it strikes the observer that his contributions lie in the area of polemical scholarship, this in no way negates his influence upon many of the country's intellectuals today.

Nature of Reality

The basis of reality (ontology) is, according to Shariati, the unity of God, nature, and man. Shariati alternatively expresses the integration of these three elements as "the embracing of the entire world in a unity." This notion of the fusion of God, nature, and man is the central concept in his "integralist world view" (*jahanbini-ye tauhidi*). He insists that his world view permits a good deal of room for man as an autonomous individual who bears responsibility for his actions.

Yet, Shariati falls into the trap of the logical fallacy of misplaced concreteness (reification). In other words, he attributes tangible and human characteristics to what is a concept in his own mind. In this case, the concept is the world seen as the fusion of God, nature, and man. That he succumbs to this fallacy can be seen in his assertion that such a world is "alive, willful, self-aware, endowed with feelings and an ideal."[1]

Shariati's doctrine of first principles—or ontology—may be pursued one step further. For him *tauhid* (the integration of God, nature, and man) means the rejection of contradictions. If what exists prior to everything else is the unity of God, nature, and man, then contradictions are impossible. As he puts it: "the structure of tauhid cannot accept contradictions or disintegration in the world. Therefore, the world view of tauhid does not contain contradiction[s] in existence, in man, nature, spirit, body, the world and the hereafter, matter, and meaning. Contradictions are not to be found, according to tauhid, in the legal, class, social, political, racial, national, terrestrial, lineal, genetic, subjective, inherent, or even economic realms."[2]

Despite his apparently emphatic rejection of contradictions (seemingly based on his perceived need to contend against the dialectics of Marxism), they actually are an important element in his social thought after all. Here, a paradox emerges. On the one hand, he applies the logic of dialectics—which rest fundamentally upon the constant interaction of mutually contradictory forces—to general historical evolution. On the other hand, he claims that contradictions do not operate in a genuine Shi'i historical community. The strong implication is that God, nature, and man are integrated into a unity only for Shi'i Muslim experience. For non-Shi'is, the doctrine of first principles decidedly features contradictions.

Shariati does not explicitly enter into a discussion of Ash'arite ontology, which has dominated Sunni Islamic thought over the centuries. According to the Ash'arite doctrine of reality, the universe is believed to consist of millions of monads or atoms that are not bound in time or space. It argues for the formlessness of things and the lack of any causes other than God's will. Such a position underscores the omnipotence of God in the Ash'arite view, since a doctrine of cause and effect permits human beings to fix in time and space phenomena that only God can identify and shape. Cause and effect imply some degree of natural law, limiting God's absolute power to do what He wills with the world at every moment.

Shariati by implication rejects this Ash'arite occasionalistic world view in his stress upon a doctrine of causality. Especially important in this connection is Shariati's concept of *jabr-e tarikh*—historical determi-

---

1. Ali Shariati, *Islamshenasi* (Tehran: Hosainiyeh Ershad, n.d.), p. 47.

2. Ibid., p. 53. There are nettlesome problems of translation, here. The word *khaki* as an adjective I have translated as "terrestrial," although an alternative may be "territorial"; *khuni* I have rendered as "lineal" (there being to my knowledge no satisfactory English word to render "blood" in its adjectival form); *fetri* I have translated as "inherent."

nism—about which more will be said below. In other words, Shariati accepts the Mu'tazilite doctrine, which has long been the Shi'i position in explaining the nature of reality. This suggests, as against Shariati's detractors among the Iranian clergy, that his thought has more affinities to Shi'ism than to Sunnism, despite their consideration of him as a latent adherent of Sunni positions.

Strange to say, having expended much effort to unite God, nature, and man, Shariati wants simultaneously to separate them from one another. The observer cannot resolve Shariati's inclination to do this by reference to *real* unification and *apparent* separation, or vice versa. No, he decidedly wants it both ways, as is clear when he says the three elements "are separate from one another . . . [but] the source is the same. All have a single direction and move and live with one will and spirit."[3] It may be supposed that Shariati's separation of the elements which he also believes to be united has to do with the dilemma posed for him of the omnipotence and omniscience of God. In other words, his position risks diffusing the attributes of God among other entities of the universe (that is, nature and man), thus diminishing God's power.

Attempting to refine his doctrine of reality, Shariati identifies the primary force in the universe. He holds this force to be an essence (*zat*) that is both "unseeable and unknowable." He argues further that this essence is composed of matter and energy. In this context, such matter and energy are "alternating manifestations" (*jelvehha-ye motanaveb*) of the essence identified by Shariati.[4]

It will be seen that Shariati's doctrine of first principles is complex. It involves the fusion into unity, yet separation from each other, of God, nature, and man. This substance (that is, the fused elements) operates in the world as an invisible and incomprehensible force. Such a force in its turn consists of energy and matter, each of which alternately expresses it. He seems to be saying, finally, that the "unseeable and unknowable" essence is greater than the sum of its parts (energy and matter).

Shariati has thus struggled to establish a philosophical position with respect to the nature of reality. What the consequences of this position are for the consistency of his social theory taken as a whole should become clear in the last part of this essay.

Theory of Knowledge

Whereas the classic Islamic theory of knowledge (epistemology) rests on the concept of *kasb*—that is, that man's knowledge is contingent upon God's—Shariati transcends this doctrine and comes very close to Marx's

---

3. Ibid., pp. 49–50.
4. Ibid., p. 50.

position but ultimately veers off in the direction of phenomenology. Marx
argued that claims to knowledge depend upon the process of man's
interaction with his fellow man in the creation of social product. Of
central importance to Marx's theory of knowledge is the insistence upon
the actual and concrete involvement of the individual with his social and
material environment. And, of course, the knowledge that man gains as
he produces value in the division of labor permits him—in Marx's view—
ultimately to recognize his alienation and to organize to terminate it.

Shariati also envisages man as gaining knowledge by social action in the
real world. His view is that man's knowledge is coordinate with what he
regards to be the interactive relationship among God, nature, and man.
Note that he wants to emphasize the voluntaristic quality of the relationship, lest one gain the impression (false from Shariati's standpoint) that
man remains a passive entity in this scheme of things. Perhaps critical to
such voluntarism is Shariati's decisive orientation toward what he terms
entezar-e mosbat (dynamic anticipation of the return of the Imam) and
shahadat (bearing witness on behalf of and/or martyrdom for the sake of
the faith). Underpinning both entezar and shahadat is the conception of
man as someone who does, acts, makes decisions, chooses among alter-
natives. In Shariati's theory of knowledge man ought not to be seen as a
plaything of forces beyond his control and grasp. In brief, Shariati's view
of the problem of knowledge, like Marx's, seems to be rooted in a
perspective of man as *homo faber.*[5]

But is there more to Shariati's theory of knowledge? Does he give
precedence, as Marx does, to praxis, according to which claims to truth
and knowledge rest upon relations of production as they are influenced by
land, labor, capital, technology, and so forth? As a matter of fact, Shariati
appears to argue in favor of a phenomenological theory of knowledge,
whereby claims to the truth and knowledge can only be based upon
knowledge of appearances (*padidahha*). Thus, Shariati says, "nature—
that is, the world to which we bear witness—consists of an aggregation of
signs [*ayat*] and customs [*sonnatha*]." Shariati tells us that the word *sign*
is "synonymous with the term *phenomenon.* . . . A phenomenon, or
phenomenology more generally, is based upon the idea that absolute
truth, the depth of reality and the fundamental essence of the world,
nature, matter, are in no way within our grasp. *What exists, is capable of
being known,* experienced, and scientifically studied and perceived by us,
is appearance, not what is."[6]

Shariati divides existence into that which is hidden and that which is

5. Shariati, "Mas'uliyat-e Shi'a budan," in *Shi'a* (Tehran: Hosainiyeh Ershad, n.d.), pp.
229–30 and passim. As a matter of fact, the entire corpus of his work reflects these
considerations.
6. Shariati, *Islamshenasi,* pp. 51–52, emphasis supplied.

evident. But the primary reality is the hidden, what Shariati calls *zat*. This primary reality produces appearances—in fact the concrete, everyday, material objects of life—and man uses signs to refer to them. But the primary reality will remain unknown to us.[7]

Nevertheless, according to a dynamic that Shariati is convinced operates,[8] man is autonomous in regard to his social action and social choices. Man, therefore, can act independently of this essence/zat, which yet causes him to choose with respect to appearances only. It seems, consequently, that Shariati would have man operating as a self-contained entity but making decisions and choices about only the appearances of reality. These difficult considerations will be taken up below in a discussion of Shariati's philosophy of history.

Philosophy of History

Shariati's philosophy of history is rich with themes and the interplay of ideas. While eclectic in the borrowing from other traditions, notably Marxism, it contains analysis that is original in the context of existing Shi'i interpretations. According to him, the philosophy of history of Islam is based upon what he terms "scientific determinism" (*jabr-e elmi*). This signifies that science, especially anthropology, sociology, and political economy, can usefully be applied to gain a true understanding of historical development in Islam.

Influenced again by Marx, he argues that "history unfolds through dialectical contradiction[s]." History has evolved in the context of a struggle between mutually opposing forces. This struggle, he holds, "began with the first man on earth and has always and everywhere been waged."[9]

Shariati's evident historicism can be detected in his conviction that history "started from somewhere and of necessity must lead to somewhere; it must have a goal and a direction." He thus seems to be advocating a universal history[10] within the framework of which man can then choose, at various stages in his development, to follow the imams, opt for laissez-faire economics, prescribe Marxist views, and so forth.

Moreover, Shariati additionally argues that historical change occurs not only through contradictions but contradictions involving the mode of production. Couching his analysis in terms of the Cain and Abel legend,

---

7. Ibid., p. 51.
8. In my view the dynamic remains obscure, both in *Islamshenasi* and elsewhere in his essays.
9. Shariati, *Islamshenasi*, pp. 69–70.
10. Shariati, *Jabr-e tarikh* (Tehran: n.p., 1354 H. Sh./1975), pp. 56–59.

he asserts that the brothers in fact provide the archetypes of mode-of-production conflict: in the one case Cain is the agriculturalist; in the other Abel is the pastoralist. Whereas Cain's social rank and "class" position in society were anchored in his ownership of productive means, that of his brother rested on what he was capable of securing by his hands in hunting, fishing, gleaning. Ultimately, Shariati regards the conflict between Cain and Abel to be an "objective" (*aini*) one that sets the stages for all future struggles, themselves each also objective in nature.[11]

It will be recalled that Shariati had already taken a position on the nature of reality in which the basis of the universe is the unity of God, nature, and man. It is to be assumed, in light of what he now says about contradiction's being an abiding element of social change, that the alleged unity exists only in a genuinely Shi'i community. Other societies face the certainty of conflict. If this be a correct inference from Shariati's position, then the question presents itself, What is the mechanism of historical development and social change in a true Shi'i community? Shariati would likely respond that the mechanism of change would be a combination of leadership based on justice and allegiance of the people to the *velayat* (delegated rule) of Ali, the imams, and the general agency.

Despite the foregoing, Shariati's notions of historical change suggest that it is appropriate for us to see Marx's influence upon him. On this level he rebukes the ulama (clergy) for deriving a merely moral lesson from the Cain and Abel legend—that is, an admonition that "thou shalt not kill." Social science argues that this historic dispute between the two brothers must be seen as a class struggle. The methodology of the social sciences requires that we establish the causes of certain effects by eliminating constants in comparing two entities, and the only differentiating factor between the two brothers is their social occupation. They had had the same parents, grew up in the same social environment, had had the same influences brought to bear upon their personalities as infants, children, adolescents. Therefore, an ancient legend spawned by the scriptures of the great religions may now be interpreted in a new light, yielding a more powerful explanation through the use of Marxist-influenced sociology.

A major departure from Marx, nonetheless, is to be seen in his contention regarding the relations between ownership of productive means and power. Shariati asserts that it is power which determines ownership and not (as Marx says) that ownership shapes power.[12] This point of difference with Marx suggests a more deeply rooted variance between Shariati and Marx concerning free will and historical determinism, to which we shall return shortly.

11. Shariati, *Islamshenasi,* pp. 69–70.
12. Ibid., pp. 72–73.

Meanwhile, it is worth stressing that Shariati wishes to differentiate between fundamental change (*harakat-e jauhari*) and small-scale (transitional) change (*harakat-e enteqali*). All societies witness the cumulation of many discrete, small-scale changes affecting different facets of life. Hence, a social institution such as the family undergoes small-scale change if the basis of authority is transferred from age/wisdom to virility/wisdom. We can speak of fundamental social change, however, if we observe the following transformation. Suppose that at an earlier time divorce was forbidden, marriage of near relatives prohibited, polygamy sanctioned, only marriage through ecclesiastical auspices permitted, and the extended family formed the basis of the household economy. If we then perceive that at a later time, in the same society, divorce was permitted, first-cousin marriage allowed, monogamy alone was tolerated, civil ceremony became the legitimating practice, and the nuclear family formed the foundation for the household economy, then one is speaking of major social change.[13] This example is not Shariati's, but it is presented here to clarify his meaning.

Shariati is convinced that, at the level of fundamental change, all societies face the problem of the rise and decline of their civilizations. The motor force of historical change being contradiction, is there any escape from decline and disintegration? he queries. Historical determinism suggests not, he holds. But, continuous revitalization of society is possible, according to Shariati, through the doctrine and practice of permanent revolution. Shariati does not mean permanent revolution in Trotsky's sense of periodically intensifying revolutionary ardor and praxis in a society undergoing its travails. Instead, Shariati argues that the three dynamic principles of *ijtihad* (independent judgment), *al-amr bi al-ma'ruf wa al-nahy an al-munkar* (commanding the good and forbidding evil), and *muhajirat* (emigration) will protect the Islamic community from decline for an unspecified long-run period of time.[14]

How can this be so? To begin with, ijtihad, correctly applied, renews and rebuilds ideas. The problem in Shi'i society since the disappearance of the Twelfth Imam has been that ijtihad has been implemented within a narrow compass. Consequently, its scope has been limited to legal specialists deducing derivative ordinances (*ahkam-e far'i*) of law. Yet, ijtihad should be applied in its broader sense of clarifying one's ideology, Shariati remonstrates. And in this sense it becomes "an objective duty [for] every individual to exert himself through ijtihad in regard to his own ideology." With respect to the second principle in Islam that will aid in

13. This is the point made by Robert Nisbet in his "Introduction: The Problem of Social Change," in *Social Change,* ed. Nisbet (New York: Harper Torchbooks, 1972), p. 2.
14. Shariati, *Islamshenasi*, pp. 451–54.

revitalizing Islam, Shariati is just as forceful. Commanding the good and forbidding evil is "the mission and objective duty of all individuals—among the masses, the wretched, the intellectuals, the bazaar merchants—all are responsible for implementing *al-amr bi al-ma'ruf wa al-nahy an al-munkar*. This principle will rescue societies from the rise and fall [doctrine]. No one can be uncommitted or neutral on this issue."[15]

The third principle is not clarified by Shariati, except to say that the emigration he speaks of may be internal to the person or may involve his external relocation. The implication, however, is that emigration prevents routinization and keeps one in touch with newness in existence.

Is Shariati then arguing for free will? Emphatically so. He accepts Sartre's point that man is free to choose; the only limiting factor upon man's will is his own mortality and the requirements of food, shelter, health, and the biological necessities associated with these. In all other respects, man is absolutely free to make his own decisions and consequently absolutely responsible for the choices he does make.[16]

Shariati argues against the materialists, whom he charges with viewing man's will as being determined and therefore not autonomous. He believes in historical determinism, but he prefers the French *déterminisme historique*—to him a more flexible concept—to jabr-e tarikh. The latter concept has, at the hands of Iranian intellectuals, led to the caricature of man as an automaton. For Shariati, however, historical determinism means that history "is a single, ongoing and uninterrupted phenomenon in time which is influenced by specific [*mo'ayyan*] causes (mo'ayyan is not *jabri*)."[17]

Man in history is like a fish in a river. Now, the river courses its way through shallows, rapids, narrows, wide gorges, and over waterfalls in a bed shaped by geological formations over time. Yet, the fish can go in various directions, even upstream. Man, for his part, is influenced by scientific laws of causation; yet, man is free to choose his own course, even to the point of taking his own life.[18]

Sometimes, Shariati seems to be saying that history is the motor of change rather than man. For example, he declares, "History is the factor that changes man from a quasi-savage being into contemporary man. The latter has reached a certain degree of perfection up to the present and will be, in the distant future, the ideal person, noblest of all creatures in the material world." At other times, history for him is a "crucible" in which man is transformed.[19] Interestingly, he hearkens to Greek notions of man

15. Ibid., pp. 453–54.
16. Shariati, *Jabr-e tarikh*, pp. 47–49.
17. Ibid., pp. 51–52.
18. Ibid., pp. 53–54.
19. Ibid., pp. 61, 65.

as a social creature in the process of realizing the best that is in him—
"man is a being in the process of becoming."[20] The goal defines the
individual, then, and we have here a teleological conception of man's
growth toward a certain end. This parallels Shariati's teleological view of
historical development which has already been identified above as his
historicist philosophy of history.

With respect to the question of free will versus determinism, Shariati
believes that he has established an interpretation of Islam which differs
from both idealism and materialism. Whereas both of those philosophies
of life denature man (in the case of idealism by making man the object of
an abstract and disembodied Absolute Idea; in the case of materialism by
making man derivative to matter), Islam ennobles him. Shariati's view is
expressed in the following passage:

Islam's doctrine of first principles [ontology] is based upon belief in the hidden.
By "hidden" I mean that unknown reality that exists in the base material, natural
phenomena which are accessible to our senses and mental, scientific, and expe-
riential comprehension. This unknown reality is reckoned as a higher grade of
truth and the fundamental focus of the totality of movements, laws and manifestations of this world.

This "hidden" is in reality the absolute spirit and will of existence. Contrary to
idealism, which supposes phenomena of the material world to be the product of
the Idea; and in contrast to materialism, which imagines ideas to be the emanation
of the material world; Islam counts both matter and idea as different appearances
(signs) of that "absolute hidden being." Thus, Islam rejects both idealism and
materialism simultaneously; Islam recognizes the existence of the world of nature
beyond our ideas; and it holds that man, as a being having ideas in the face of
material nature and the material social environment and material production, is
autonomous and genuine.[21]

Yet, we also have a Shariati who, as we have seen, believes in historical
determinism. Rejecting happenstance and disjunction in historical progression, Shariati equates historical determinism with God's will. But
that, in turn, is integrated into the principle of entezar. The exact linkage
between causation, God's will, historical determinism and entezar are not
clarified by Shariati, but we are told that ultimately the Shi'i philosophy of
history places man in the forefront of change.[22]

20. Ibid., p. 64.
21. Shariati, *Ensan, Marksizm, Islam*, 2nd ed. (Qom: n.p., 1355 H. Sh./1976), p. 29.
22. Cf. his comments in *Entezar, mazhab-e eteraz* (Tehran: Hosainiyeh Ershad, 1350 H.
Sh./1971), pp. 41–42: "Entezar is a historical determinism. . . . I, who am waiting in this
corner of the world and this moment of history—it is possible that tomorrow or at any other
moment a revolution will occur over the surface of the globe on behalf of truth, justice, and
the oppressed masses in which I, too, must play a role. This revolution will not be [through]

Political Community and Authority

What kind of political community does Shariati envisage for Islam, and more particularly for Shi'ism? In the first place, its members dynamically orient themselves to matters of social existence, such as allocation of goods, rendering services, maintaining appropriate standards of health, education, and welfare. The very word *umma* (Islamic community) derives from an Arabic root meaning to go, to betake oneself. Shariati alleges that other words used by other peoples to signify community, such as nation, society, race, people, tribe, sect, lack "progressive spirit, social perspective, dynamism, commitment . . ." The social system of the Islamic community, according to him, is based upon justice and equitable allocation. It is a community in which the people collectively hold property (*malekiyat-e mardom*), and no class differences exist (*jam'eh-ye bi tabaqeh*). And, contrary to Western variants of socialism (in his interpretation), the Islamic community is goal-oriented. The political order of this community is not a democracy of the elite; not a liberalism that is bereft of purpose and is the plaything of the establishment (*qodratha*); not one based on a "fetid aristocracy"; not one founded upon a dictatorship against the people; not one rooted in an oppressive oligarchy. It is rather "based upon true leadership (and not leader, since that would be fascism)."[23]

The weight of Shariati's writings makes clear that such leadership must derive from the group in society that he terms "enlightened thinkers" (*raushanfekran*). Care must be taken to remember, upon considering Shariati's social thought, that while Imam Ali is the archetypal leader of the Shi'i community, (1) he is not available to contemporary Shi'ia (i.e., they must rely upon more than one individual to lead them); (2) Shariati's model is that of an enlightened intellectual, not a clergyman. Now, it is true that for Shariati a clergyman may also be simultaneously an enlightened thinker. However, the burden of this writing is to show how the clergy has either wittingly or unwittingly cooperated with oppressors over

---

praying and dying but instead by the flag, sword, armor, and true jihad . . . thus I believe in historical determinism, not chance historical occurrence. . . . I here believe that history is moving deterministically toward the victory of justice, the decisive salvation of the oppressed masses, and the inevitable annihilation of oppression and oppressors." Within this formulation of historical progression, Shariati draws a contrast with Marxism, for which—he claims—"history, itself, like a living society, is independent of individuals"(ibid., p. 42). In his view, if Marxism may be said to have accorded any role to man in historical progression, it was really with Lenin and Mao that a break was made with the "dogmatic and dry" scientism and "sociologism" of the nineteenth century. For this notion see Shariati, "Khod Sazi-ye Enqelabi," in *Khod sazi-ye enqelabi* (Tehran, Hosainiyeh Ershad, n.d.), pp. 131–32.

23. Shariati, *Islamshenasi*, pp. 98–99.

the centuries.[24] The enlightened thinker, by contrast, opposes himself to, protests against, struggles with, oppressors and oppression.

The enlightened thinker, indeed, has the task of creating what Shariati unabashedly terms an "Islamic Protestantism" for the sake of cultural engineering, stimulating the political and class consciousness of the masses, building bridges between the intellectual stratum and the masses, defrocking false priests and, in a word, ushering in a Renaissance.[25] Shariati's preference for the raushanfekr over the clergyman, more affirmatively speaking, has to do with his deep awareness of the problems affecting the real life chances of the Islamic community. The members of the ulama stratum are learned, to be sure, but mainly about subjects (*kalam, fiqh, usul*) far removed from the daily needs and social action of Muslims.[26] In many respects the raushanfekr is an emanation of something that Shariati has insisted perhaps plays the key role as the motor force of historical change: *an-nas* (the people).[27]

But what role do the *nas* play in the community when it comes to questions of authority, legitimacy, sovereignty, the state? Shariati posits that they are critical in designating the deputy of the Imam as the leader(s) of the community. Shariati joins the issue in his discussion of the periods of Islamic history. These he divides into four: (1) the era of prophecy; (2) the era of the Imamate (the rule of Ali and the eleven imams who succeeded him); (3) the period of occultation (i.e., Muslim history since A.D. 874) of the Imam; (4) the era of resurrection and true justice. Shariati

24. He defended himself against the charge that he envisages no social role for the ulama by responding that that was a distortion of his views; and that he had said many good things about clergymen, not least of which is that they have never signed any treaties assigning the resources and territory of Iran to foreigners. For his position, see his comments published in the proceedings of a roundtable on interrogatories and criticisms directed against the Hosainiyeh Ershad by its opponents entitled *Pasokh be so'alat va enteqadat* (Tehran: Hosainiyeh Ershad, 1350 H. Sh./1971), pp. 121–31.

25. Shariati, *Az koja aghaz konim?* (Tehran: Hosainiyeh Ershad, n.d.), pp. 55–56.

26. Shariati, *Ravesh-e shenakht-e Islam* (Tehran: Hosainiyeh Ershad, 1347 H. Sh./1968), p. 5.

27. Ibid., pp. 14–16. In this essay Shariati has yet another opportunity to discuss matters in the context of Islam's philosophy of history. Here, he stresses the importance of al-nas (which he considers the primary factor), personality, customs, and chance. (In other words, happenstance is an aspect of the progression of history in Islam after all!) Islam, he says, has its *sunna*—its customs and traditions. "Islam has a definite origin, a definite way, a definite path and nature. Basically, all societies have fixed and definite immutable [social] laws. A society is like a living thing which, like any other living being, possesses fixed, immutable laws upon which the life of society is made stable. Thus, we seem to be approaching a historical determinism, a sociological determinism. But Islam has something else to say about this that rectifies it, and that is that in Islam the people and the human individual are both responsible for their own fate." If the juxtaposition of fixed laws and social responsibility of individuals appears contradictory in sociological science, the Qur'an accepts the two principles as complementary nonetheless, he declares.

argues that the first and fourth periods of Islamic history are those of the mission of the prophet and his legatee and as such designated by God. The prophet and the Mahdi (the Imam *cum* messiah whose return to the world signifies the end of corruption and commencement of the golden age) are God's appointees. They have been commissioned by Him to be the leaders of the Muslims. The prophet had designated Imam Ali to be his successor, Shariati holds, but the usurping companions of the prophet illegally appropriated the velayat from Ali and wrongfully established their own authority over the community. Despite this usurpation, the principle of designation by a particular source was clear, Shariati maintains. However, in the third period of Islamic history—that since the occultation of the Twelfth Imam—since neither the prophet exists nor is the Imam present, the mission of the prophets and imams is charged to the people themselves. And it is the people (al-nas) who must teach Islam, discern the right, implement Islamic laws, establish an Islamic society in place of the false one maintained by tyrants, defend the power and unity of the Muslims in the face of their enemies, undertake jihad, implement ijtihad

The people must designate (*tashkhis*) the best among them to lead the community. This designated group (sometimes referred to as a single individual, despite his own warning of the lurking dangers of fascism when one individual rules!) will exercise leadership responsibilities; but the people will continue to be in direct contact with the leadership, "and they should secure the government of knowledge . . . just as Plato had urged."[28] The reference to Plato is not the only allusion to Western thought and practice with respect to the role of government and the state. For Shariati then proceeds to a conception of popular sovereignty that is virtually indistinguishable from that issuing from the French Revolution:

The responsibility of leadership lies with those who hail from the people and are elected [*montakhab;* cf. *moshakhkhas*] by the masses of the people. . . . In Alavi Shi'ism there is a period of occultation that is a period of democracy. Contrary to the system of prophecy and Imamate, which are designated by God, the leadership of society during the period of occultation is based upon the principles of study, designation, *election* and consensus [ijma] of the *people. The power of sovereignty [hakemiyat] originates from . . . the community.*[29]

Shariati blames deviations from the true Shi'i community upon three social groups: (1) despotic rulers; (2) collaborating clergymen; (3) the passive masses of the population. The political community of Ali having

28. Shariati, *Tashayyo'-e alavi va tashayyo'-e safavi* (Tehran: Hosainiyeh Ershad, n.d.), p. 273.
29. Ibid., p. 274.

been destroyed by his assassins, the structure and principles underlying that community have never since been restored. Since then, people who have craved justice have preferred cautious dissimulation of belief (ta-qiya) and inert waiting for the Mahdi (termed entezar-e manfi, or passive anticipation of the return of the Imam). But Shariati has other things in mind for the masses. These include enlightened thinkers to stimulate their political consciousnesses in active interaction with them. Such thinkers have to bring the contradictions in the structure of society to the attention of the people lest no action be taken to resolve them to the advantage of the masses. The enlightened thinker must accept the advice of Francis Bacon to smash the idols of ignorance as the necessary preliminary to new conceptualizations in dealing with persistent social problems.[30]

The activist, responsible, revolutionary-minded enlightened thinker will expel the "official clergy" (ruhaniyat-e rasmi), the "co-opted clergy" (ruhaniyat-e vabasteh) from their entrenched positions of authority and influence. There is no doubt that one mechanism for implementing this purge of the clergy is through what Shariati has called cultural engineering and a new social psychology of Shi'i man. Moreover, although it is a Shi'i Islamic community that Shariati holds up as the ideal, it is clear that he wishes to restore Islamic unity. Therefore, much of the burden of his argument against the "false clergymen" is directed at their willing cooperation with rulers whose behavior created cleavages in the umma.[31]

Shariati is particularly upset at what he terms the "official administrators" (motavalliyun-e rasmi—specifically including some grand mujtahids) of Iranian religious institutions. They have, he argues, converted the "socially progressive, this-worldly" aspects of Islam into "private morality, attachments purely to the hereafter, and oblivion to reality."[32] If the

30. Shariati, Az koja aghaz konim? pp. 38–41.
31. Shariati, Tashayyo, pp. 51–52. His defense of Islam as a whole and hearkening to Sunni Islamic doctrine, practice, sources, etc. embroiled Shariati in polemics with Shi'i ulama. Such conflicts over details of interpretation of Islamic history and ideas cannot really be examined in an essay on Shariati's social thought—see, however, Shahrough Akhavi, "Shi'i Social Thought and Praxis in Recent Iranian History," in Islam in the Contemporary World, ed. C. K. Pullapilly (Notre Dame, Ind.: Cross Roads Press, 1980), pp. 171–98—it is worth noting that he upheld shura (collective decision-making) as the basis of Islamic democracy and stressed that the people implement ijma (consensus). For some of the polemics between Shariati and the ulama, consult Pasokh be so'alat, passim; and Shariati, "Nameh'i be agha-ye Naser Makarem," in Haft nameh az Mojahed-e Shahid Dr. Ali Shariati (Tehran: Entesharat-e Abu Zarr, 1356 H. Sh./1977), pp. 27–39; and Naser Makarem Shirazi, "Aya Hokumat-e Islami bar Pay-e Shura Ast?" in Darsha'i az Maktab-e Islam (Qom) 13, no. 1 (1392 H.Q./1972): 76–78.
32. Shariati, Tashayyo, pp. 140–41 and passim; Shariati, Hajj (Tehran: Hosainiyeh Ershad, 1350 H. Sh./1971), p. 6; Shariati, Cheh bayad kard? (Tehran: Hosainiyeh Ershad, n.d.), pp. 8, 14–15, 42; Shariati, Shahadat (Tehran: Hosainiyeh Ershad, 1350 H. Sh./1971), pp. 5, 27–28 and 9–10 following p. 78 in text; Shariati, Bazgasht be khuishtan bazgasht be

clergy are once again to play their potentially revolutionary role, they must be made to understand that fiqh (jurisprudence) amounts to the sociology of Islam (sic).[33] The problem is that certain of the grand mujtahids lack knowledge, even knowledge in the traditional, transmitted sciences, such as *hadith* (sayings of the prophet and the imams) and kalam (systematic theology). The only knowledge that they have is that of derivative ordinances: in other words, *vuzu* (ablution), *haiz* (menstruation), and *nefas* (childbirth). Yet, these very same high-ranking clergymen have the nerve to tell the enlightened thinkers to silence themselves about religion because they are not mujtahids and must emulate (*taqlid*) their "betters." But Shariati ripostes that taqlid must only be based upon narrow, technical issues. In all other respects, "Every person must do his own analysis, commensurate with his mental capacity and intellectual reserves . . . since taqlid is not a matter of intellect, it is—therefore—a technical or special matter. . . . *What is dangerous is intellectual emulation.*"[34]

Shariati's anti-elitist emphasis in regard to knowledge weaves like a leitmotif through his various essays and lectures. The raushanfekr, it will be understood, is not at all a monopolist of knowledge. If anything, Shariati values his activism and social commitment above discrete bits of information that he may have tucked away in a corner of his mind. Certainly the raushanfekr knows that in historical progression and social change man has an active part to play. It is not a question, as the "official clergy" would have it, of holding classes where students and teachers engage in intellectual casuistry. He berates the "co-opted clergy" for promoting two cancers that have enervated the body politic of the Shi'i community over the centuries: (1) an eternal optimism on their part that God, because he is just, may forgive even the *prétendu* Muslims who are the real enemies of Islam; such forgiveness is possible, according to them, despite even treasonous behavior to true Islam; (2) a fatalism (jabr) which has led the clergy to accept the appropriation of the velayat of Imam Ali as God's will. No, the raushanfekr will not permit the clergy to get away with such duplicity. Shariati argues that the Shi'i community can only be resurrected in its genuine form if the contemporary generation were to emulate the example of Imam Husain at Karbala. Shariati agrees that Husain sought to establish a political order for the Shi'i community. But the meaning of his act goes beyond the idea of restoring the velayat to the *ahl al-bait* (household of the prophet). Husain's action was a prototype for all societies and all cultures. Therefore, Shariati is urging, here, that

---

kodam khuish? (Tehran: Hosainiyeh Ershad, n.d.), p. 325—where he speaks of the "nationalized clergy" (*ulama-ye melli-shodeh*).

33. Shariati, *Tashayyo*, p. 225.

34. Ibid., pp. 313–14. Emphasis supplied.

the raushanfekr follow the path of Husain by bringing all oppressed peoples together as the final act before the return of the Mahdi. The Imam would surely return to introduce the golden age of justice in the face of this outstanding manifestation of what Shariati terms *entezar-e mosbat*.[35]

This is Shariati the anti-imperialist speaking. Establishment of the Shi'i political community can only occur through the uprooting of foreign domination in all its forms. But Shariati somehow transcends his role as fighter for the restoration of Alid Shi'ism and becomes very much a spokesman for masses everywhere who have suffered from the depredations of imperialism. No analysis of Shariati's political and social thought may ignore, consequently, his clarion calls for third-world revolution.

Critique

Shariati had little to say about the structure and organization of the true Shi'i political community and its wider social order. Therefore, we have only inferences as to his preferred arrangements for political economy, bureaucracy, law, parties, elite-mass relations, finance, and the like. Certainly he believed that the true Shi'i community would be classless, founded on social justice, equity, harmony of interests, and fraternity.

One may find, in his social theory, much attention—even if diffused—to such questions as the nature of reality and doctrine of first principles; theory of knowledge, philosophy of history; and political community and authority. A number of inconsistencies and logical lacunae need to be indicated. At the same time, it should be clear that were Shariati alive to respond to these criticisms, he would almost surely deny that they pose any intellectual problems of this sort.

With respect to his doctrine of first principles concerning the nature of reality, the relationship he underscores among God, nature, and man is not clear. Is the primary reality the "hidden," as he puts it? Or is it the unity in which man plays a decisive role? If it is the "hidden," then he would seem to accept revelation and God's will as the primary reality. However, he often holds out the basic truth—for him—that man is autonomous. At one point he argues that man acquires his freedom and elects to act based upon God's entrusting (*tafviz*) such freedom and action to him. This, he submits, makes man the surrogate (*janeshin*) of God in nature. Ultimately, "[i]n the Islamic world view man, in relationship to nature, is the sovereign will and, to use an expression, the god of nature."[36] Nevertheless, we had been given to believe elsewhere in his writings that a unity exists among God, nature, and man in which an

---

35. Shariati, *Shahadat*, pp. 35ff.
36. Shariati, *Ensan, Marksizm, Islam*, p. 31.

invisible essence is determinative of development and change. On this level, if the integration of these three elements indeed obtains, can Shariati consistently argue for a prioritization of God, nature, and man in descending order of power, control, and sovereignty? In other words, where is God and where is man in the ultimate scheme of things?

Shariati's conceptualization of knowledge rests upon a phenomenological foundation. The enlightened thinker is socially aware and must illuminate the contradictions in society, especially class contradictions. Yet, are these contradictions the surface appearance of a reality that is more basic and which we cannot know? Shariati's affirmative answer leads us to wonder what underpins the class conflicts. Is Shariati saying that the world is so complex that we can only hope to know certain aspects of it? If so, we can identify him with the methodology of Husserl, Weber, and Schutz, who all argue the impossibility of generating covering laws to explain causal forces in the universe. But if Shariati is saying that class conflict is an appearance of a reality that is more substantial and immanent in man's world, is he not saying that man is not an autonomous being, and are we not back to the doctrine of *iktisab,* or the contingency of human knowledge upon divine? Eventually, this leads one down the road to the Qur'anic admonition that "God knows and you do not know."

With respect to the philosophy of history, the shifts in Shariati's views will already have been apparent to the reader. Sometimes, in Islam, the rise and fall of civilization is said to be the motor force of history (which nonetheless may somehow by regulated and fine-tuned by the skillful manipulation and application of ijtihad, *al-amr bi al-ma'ruf wa al-nahy an al-munkar,* and muhajirat). But at other junctures, the motor force of history is said to be contradiction. And at yet other instances Shariati tells us that the motor force of history is the combination of the people (al-nas), social customs, personality, and chance. In his discussion of philosophy of history, additionally, Shariati reveals his historicism and teleological perspective. The problems with historicism have been vented by Popper, but it may here be mentioned that one of the greatest difficulties lurking behind Shariati's analysis is his tendency toward endowing concepts with actual attributes (what has been termed the fallacy of misplaced concreteness, or reification). Apart from this, Shariati's discussion of free will seems somewhat diffuse because of unclarified relations among man's will, contradictions in society, God's sovereignty, the unity of God, nature, and man, and the "hidden essence" (zat), which apparently is the primary reality of the world. Moreover, by what particular dynamic do potential contradictions become dissolved and resolved in a true Shi'i historical community, whereas they are inescapable elsewhere?

On the matter of political community and authority Shariati has a problem reconciling belief in the rule of the Imam and his more democratic inclinations. The contrast may be appreciated if two sets of his comments concerning the election of the deputy[ies] of the Imam by the people during the period of occultation are contrasted. In one place, as noted above, he emphasizes the people's role so as to suggest popular sovereignty. He even uses the highly specialized term *ijma* in the context of this discussion. Elsewhere, however, he acknowledges that only those who know enough to evaluate the candidates have the right to elect the leader(s) of the community. And he goes so far as to say explicitly that the Imam has given the responsibility to lead the community during his absence to the ulama.[37] Nonetheless, Shariati hedges even here, as he permits two contingent elements to enter into his discussion. The first contingency is his assertion—in the very act of claiming that the clergy comprise the general agency—that "we see that in the period of the Greater Occulation a system of election has come into being. These elections are democratic for the leader[s], but it is not a free domcracy. Although the elected leader[s] *is [are] elected by the "people,"* he [they] is [are] responsible to the Imam as well as to the people."[38] In other words, Shariati is very ambivalent about according the authority to designate the leader(s) of the community to the clergy. And while in the very next breath he does admit· that everyone does not vote in the election, the second contingency enters in: namely, it is "enlightened" clergymen who play the decisive role. As has already been shown, Shariati uses the term *enlightened* in the great body of his works deliberately to make invidious distinctions between social activists, of whom he highly approves, and scholastic pedants, whom he excoriates.

Nevertheless, Shariati's hostility to the "false clergy's" longstanding influence in politics should not blind the observer to the fact that Shariati equivocates on the question of community authority. Furthermore, it must be recalled that he asks us to take it on faith that leaders elected by enlightened intellectuals will doubtless be faithful to the Imam's interpretation of justice, righteousness, equity. His formulations resemble the model of the philosopher/king, and he assumes, with Plato, that it is not necessary to pose the question, Who guards the guardians?

Ultimately, a critical analysis of Shariati's writings faces the issue of his ardor and commitment as a Shi'i. His father, Mohammad Taqi Shariati, revealed the depth of his son's loyalty to his faith in a statement he issued

---

37. Shariati, *Entezar,* pp. 14–16. For a rejection of the view that the clergy collectively may be considered the general agents of the Imam in accordance with the alleged principle of *ex ante* appointment, see Joseph Eliash, "Some Misconceptions Concerning Shi'i Political Theory," *International Journal of Middle East Studies,* 9 no. 1 (February 1979): 9–25. In other words, the debate continues as to whether explicit doctrinal authorization exists for the ulama to stand in the stead of the Imam.

38. Shariati, *Entezar,* pp. 14–16.

during mourning ceremonies at the time of the younger Shariati's death. At one point (presumably after his arrest and exile by the regime in 1973) the elder Shariati had been startled awake by sobs in the middle of the night. He soon discovered that it was his son who was crying as he was sitting at his desk during a long night's study and writing. When the father asked his son why he was so afflicted, Shariati told him that that night he had bid his farewells to the Prophet and to Imam Ali (as a preliminary to facing death.)[39]

This story highlights the problem of analyzing Shariati's works. For ultimately Shariati is committed to revelation and to the doctrine of the Imamate. There is a threshold, therefore, beyond which certain positions must be accepted a priori. A critical analysis may point to these as assertions, rather than logical demonstrations. Very likely, to Shariati the quest for logical rigor becomes, after a certain point, a sterile intellectual exercise. The sociologist may ask Shariati to provide the causal links in the formulation that class conflict will not or cannot occur in a true Shi'i historical community. But Shariati's answer would no doubt be that they could not occur *by definition*. Ultimately, then, claims to knowledge based on revelation will not yield to analysis of this sort, despite Shariati's determination to bring sociology to bear on Islam.

39. For this episode, see *Vizhehnameh* (Tehran: n.p., 1357 H. Sh.?/1978?), p. 11.

CHAPTER EIGHT

Shi'ism and Islamic Economics: Sadr and Bani Sadr

HOMA KATOUZIAN

The Wider Dimensions

Islamic economics has been attracting increasing interest in recent years. A distinguishing feature of modern Muslim writing, dialogue, and discourse on economics is the awareness it displays of modern Western theories of political economy. Already, some Sunni (Indo-Pakistani and Arab) economists have published books and articles and held conferences on Islamic economics.

The Iranian contribution to the subject has been limited to a few books, articles, and (recorded) utterances and statements by Muslim theologians and activists such as the late Sayyed Mohammad Baqer Sadr, Abol Hasan Bani Sadr, and the late Ayatollahs Taleqani and Motahhari, rather than by trained economists (although Bani Sadr had some economics courses). This is an aspect of a more fundamental difference between Sunni and Shi'i approaches to the problem: Sunni writers tend to assume that contemporary Muslim societies and the past civilizations from which they evolved are—even though with important qualifications—Islamic, whereas Shi'i views assume that—apart from the short periods of Muhammad's and Ali's rule—the Islamic state and political economy have no precedent in history. Many of the strengths *and* weaknesses of the specifically Shi'i Islamic economics arise from this basic point of departure.

The Theoretical Framework   An exposition and appraisal of any system of political economy inevitably involves questions concerning theory, method, sources, as well as social context, historical experience, and current practice. However, Shi'i Islamic economics lacks such a framework because it claims not to be a science of existing reality but an ideology, a universal vision, which would establish a completely different framework for economic activity and social relations. In the words of a

145

contemporary Shi'i *faqih* (jurist) and leading writer on Shi'i political economy, "Islamic economics is not a science of political economy. [Rather,] it is a revolution [i.e., a revolutionary ideology] for changing the corrupt [*fased*] reality, and turning it into pure [*salem*] one—it is clearly not an objective analysis of existing reality."[1] Indeed, the view that there is no major past or present example of a Shi'i Islamic political economy is sometimes used as one explanation of why a science of Shi'i Islamic economics does not exist.

Islamic economics has not yet been applied to, nor is it being currently experienced in the real world.[2] . . . Therefore, it will be impossible for Islamic economics to reveal itself in its true sense unless it is applied to the real world, passes through all its vicissitudes, and systematically studies all the events and experiences which it comes across.

In fact, while lack of past experiences may justify the absence of many details, it does not explain the lack of an integrated network of ideas and policies.

Approach, Method, and Scope These points are a part of the wider methodological characteristics of recent writings and preachings on Shi'i Islamic economics: for example, their combination of strong elements of both idealism and pragmatism. Their *idealism* (in the sense of romanticism) tends to ignore or underemphasize major problems, which are simply attributed to the existing "corrupt reality" without a clear program for their resolution. Their *pragmatism* tends to explain away doctrinal difficulties by means of ad hoc interpretations, and by the explicit admission of "expediency" in matters that do not involve basic Islamic commandments. For example, what is neither specifically mandatory (*wajib*) or permitted (*halal*) is left to the arbitrary measures of Shi'i Islamic government, even if such measures could contradict the precedents set by the Prophet and the Shi'i imams.[4]

Also, since Islam has a claim to universal conversion, it follows that its system of political economy is likewise universal:

Islamic production planning is cosmopolitan. . . . There will be no solution for the salvation of man and nature other than the internationalization of land and natural

1. Sayyed Mohammad Baqer Sadr, *Iqtisaduna*, Persian trans. *Eqtesad-e Ma* (Tehran, 1350/1971), vol. 1, p. 403. For a more competent and coherent statement of Sunni Islamic economics see M. A. Mannan, *Islamic Economics, Theory and Practice* (Lahore: Ashraf, 1970). See further, Sadr, *Eqtesad-e Ma*, vol. 2, pp. 9–17.

2. Sadr, *Eqtesad-e Ma*, vol. 1, p. 406.

3. Ibid., p. 408.

4. This rule includes the category of *mubahat*, which affects many aspects of life and labor in society. See further ibid., vol. 2.

resources on the basis of the fine principles of [Shi'i] Islam. The future will witness the struggle of conscious human beings to end destructive [i.e., non-Islamic] activities and universalize nature on the basis of the principles of Islam—or there will be no future at all.[5]

Yet, even assuming that the whole world suddenly converted to Shi'i Islam, there seems to be no provision for the application of Shi'i Islamic economics to lands with diverse living standards, economic endowments, and technological characteristics, not to mention culture, history, and so on. The concrete setting and social context of many Shi'i economic arguments is a traditional, rural, and commercial society. Such a social and economic context is not even an accurate description of contemporary Islamic, let alone many non-Islamic, countries. Given this background, it is not surprising that there is no discussion of international economic relations in Shi'i Islamic economics.

Sources, Citations, and References A striking feature of recent Shi'i economic works is their display of awareness (though in a different way from Sunni writings) of modern—both capitalist and Marxist—systems of political economy. For example, the first volume of a leading writer's book is almost exclusively devoted to a (purported) description and refutation of these—and especially the Marxist—systems of economic thought.[6] The greater preoccupation with Marxism may be explained as follows: Shi'i ideas and precepts are (at least immediately) addressed to Iran and, to a lesser extent, other Islamic countries. The political oppositions in these countries, to which many Shi'i religious leaders and intellectuals have belonged, inevitably oppose their social system, which is usually (though wrongly) believed to be capitalist. Hence, Marxism appears to be the main alternative, and Shi'i Islamic writers develop a dual attitude toward it: on the one hand, they tend to argue their own case through attempted refutations of Marxism; and, on the other hand, they try to interpret Islamic laws and traditions so they seem no less revolutionary, just, and so on, than Marxist ideals. In fact, even the attacks on capitalist economics (which is not regarded as a serious rival) seem to be part of the attempt to prove to the Marxists that Shi'ism is not a capitalist system.

The sources and citations of Shi'i Islamic economics consist of a mixture of Qur'anic verses, quotations from Traditions and classical theological interpretations, and references to (secondary) writings on liberal and Marxian economics. There being no theoretical framework, no major historical or contemporary experience, no clear social context, and no systematic method, existing writings on the subject tend to combine

5. Abol Hasan Bani Sadr, *Eqtesad-e Tauhidi*, n.p., n.d. (1978).
6. Sadr, *Eqtesad-e Ma*, vol. 1.

abstract norms and values with assertions on what will happen once the system is put into operation, interspersed with a rather haphazard discussion of property, production, distribution, trade, and so on. Shi'i Islamic economics is part of the growing effort to demonstrate that Shi'i Islam contains all the ideas necessary to build a just polity, in reaction against the move of many Muslim intellectuals toward Western liberal or communist ideologies and of rulers like the late shah to implement iniquitous Western-inspired policies. For many of its perpetrators, intellectual rigor is less important than an appeal to indigenous tradition, and this appeal gains from being simplified, as it is accessible to more people than a rigorous economic discussion would be.

The Main References of this Chapter Apart from little pamphlets, newspaper articles, utterences, and the like, there exist two (purportedly) comprehensive treatments of the subject, which make up the main direct references of this chapter: Sayyed Mohammad Baqer Sadr's *Eqtesad-e Ma,* and Abol Hasan Bani Sadr's *Eqtesad-e Tauhidi.*[7] Sadr's book was published first and is used as a main reference by Bani Sadr; it goes into greater detail, takes up more concrete cases, is relatively less abstract or idealistic, and has a wider coverage of topics than Bani Sadr's. The background economic knowledge and the degree of awareness of actual economic problems displayed in these books are comparable, although Bani Sadr has other writings (especially in French), which demonstrate an appreciably higher standard of knowledge and argument in the social sciences. However, apart from coverage, there are—sometimes significant—differences in expression and emphasis, which may be explained (a) by the different intellectual background and placement of the two authors (Sadr was a theologian living in Iraq, whereas Bani Sadr was, at the time of writing his book, a social scientist living in Paris); and (b) by the fact that, whereas Sadr was what is now described (not wholly accurately) as a Muslim fundamentalist, Bani Sadr's roots are in the Muslim wing of the popular movement of Iran once led and symbolized by Dr. Mohammad Mosaddeq.

Born in 1933, Bani Sadr later studied sociology at Tehran University, where—in the period 1960–63—he became an active member of the Freedom Movement group of Muslim Mosaddeqists led by Mehdi Bazargan. In 1963, he went to Paris, where he continued his studies in

7. Ibid., and Bani Sadr *Eqtesad-e Tauhidi.* The late Ayatollah Taleqani's *Islam va Malekiyat* is less comprehensive than these two works and its arguments on private property in Islam are generally in keeping with the two of them. The semiofficial daily newspaper *Keyhan* published a series of articles in May–June 1980 described as "Unpublished Economic Notes" by the late Ayatollah Motahhari. It may be significant that the main purpose of these notes is to argue that labor alone is not the source of value.

economics and sociology, and participated in exile political activities against the shah's regime, until his return to Tehran—in January 1979—as an aide to Ayatollah Khomeini; he was later elected president of Iran but was deposed in June 1981 and fled Iran in July. He wrote and edited a number of books and pamphlets in Persian and French, including *Pétrole et violence*, of which he was co-author with Paul Vieille. Bani Sadr's father was a relatively conservative ayatollah, whereas he himself is a broadly radical Muslim intellectual and politician. His political activities help explain the differences both in the type and level of argument between his book on Islamic economics and some of his other publications, and also the ambivalence between the democrat and the authoritarian-populist that is observed in the latter book. They also explain his conflict with the dominant Islamic Republican Party on a number of basic social and political issues.

Mohammad Baqer Sadr was an Iraqi Shi'i who was an influential writer and politico-religious thinker. He was born in Najaf in 1930 and executed by the Iraqi Ba'th regime in 1980.

Property and Property Ownership

According to Bani Sadr, God is the sole creator, owner, and arbiter of everything on earth and in heaven. He is therefore the monopolist of all property on earth from the Fall till the Day of Judgment. But, this eternal truth has a "negative" (*salbi*) and a "positive" (*ijabi*) aspect to it. The "negative" aspect is explicit, namely, that everything is God's and no one else's. The "positive" aspect is, however, implicit, and it shows that "in benefiting from what belongs to God, all men are equal, and there can be no discrimination among them."[8] Here, the liberal concept of "man in the state of nature" and the Marxian category of "primitive communism" seem to have been mixed together in order to provide (though without further elaboration) a "historical origin" for the doctrine: "The positive aspect of 'God as the (sole) owner' is that the (same) relationship which had existed between God and all men *in the early days of human free living—that is, before the emergence of power centers—would, once again, be established.*"[9] This being the origin and the foundation of all wealth, it follows that "the only basis recognized in Islam for property ownership is (human) labor. That is, Islam has only recognized relative (not absolute) property ownership on the basis of labor and its fruits."[10] It is difficult to know (a) what is so peculiarly Islamic about the "negative"

8. Bani Sadr, *Eqtesad-e Tauhidi*, p. 114.

9. Ibid., emphasis added. There is no discussion of how these "power centers" emerged, how they can be removed, and how they can be prevented from reemerging.

10. Ibid., p. 117.

aspect of the statement; (b) on what, other than personal interpretation, the "positive" aspect is based; (c) what will be the position when, in their "equal" attempts to benefit from God's property, people end up with *unequal* results and/or manage to accumulate more or less of their products; (d) what went wrong in that original state of bliss, and—especially—what (other than mere sinfulness) led to millenia of great individual and social inequalities; (e) why it was not possible to restore "the same relationship which had originally existed between God and all men" as a result of the Prophet's mission; and (f) what real chances there are for its restoration between now and the advent of the Twelfth Imam.

Bani Sadr himself acknowledges Sadr's priority in describing labor as the sole foundation of wealth in Islam. But the implications of Sadr's view seem more authentic, and can be significantly different from Bani Sadr's. Sadr, too, repeatedly states that "labor is the source of private rights and ownership of natural riches"; but his greater regard for Islamic sources and traditions tends to give his view a distinct flavor of its own. According to Sadr, the "real meaning" of *the negative aspect* of the above principle is in its "negation of personal ownership and private rights *concerning those natural riches and raw materials which are acquired* [sic] *without the use of labor.*"[11] And his further examples and references show that such rights may result from the application of human labor to "this kind of property," especially if this is done by permission of the Islamic government. Indeed, this is what he then describes as *the positive aspect* of the principle, which he further qualifies by pointing out that the differences in various activities as well as natural resources must be taken into account.[12]

Both writers emphasize that private ownership of wealth and property in Islam is "relative," either—as in Bani Sadr—mainly because God's total ownership is perpetual "until the Day of Judgment," or—as in Sadr—mainly because of the more concrete limitations imposed on it by legal and doctrinal rules and regulations. Sadr classifies property ownership into three categories: state ownership, public ownership, and private ownership. The difference between state and public ownership is that "although from the social viewpoint they are similar, in one of them, i.e., public ownership, the owner is the people, and in the other, it is the authority and the apparatus which has been commissioned by God to take charge of the people's affairs."[13]

In practice, there are two aspects to this distinction between public and

11. Sadr, *Eqtesad-e Ma,* vol. 2, p. 137, emphasis added.

12. Contrast with Bani Sadr, *Eqtesad-e Tauhidi,* p. 114: "If Islam allows the slightest inequality, even as much as a grain, then these inequalities will grow and become a general and universal phenomenon." But this abstract argument is seldom borne out by the rest of Bani Sadr's statement (see, e.g., n. 17, below).

13. Sadr, *Eqtesad-e Ma,* vol. 2, p. 82.

state property: descriptive and functional. The *descriptive difference* is laid down by Islamic laws and traditions, for example, virgin lands, mines, and so on, belong to the state, whereas *the public revenues* from land under cultivation are common property or wealth. The *functional difference* is that while public wealth must be spent only on social services, state property and income may be used directly by the state or assigned to "needy persons" for investment in productive activities.[14] However, it is difficult to make much *operational* sense out of these distinctions, which, in application to any contemporary society, may lose all meaning and/or cause many unnecessary problems. In fact, they are entirely due to political and theological classifications at the time of the Islamic conquests.[15]

We saw earlier that both authors regard labor as the foundation of all (human) property, although the implications of their views can be significantly different. Furthermore, both emphasize that Islamic private property, income, and wealth are not absolute, that is, they cannot be held and disposed of with complete freedom. For example, Islamic taxes must be paid, private charity is strongly recommended, and ostentation is denounced. However, Sadr's detailed discussion of the subject gives rise to problems that Bani Sadr's silence simply avoids. For example, Sadr locates the concrete (as opposed to abstract) origin and point of reference of Islamic property in the early Islamic conquests, but he says nothing about the status of private wealth in contemporary Muslim societies before or after the establishment of Islamic government.[16]

Yet, an indirect insight may be gained into this question from Sadr's discussion (and Bani Sadr's brief mention) of Islamic inheritance laws. Both of them emphasize the inability of the deceased to impose his own will regarding the beneficiaries from two-thirds of his estate. Indeed, Sadr goes further and claims (with little evidence) that even the free will permitted for the remaining one-third of the estate has been an "expedient" which it is advisable not to practice.[17] This would tend to *inhibit,* not prevent, the concentration of private wealth and property, but it does

14. Ibid., p. 83.

15. For example, warriors could keep four-fifths of the personal booty, state revenues would be used for "social services," while virgin lands, etc., would be given to "needy persons" to develop against the payment of various taxes and dues. In practice, however, these theoretical demarcations began to disappear after the first few decades of the early Islamic conquests.

16. Sadr, *Eqtesad-e Ma,* vol. 2, pp. 86ff. See also n. 15, above.

17. Ibid., pp. 185–86. Cf. Bani Sadr, *Eqtesad-e Tauhidi,* pp. 150–51: "Let us say in passing that in this way, and with the Islamic rules for the distribution of inheritance, the fruit of a person's permitted [*halal*] labor, however considerable it may be, will be spread, and the creation of a wealth complex through inheritance will be avoided." He does not explain how this will be obtained, but the admission of "considerable" private wealth is worth noting (contrast with n. 12, above).

leave a "permitted" mechanism for the perpetuation of wealth, property, and associated privileges. Neither of the two authors discusses this important issue or the mandatory inequality of the shares of men and women in Islamic inheritance laws.

In general, it is difficult to discover a systematic and consistent statement on the origin, status, and prospects of private property in a Shi'i Islamic state. Fortunately, however, the authors' discussions of other aspects of economic life make the status of private wealth and property a little clearer.

Production, Distribution, and Exchange

There is little or nothing in the works of Sadr, Bani Sadr, and others on the theory, technology, and growth of output and income, on relative prices and the pattern of consumption, or on the organization and structure of production, employment, and the like. This is partly due to a lack of realization that every system of political economy, tried or untried, should address itself to such questions; and partly because Bani Sadr tends to avoid precise formulations and awkward questions that may weaken the radical tone of his utterances, while the point of reference of Sadr's *concrete* examples and statements is a traditional, rural, and commercial society. But there exists a rather extensive discussion of the distribution of income, trade, business partnership, and so forth.

Wage, Profit, and Rent   Both Sadr and Bani Sadr open their discussions of the distribution of income by reiterating the abstract principle that the whole produce of labor belongs to the laborer. In this connection, Sadr launches an attack on capitalist economics for putting the means of production "at the same level as labor," and claiming a share of the product for the former too. The argument is unconvincing, however, because capitalist economics does not put the means of production but *their owners* "at the same level as labor" and, *on the assumption that private property is legitimate,* it assigns a share of the income or output to private proprietors. There seems to be no real (as opposed to verbal) conflict between this and Sadr's own views. Pointing out that the means of production "are also a kind of *labor,* only embodied labor, the use of which results in their depreciation,"[18] he states: "Productive labor can take [sic] the means of production from someone else and, in return, *pay a reward consistent with its services to its owner, [likewise] land can be rented out against a certain sum and used for productive purposes.*"[19]

Capitalist economics also describes the returns to land, labor and

---

18. Sadr, *Eqtesad-e Ma*, vol. 2, p. 233, emphasis in the original.
19. Ibid., p. 214, emphasis added.

capital as *rewards for their services,* and it makes no real difference if "the whole produce or income" is "owned by the worker" who is then required to pay a share of it for the "services" of private property, or private property's share is put aside and the rest of the output (income) is paid to the worker. The "difference" is merely one of *wording.*

This position is further clarified with respect to merchant profit. There is a vague implication in Sadr's discussions that merchant profit is justified on the grounds of the costs (including his own labor time) incurred by the merchant in his trade. But it is commonplace that a (sometimes considerable) part of the merchant's income is a pure return on the use of his capital. And if this were not to be allowed then consistency would require the Islamic society to compensate the trader whenever he makes a *net loss,* just as the manager of a state firm or trade agency would receive his salary even if the firm loses in a given year. Alternatively, if the merchant were to be compelled (by an unknown mechanism) to earn no more than the value of his financial and labor costs, what could prevent the traders from transferring their capital to the ownership of urban or rural property and enjoying its rent—as is clear from Sadr's discussion—with the blessings of the Islamic state? Note, however, that all this is wholly unrelated to Sadr and Bani Sadr's scattered references to the illegality of "buying cheap and selling dear," for this concerns not merchant profit but speculative surpluses.

Bani Sadr seems to be somewhat more conscious of the ideological aspects of these issues. His discussion of them is brief and ambiguous, though still inconsistent. Contrary to Sadr's view is that of Bani Sadr, who categorically states that—for a long list of both moral and pragmatic reasons produced in his text—physical capital cannot be regarded as accumulated labor.[20] But, he says, even when it can (for example, as a result of inheritance) it should not be considered "at the same level as the living labor of the worker": "The correct method is for the worker who uses such means of production to own the produce of his labor and pay a rental [*ojrat*] to the owner of the depreciated means of production."[21]

This statement is ambiguous, and it could mean that only the depreciation costs should be paid as "rental" to the proprietor: if so, then the term *rental* is a misnomer, and there will be no profits and rents in productive (as opposed to trade and service) activities; if not, then rents and profits are allowed even in these activities.

Suppose that in a Shi'i Islamic economy the proprietor's "rental" was

---

20. Bani Sadr, *Eqtesad-e Tauhidi,* pp. 132–34.

21. Ibid., p. 134. This is qualified in the case of a proprietor who "somehow" cannot directly employ his own means of production, but no further explanation or examples are provided.

to be no more than the depreciation costs of his property. What would or could prevent him from using his capital either directly or through partnership in trade, agriculture and, by extension, manufacturing production—in various "permitted" ways, which are extensively described by Sadr—and enjoy a real return on it; buy and rent out a row of houses, or, failing all these possibilities, keep it in liquid (money) form and *spend* it as he pleased? In general, the root of these and other loopholes and inconsistencies is a failure to recognize the fact that where, as in the Shi'i Islamic economy, private property is permitted, there would be no way of organizing economic life that would exclude real earnings from it: to say that a return on private property will not be allowed is to negate the institution of private property itself.

Besides, Bani Sadr states that in the ultimate kingdom of the Twelfth Imam, "profit taking, even in trade, would be forbidden [*haram*]." Although the claim has not been substantiated, it shows that in the Islamic state prior to the Imam's ultimate kingdom profit taking *is* permitted. Incidentally, the emphasis on profit "even in trade" is due to the writer's implicit belief that merchant profit (no doubt because it is explicitly allowed by the Qur'an and the Traditions) is somehow "more legitimate" than other types of property income in the modern world, whereas it makes no material or moral difference *how* an earning is made by the use of private property, but whether or not private property itself is permitted, and it can earn a return one way or another.

The upshot of the discussion of these two books is that both private property and (therefore) property income are allowed in the Shi'i Islamic political economy.

Riba, Interest, and Money

Riba and Interest   Islamic economic statements, be they Shi'i or Sunni, would seem to be on their surest grounds on the subject of *riba,* which is explicitly prohibited in the Qur'an. Both Sadr and Bani Sadr emphasize the prohibition of riba and, like many other Islamic writers, assume that it is the same as modern interest charged on monetary loans. This, however, is debatable. For example, it has been argued that riba is more comparable with usury, or "excessive" interest, but the argument makes little or no economic or theological sense: economically, an "excessive" rate of interest at a given time or place may be regarded as "normal" at another; theologically, the prohibition of riba is total and categorical, leaving no room for argument about specific rates. Alternatively, it may be suggested that in the social and historical context of its prohibition,

22. Ibid., p. 23. See also chap. 13.

riba must have referred to charges paid for borrowing money and, especially, goods for *consumption* rather than for trade and production. This is a more persuasive argument but it is not completely convincing, at least for those who wish to insist that riba and interest are identical.[23] In any case, there are more important considerations from the realm of political economy that have seldom been recognized.

Suppose that, according to Islamic law, the taking of riba on gold, silver, and *all other commodities* is forbidden. However, this would say nothing about *paper money,* which is neither a commodity nor a *commodity money* such as gold and silver; gold, silver, and other commodity monies are, like all commodities, produced at a certain cost, and for that reason they may be said to have an "intrinsic value"; but paper money is issued at hardly any cost and therefore has no intrinsic value—it is "valuable" only for as long as it is (contractually) accepted as a medium of exchange. This has various implications for the present problem, only the simplest of which will be taken up here.

Writers on Islamic law and Islamic economics agree that the prohibition of riba means that the borrower must return to the lender the exact equivalent of the loan when it falls due. In a modern political economy the "value" of paper money—its purchasing power in terms of commodities, *including* gold and silver—changes, and, in recent times, is likely to fall. For example, a certain sum of money lent (for a year) in 1979 would have a commodity equivalent or purchasing power *less* than it did in 1979 when it falls due for repayment in 1980. This is comparable to the case of lending, say, three sacks of wheat and receiving, say, two sacks in return, which would be against the letter and the spirit of the law. It follows that, to be consistent with Islamic law, a rate of interest equal to a rate of inflation agreed between the lender and borrower would have to be paid.[24] For example, when in 1975 some bank interest rates in Iran were 6 percent, the general rate of inflation was not less than 20 percent; therefore *the principal sum plus interest* paid on an annual loan at the end of 1975 would have lost 14 percent of its purchasing power, and

---

23. In his *Islam and Capitalism* (London: Allen Lane, 1974), Maxime Rodinson makes a few similar points, but seems unsure of his argument: he uses the terms *riba, usury,* and *interest* almost interchangeably, although he says that riba may not have been the same as interest; his argument (p. 14) that riba seems to signify "the doubling of a sum owed (capital and interest . . .) when the debtor cannot pay it back at the moment when it falls due" is unconvincing; and his (alternative) arguments that the pagans, Jews, or Christians may have been the target of the prohibition, or that it may have aimed at uncooperative converts, sympathizers, etc., involve too many unresolved possibilities (chap. 2, pp. 14–15). In chapter 3 the arguments concerning the *practice* of the law in past Islamic societies carry more conviction.

24. The reference to a "mutually agreed" rate of inflation is in order to ensure relative justice.

consistency with the Islamic law would have required the borrower to compensate the lender by a rate of interest of 20 (*not* 6) percent.[25]

Assume for the sake of argument that the purchasing power of money stays constant. This unrealistic assumption would ensure that a sum of money lent without interest would have the same commodity equivalent when it is returned by the borrower. Suppose that in such a situation a person borrows from the state or private individuals, uses it in trade or other activities, enjoys the profit or rents made on the investment, and returns the principal of the loan when it falls due. If the money has been borrowed from the state, this would mean that those who obtain such loans could earn a living at the expense of the public, because, for both economic and social reasons, it would be *impossible* for everyone to have equal access to state loans. If, on the other hand, these are entirely private loans, then it would mean that, because of personal, social, educational, or legal barriers, the lender is unable to use his own money in a like manner, and *if* he lends it, he would have to let the borrower alone enjoy the entire proceeds of the investment. But it is more likely that he would simply keep his money for his own use because this would at least ensure liquidity (i.e., ability to spend *whenever* he likes) and exclude the risk of the borrower's default in repaying the loan.[26] In sum, the least that can be claimed is that the law of riba is not applicable to cases where inflation results in a fall in the purchasing power of money.[27]

The Case of Partnership in Trade and Investment   If two or more business partners are *active* in running the business, then—as in all systems in which private property is allowed—they can share equally in the profits or losses relative to their shares in the company's capital. But if a person lends his money to another for the purpose of a given business investment without his own participation, that is, if he is a "sleeping partner," then he could enter a *prior contract* with the active "partner" to pay him a mutually agreed share of the profits; but he would have to bear all the losses if the venture fails. This arrangement, known as *mudhariba*, is described by Sadr, who praises its justice and morality: because the passive "partner" is not involved in the business (or "does not work" for

25. An analogous difficulty is posed when prices fall and the purchasing power of money *rises*. In this case a sum of money returned *without interest* has a *greater* commodity equivalent than when it was lent, and the lender gains at the expense of the borrower.

26. An examination of the text and context of the law of prohibition of riba in the Qur'an (especially the *Ayat* 262 through to 276 of *Surat al-baqara*) supports the view that the law refers exclusively to loans given for the subsistence of the poor and the needy. See H. Katouzian, "Riba and Interest in an Islamic Political Economy," *Peuples Mediteranéens* no. 14 (1981): 97–109.

27. Cf. Sadr, *Eqtesad-e Ma*, vol. 2, pp. 218–19, 231 and 239–40, and Bani Sadr, *Eqtesad-e Tauhidi*, pp. 193–99, who take for granted that riba is the same as interest on money.

it), he has to bear *all* the losses.[28] On closer examination, however, it looks as if there is not much that is peculiarly just or moral in this rule.

First, if the passive "partner" provides the whole of the capital while the active "partner" merely runs the business (*which is the only example mentioned by Sadr*), then this would be tantamount to the owner of capital *employing a worker* for using his capital in a business of his own choice, and paying him a *mutually agreed* share of the firm's proceeds as his *wages;* but if the business failed, the capitalist would have to bear all the losses *without having to pay a wage to the worker*. Compare this with a capitalist economy where (a) the capitalist—whether or not he himself is active in the business—would have to pay the wages and salaries of workers and managers even if he made a net loss; and (b) wage rates often must be at or above a legally enforced social minimum, and negotiated not by a "mutual agreement" between the capitalist and the *individual worker*, but by *collective bargaining*, which is bound to increase the workers' share in the firm's income. If the passive partner provides only a part, say 50 percent, of the capital, a case not discussed by Sadr, then the rule must mean that the passive partner should pay a "mutually agreed" percentage of *his own* (50 percent) share of the profit to the other, but fully bear *his own* (50 percent) share of the loss. This is no more, but *could* be less, just than similar contracts and institutional relationships in a capitalist economy. This type of arrangement for employment and partnership is not confined to trade and other urban activities and its extension to agricultural investment and production is called *muzari'a*. The implications of muzari'a are the same as the previous case; hence it does not call for a separate discussion.[29]

The discussions in the above sections—based on the statements, arguments, and examples of the Shi'i writers themselves—lead us to conclude that: private property is legitimate, and labor is entitled to a share (not the whole) of the national income. All claims to the contrary would seem to be due *either* to isolated abstract statements (such as "labor is the foundation of all wealth") which are inconsistent with the concrete rules for trade, partnership, and so forth; *or* to an apparent belief that mere verbal forms (e.g., "the worker owns the whole of the produce, but should give a rental to the owner of the means of production") alter the social and economic *substance* of these relationships.

Money and Accumulation   Both Sadr and Bani Sadr emphasize that holding "excessive" money is prohibited by Shi'i tradition. Bani Sadr goes further and speaks of limits to wealth as well: on page 132 of his

28. Sadr, *Eqtesad-e Ma,* vol. 2, pp. 216–18 and 220–28.
29. Ibid. and pp. 243–45.

book, he cites "the Imam" (presumably Ali) as saying that "it would be
impossible for anyone to accumulate more than 20,000 dirhams [silver
coins] through permitted activities"; but on page 207 he quotes the Sixth
Imam, Ja'far as-Sadiq, that "no one has ever managed to accumulate
10,000 dirhams by permitted activities," and he adds that a dirham is
"equal to one toman." The problem is that (a) the authenticity of these
related Traditions is open to doubt; (b) they are contradictory, the earlier
putting the limit at twice the level of the later Tradition; (c) Bani Sadr's
claim that a dirham is equal to one contemporary toman is doubtful
because (d) the *purchasing power,* not the nominal value of money, is the
relevant datum, and this may have been *less* in Imam Ja'far's time than in
Imam Ali's, and is bound to be much less now; and (e) personal wealth
must be judged relative to collective wealth: up to two centuries ago there
were very few millionaires in the world, but this does not mean that the
distribution of wealth was more just than at present, because *total* wealth
has been continuously rising. Therefore, it is hard to know what the
relative significance of the above figures were in Imam Ali's and Imam
Ja'far's times; and if anything more than 10,000 or 20,000 tomans' worth
of a household's wealth (*not* income) were due to "forbidden" activities,
then most Iranian families—traders, shopkeepers, civil servants, politicians, religious leaders, and so on—would have to be described as sinful
and corrupt.[30]
    So much for limits to wealth. Similar problems are encountered on the
question of limits on liquid cash holdings: on page 203 of Bani Sadr's
book, Imam Ali is said to have put the limit on cash holding at 4,000
dirhams and in the immediately following lines the Fifth Imam, Muhammad Baqir, is said to have put the limit at "2,000 dirhams, that is 20,000
tomans of today." All the above points are again applicable: the Traditions cited contradict each other; they may not be authentic; the proposed
rate of exchange between the dirham and the toman (now ten times the
previous case!) is arbitrary; changes in the purchasing power of money
are ignored; and it is overlooked that the aggregate stock of money
increases with the growth of total wealth, resulting in higher levels of cash
holding by most members of society.
    The *Ayat* of the Qur'an quoted by both Sadr and Bani Sadr in denounc-
ing excessive cash holdings are, as they acknowledge, directed against the
holding of *treasure,* and are therefore not against wealth but against
hoarding. Sadr (though not Bani Sadr) is explicit on this latter point when
he says that "Islam has opposed the hoarding of cash, its idleness, and its
withdrawal from the flow of production."[31] His further critique of "capi-

30. At the current official rate of exchange, 20,000 tomans is about $2,500.
31. Sadr, *Eqtesad-e Ma,* vol. 2, p. 268.

talist economics" for not realizing that idle cash balances could result in depression and unemployment owes something to J. M. Keynes's analysis of this problem, although he seems to believe that *in all circumstances* it is better to spend rather than hoard.[32]

Even assuming that Bani Sadr's personal cash limits of 2,000 or 4,000 dirhams, or Sadr's limit of 20 dinars (!) is *literally* applied, it could only mean that in a Shi'i Islamic political economy, people should constantly spend their money (liquid assets) on goods and property (real assets), and let the state deal with the inflationary consequences of such spending. It says nothing about accumulation in *real* terms or the distribution of wealth and property among individuals and social classes that the authors believe they are discussing.

The Islamic State

The Islamic state is given wide economic powers by both Sadr and Bani Sadr: it owns, organizes, and spends "state" and "public" properties and revenues, imposes taxes on the private sector, lends money and property to "needy persons" for them to invest, and (at least implicitly) it can nationalize private property when this is in the public interest. Given these wide-ranging powers it is important to know, both in theory and in practice, what constitutes the basis of the authority, legitimacy, and authenticity of a state calling itself Islamic on Shi'i lines.

Bani Sadr devotes the penultimate chapter of his book to a description of "the perfect Islamic society"—the universal Kingdom of the Twelfth Imam—which, according to him, citing Ali Shariati, would take "twelve generations" to reach after the inception of the first Islamic state. This is the society in which all divisions, "vindictiveness," self-seeking, coercion, domination, alienation, and inequality disappear from experience: "it is the world of equality and economic oneness."[34] It is implicit in the above, and explicit elsewhere in the book, that, before the Perfect Society has been reached, it is both possible and necessary to establish Islamic government.[35] Sadr, on the other hand, does not separately or extensively discuss the characteristics of the Perfect Society but concentrates on the more readily available Islamic state, or what Bani Sadr calls the "period of purgatory."

No method or mechanism is proposed for the realization of the Islamic

---

32. Ibid., pp. 269–72. See also pp. 325–26.
33. Bani Sadr, *Eqtesad-e Tauhidi,* chap. 13, pp. 315–40.
34. Ibid., p. 319: both here and elsewhere, the author uses the word *tauhid* (unity, and monotheism) as opposed to *shirk* (multiplicity, and polytheism); but he usually means *vahdat* (oneness) as opposed to division.
35. Ibid., p. 255.

state except (in Bani Sadr) by saying that the Muslims should act. There are, however, two stages to revolutionary action—the seizure of power and social reconstruction. The latter presumes the existence of the appropriate Shi'i authority and leadership. Historically, Shi'i religious leadership has been dispersed, partly because the faith and its leaders have had no claim to government (as opposed to communal autonomy and political participation). However, following Ayatollah Khomeini's innovative arguments in his *Velayat-e Faqih,* both Sadr and Bani Sadr think differently, although—once again—there are some differences of tone and approach between them. The question is, who and what determines the legitimacy of an Islamic government from the viewpoint of these authors?

It is difficult to find a clear or consistent answer to this all important question. They both speak of "the Imam," frequently referring to a historical Shi'i imam, occasionally meaning the Twelfth Imam (the Qa'em or Mahdi), but sometimes meaning the leader or "government" of the Islamic state before the Perfect Society. In addition, Sadr uses the term *Vali-ye Amr* (Guardian of the Cause)—a term historically applied to the twelve Sinless Imams—to mean the leader of the (Shi'i) Islamic state. He describes the Islamic leader and government as "the authority and apparatus chosen by God to take charge of the people's affairs"[36] but says nothing about how God's choice is to be known and recognized. Yet, this authority is entitled to wide-ranging powers, including the use of "expediencies" even in contravention of Traditions set by the Prophet, the Sinless Imams, and all the classical Shi'i theologians.

Bani Sadr devotes many pages to the concept, position, and powers of "the Imam" in the Islamic state—i.e., in "the period of purgatory" before the realization of the Perfect Society. Unfortunately, however, his is a rather abstract concept that is not easy to grasp. The Imam can be anyone, he is the "representative" of the "consensus" (ijma'), but this does not mean a democratically elected political *or* religious leader, nor (necessarily) one who has been chosen by popular acclaim. He describes the Imam as "the symbol of the consensus of the present as well as the future generations,"[37] but he does not say how *in practice,* the consensus of present *and* future generations is reached.

Bani Sadr insists on some important limitations on the powers of the Imam. He does not emphasize, in contrast to Sadr, his authority to resort to "expediencies," and, though this is self-contradictory, he tries to guard against the possibility of "the symbol of the consensus of contemporary and future generations" being turned into a coercive force, in order to

36. Sadr, *Eqtesad-e Ma,* vol. 2, p. 82.
37. Bani Sadr, *Eqtesad-e Tauhidi,* p. 263.

ensure "that the Imamate is not alienated from itself and turned into a [coercive] state."[38] It would be opportune to quote a passage from Bani Sadr on the subject of the limitations on the powers of *any* (apparently even a Sinless) imam:

> The society has never been given the right of owning the individual, and is not allowed to deprive anyone of the right to live, work, think, etc. That is, Islam has not elevated the public [Jam'] to the position of the Deity nor does it recognize such a right for any Imam. If a free hold over the life and death of the individual falls into the hands of the Imam (the party or whatever), then he is no longer the Imam: he is a *Taghut,* an absolute and arbitrary holder of the reins of power.[39]

This and similar passages show the commitment by Bani Sadr to a basic democratic framework which goes beyond the letter, if not the spirit, of the concept of velayat-e faqih.

From Theory to Practice?

The above summary exposition and assessment of Shi'i Islamic economics is based on writings and statements prior to the Iranian Revolution of 1977–79. It may therefore be appropriate to make a few comments on events and policies since the fall of the shah's regime.

Postrevolutionary Developments   The blunders of the shah's regime, and their damaging consequences for the Iranian political economy, resulted in the development of a few basic socioeconomic views shared by most of the political tendencies represented in the revolution. These included, for example, the need for a redistribution of income and wealth, greater support for Iranian agriculture and peasantry, elimination of wasteful "prestige" projects, the application of a more appropriate technology for industrial development; and so on. Some of these views have found expression in official and semiofficial policies since the revolution, but their forms, as well as methods of application have increasingly assumed an unsystematic and arbitrary nature. The latter tendency is at least partly explained by the general movement toward the more exclusive framework of Khomeini's *Velayat-e Faqih.*

In the first few months, some economic disorganization resulting in a loss of output and employment was unavoidable. However, further developments have led to worsening depression and unemployment. On the demand side, the *sharp* decrease in oil revenues and in incomes has led to a significant fall in aggregate consumption; and—in addition to the decline of oil revenues and incomes—social insecurity and the lack of a

38. Ibid., p. 264.
39. Ibid., p. 231.

state investment policy have reduced aggregate investment to an insignificant level. On the supply side, the precarious position of the educated labor force has persuaded many to leave the country, and the purge of state departments and industries has deprived them of adequate managerial and technical staff. Also, the deterioration of political and diplomatic relations with the West has robbed the urban economic sector of vital equipment, spare parts, and technical assistance, on which it still depends.

As of 1982, the general rate of unemployment is over 30 percent, while that of the urban sector is above 50 percent. The rate of inflation is high and increasing, and, although accurate statistics are not available, it is probably above 50 percent overall and much higher in the case of food and other necessities. Also, there is a chronic shortage of basic consumption goods, and a thriving black market for those who can afford to meet its exorbitant prices.

The agricultural sector has tended to do better because of (a) the automatic decline in direct bureaucratic interference in that sector; (b) the automatic breakup of many of the unproductive agribusinesses and farm corporations; (c) the automatic as well as officially encouraged switch to the production of more food crops; (d) the doubling (and now, apparently, quadrupling) of the state purchase price of wheat and barley; and (e) good weather conditions for two consecutive years. For these very reasons, the agricultural "boom" is likely to be deceptive, and the absence of a coherent and comprehensive agricultural strategy will not help matters in the future.

The nationalization of private banks and insurance companies, heavy industrial plants, and some import-substitution firms is one of the few concrete economic decisions taken by the postrevolutionary regime. Such a move should have expropriated the main shareholders of these businesses, many of whom had been clients of the shah's regime; and it would go some way toward meeting the ideological challenge of leftist tendencies. However, many of the major shareholders of these firms owed massive debts to state and private banks, and, therefore, their "expropriation" has merely resulted in the cancellation of their debts. In addition, the mode and consequences of such "nationalizations" are reminiscent of the age-old etatism of the Iranian system, and they have so far led to no social and economic benefits worth noticing. In any case, in the current state of economic depression and political disorder, there must be very few state or private firms that are not experiencing substantial losses.

From the beginning, there has been much talk about the economic and political rehabilitation of "the downtrodden" (*mostaz'afin*). This has led to the establishment of the Foundation for the Downtrodden (*Bonyad-e*

Mostaz'afin) with extensive powers, including that of confiscation of property (ostensibly) belonging to the elements of the previous regime. Yet, here as elsewhere, (a) the policy has been applied in an arbitrary fashion, excluding many likely candidates, and including many unlikely ones; and (b) it has been further used for settling personal or official accounts with a number of actual or potential dissidents. It is difficult to know the extent to which the "downtrodden" have benefited from the activities of this and similar organizations, but it looks as if such benefits, too, have been distributed in an uneven and selective way.

An Islamic System of Political Economy?   In principle, very little in the above decisions and policies may be regarded as exclusively Islamic. The same goes for the decision to bring import trade under state control. In practice, this has led to the creation of a tight licensing system for private importers, rather than the direct monopoly of import trade by the state which, in the circumstances, would have been unfeasible. The fact that domestic wholesale and retail trade have been thriving is explained partly by the fact that traders have tended to do well out of frequent supply shortages.

The attack on riba—interest on bank loans and credit—is apparently consistent with the Islamic view, although, in the case of interest paid on bank *deposits,* a formula has been sought in a system of giving "prizes" to private depositors, who might otherwise have withdrawn their deposits and used them in other ways. It is not clear whether a similar method of *implicit* interest payment has also been devised for bank *loans*; if not, then—given that the banks are all owned by the state—the borrowers would benefit from such loans at the expense of the general public.

A policy reminiscent of Sayyed Mohammad Baqer Sadr's discussion of the uses of state property has been the granting of special investment loans to "needy persons." In general, these "needy persons" have come from the ranks of unemployed school and university graduates, and they have used the funds in retail trade and similar activities which are ideologically right, politically safe (for example, they do not employ industrial wage-labor) and economically rewarding. Since May 1980, rumors have been circulating that private bank deposits above one million rials (roughly about $12,500, at the official exchange rate) would be confiscated. Although officially denied, these rumors are consistent with the idea of enforced limits to liquid cash holdings, and there has been a general move by the public to withdraw or reduce the size of their bank deposits. More recently, and more significantly, there have been some official proposals for the complete exclusion of the private sector from manufacturing. Such a policy might simply result in the diversion of private investment to trade and private-service activities. If so, (a) profit margins in these activities would decline so that, eventually, surplus investment funds would have to find other outlets, including greater *consumption* expenditure; and (b) a much larger proportion of the labor force would be dependent on the state, the political and economic consequences of which are bound to be complex.

It is too early to say that any *system* of political economy has yet been established in the country. The currently dominant trends in ideas, and in policy and practice, if they continue, would result in a social and institutional framework which is, by some definition, Islamic. But an institutional framework—a network of rules and regulations, a given structure of government administration and, in general, the purely ideological context of political and economic relations—by itself, will not be sufficient to describe the system of political economy on which it is based. For example, in the nineteenth century, Iran was poor and traditional, while under the former shah (from 1963) it was relatively rich, and pseudomodernist. Thus, on the face of it, there was very little similarity between Iran before the Revolution of 1905–09, and before the Revolution of 1977–79, but both systems were, in different ways, despotic.[40]

While one may empathize with the desire to construct an indigenous ideology that can be identified with the Islamic beliefs and practices of its advocates, particularly in view of the havoc caused by selective application of Western ideas under the late shah, it is no more to be expected that Islam can provide a comprehensive economic system than that the latter could be based on Christianity, Judaism, or any other traditional religio-political system. The desire to have an Islamic economics is in part a comprehensible anti-imperialist one, but modern economics, whatever its weaknesses, must respond to a whole range of monetary, financial, industrial, infrastructural, ecological, and agricultural problems that were not imagined at the time of the rise of any of the great religions. These religions may provide a moral framework for economics, as most of them include calls for justice and equity, but the specifics of any economic system should primarily arise from an analysis of existing economic conditions and problems. An analysis based on new interpretations of the Qur'an and Traditions (interpretations often influenced by Western socialism or liberalism) may provide partial answers to Iran's pressing problems, but can hardly, unless these interpretations stray much farther than they already have from their referents, provide a comprehensive system that will begin to meet Iran's serious and growing economic problems.

Shi'i economics lacks a general theoretical framework and an integra-

40. For a comprehensive discussion of this topic see H. Katouzian, *The Political Economy of Modern Iran* (London: Macmillan, and New York: New York University Press, 1981). See further H. Katouzian, "The Aridisolatic Society: A Model of Long-Term Social and Economic Development in Iran," mimeo.

ted network of proposals for economic action. It combines traditional Islamic doctrines and practices with elements of modern radical ideologies. It permits private property in trade and agriculture, and very little in its arguments would exclude it from other spheres of economic activity. It identifies riba with interest, but this is debatable in theory, and may be inconsistent with other Islamic principles in practice. It emphasizes limits to cash holdings, meaning that personal wealth above certain limits must be held in nonmonetary forms such as property and consumption goods, and overlooking the fact that a legal limit to cash holdings would be highly inflationary if economic resources are fully employed, or if there exist supply shortages and technological constraints.

There are strong indications, however, that in the proposed Islamic system, private property—regardless of the forms in which it may be held and used, and irrespective of its distribution among the people—would have the same *functional* weakness as private property in Sassanid, Safavid, Qajar, or Pahlavi Iran. This weakness, and the associated strength of a functionally despotic state, was neither due to, nor evidence of, socioeconomic justice and democracy; and this contains important lessons for the *actual*, as opposed to desired or theoretical, consequences of the application of the Shi'i Islamic framework.

This point is important because the nature of the Islamic state—the basis for its legitimacy, the structure of its power and power relations—is as indefinite and untestable as it has been in Iran's past. Ideologies and social programs can only hope to achieve their declared objectives so long as the social and economic base does not run against them. In the case of Iran, no ideology can succeed in realizing its social and moral values unless its application begins by an attack on the foundations of Iranian despotism.

CHAPTER NINE

Velayat-e Faqih and the Recovery of Islamic Identity in the Thought of Ayatollah Khomeini

GREGORY ROSE

Islam is the religion of militant individuals who are committed to truth and justice. It is the religion of those who desire freedom and independence. It is the school of those who struggle against imperialism. But the servants of imperialism have presented Islam in a totally different light. They have created in men's minds a false notion of Islam. The defective version of Islam, which they have presented in the religious teaching institution, is intended to deprive Islam of its vital, revolutionary aspect. . . . This kind of evil propaganda has unfortunately had an effect. Quite apart from the masses, the educated class . . . have failed to understand Islam correctly and have erroneous notions. Just as people may, in general, be unacquainted with a stranger, so too they are unacquainted with Islam; Islam lives among the people as if it were a stranger. If somebody were to present Islam as it truly is, he would find it difficult to make people believe him.[1]

In these words, and in numerous other similar passages, spoken before the revolution in Iran and afterward, Ayatollah Khomeini has provided an invaluable insight into the underlying content and structure of his revolu-

A significant portion of the research on which this paper is based was conducted by the author during a visit to Iran as a journalist in February–April 1979. Extensive interviews were conducted with religious and political figures in Tehran, Qom, Mashhad, Isfahan, Shiraz, Tabriz, Gorgon, Sari, Amol, Rasht, Gonbad-e Kavous, and Sanandaj. This material has been supplemented by private communications with the interview subjects since that time and documents obtained from sources in Iran, often by indirect routes. While every effort has been made to identify sources, the political situation in Iran has required that certain sources remain anonymous to protect these individuals and their families from reprisals.

1. Ruhollah al-Musavi al-Khomeini, *Islam and Revolution: Writings and Declarations of Imam Khomeini,* trans. and annotated by Hamid Algar (Berkeley, 1981), hereafter cited as *IAR,* pp. 28–29.

tionary agenda. These passages call attention to Khomeini's conviction that the Muslim world is confronted with a crisis of fundamental identity, a pervasive alienation in which is rooted the Muslim world's apparent political, military, scientific, economic, and moral debilitation.[2] The issue of alienation is no newcomer to Iranian radical intellectual circles, as the writings of Jalal Al-e Ahmad,[3] the *Goftar-e Mah* group,[4] and Ali Shariati[5] attest. However, Khomeini's analysis of the situation differs in two respects.

First, Khomeini regards the crisis as a threat to the very existence of Islam.[6] Second, he has assimilated the problem of alienation into a complex of philosophical and jurisprudential concerns. This underlies his program aimed at building an institutional milieu, based at least nominally on Shi'i[7] *fiqh*, for the revolutionary restructuring of the personal and social consciousness of Muslims into an ideologically configured Islamic identity. This concern for redressing the problem of alienation bears serious implications for Shi'i doctrine and practice. In particular, it presupposes the transformation of Shi'ism from a religio-political tradition into a revolutionary ideology (which, in turn, involves a fundamental shift in its logical structure). This makes imperative the creation of an alternative to the relatively diffuse authority structure of Shi'ism—an alternative more appropriate to the need for ideological uniformity.[8]

2. *IAR*, pp. 34, 38–39, 295–99; U.S. Government, Foreign Broadcast Information Service, *Daily Report: The Middle East and North Africa*, hereafter cited as FBIS, 24 September 1979, p. 3; FBIS, 12 February 1980, p. 11; viz. FBIS, 25 September 1979, p. 1, where Khomeini characterizes his struggle as one to "safeguard the features of Islam and the features of our school of thought."

3. Jalal Al-e Ahmad's brilliant *Gharbzadegi* ("Westoxication") was one of the most popular underground works circulated during the reign of Mohammad Reza Pahlavi.

4. Viz. Mehdi Bazargan's *The Inevitable Victory* (Houston, 1979), and *Work and Islam* (Houston, 1979).

5. Viz. Shariati's *Islamshenasi* (Mashhad, 1968), *Hajj* (Tehran, 1971), *Ummat va Imamat* (Tehran, 1971), and *Civilization and Modernization* (Houston, 1979).

6. *IAR*, 27–28, 295–99; FBIS, 9 July 1979, pp. 7, 9, 10.

7. The term "Shi'i" will be used to denote the *'Ithna'ashari* ("Twelver") or *Ja'fari* branch of Shi'ism unless otherwise noted.

8. Shi'i tradition since the time of the usuli-akhbari controversy of the eighteenth century C.E. has established a structure of authority, termed *marja'iyyat*, wherein a number of the most learned religious figures (pl. *maraji'-e taqlid*, "sources of emulation") provide an example of religious practice for the less learned (*muqallidin*, "imitators" or "followers"). The *maraji'* technically act independently, but practically consult with their colleagues on major issues. If one is not adequately educated in religious sciences to exercise independent judgment (*ijtihad*) on questions of religious practice, one must emulate a marja'-e taqlid, usually through consulting a manual of religious practice *(risalah al-tauzih al-'amaliyyah)* published by the *marja'*. The *maraji'* administer the religious establishment and higher religious education. They collect and disperse the *khums* tax, a source of financial, and hence political, independence unavailable to Sunni *ulama*. Since the nine-

Furthermore, Khomeini's program rests on a set of philosophical presuppositions; in particular, a variety of conceptualism derived from a Neoplatonic understanding of Muslim peripateticism and *hikmat-e ilahi* (speculative theology) and a notion of spiritual power derived from *'irfan* (gnosis). These presuppositions greatly influence the array of political and social policies that he advocates and the instruments available to him for their realization. Finally, an analysis of the positions which Khomeini has adopted under the influence of these presuppositions suggests that he advocates, in fact, a radical departure from Shi'i tradition under the guise of radical traditionalism. This is not to say that Khomeini's sources and his program are intrinsically that radical a departure; rather, it is the way in which Khomeini uses these sources and the purposes which underlie his program that place him as a strikingly original thinker.

Nowhere are these issues better illuminated than in the concept of *velayat-e faqih,* the purported authority—or "governance"—of the jurisprudent[9] over the affairs of the Muslim community. However, before examining Khomeini's views in detail, it would be useful to survey the history of this concept in Shi'i fiqh to provide a framework for evaluating Khomeini's contributions to the question.

Shi'i tradition holds that velayat derives from the "universal authority [*siyasa*]" of the twelve imams, descendants of the Prophet through his daughter Fatima and his son-in-law Ali, each designated by his predecessor, all immaculate and infallible, who possess a "universal authority . . . in the things of religion and of the world."[10] Since the occultation of the Twelfth Imam in A.H. 260/874 C.E., the degree to which Shi'i religious leaders—*ulama, fuqaha'*, and *mujtahids*[11]—enjoy his deputation to exorcise a velayat has been a matter of debate.

---

teenth century C.E. there have been periods in which a most learned *marja'* has risen over his colleagues to become sole marja'-e taqlid. Among those who have held this high honor were Shaikh Mortaza Ansari (d. A.H. 1281/1864 C.E.), Ayatollah Mirza Mohammad Hasan Shirazi (d. A.H. 1312/1894 C.E.), Ayatollah Fathollah Isfahani (d. A.H. 1339/1920 C.E.), and Ayatollah Husain Borujerdi (d. A.H. 1381/1961 C.E.). After Borujerdi's death a claim was put forward on behalf of Ayatollah Mohsen Hakim, but it was not generally recognized. Concern with reform of this leadership system emerged after Borujerdi's death, and a number of reforms emphasizing greater collegiality and division of responsibility among the maraji' were proposed by the *Goftar-e Mah* group's participants, including such figures as Mehdi Bazargan, Mortaza Motahhari and Mohammad Beheshti, who rose to prominence during the revolution; viz. S. Muhammad Husain Tabataba'i et al., *Bahsi dar bareh-ye Marja'iyyat va Ruhaniyyat* (Tehran, solar A.H. 1341).

9. "Jurisprudent(s)" will be used to translate faqih (pl. *fuqaha'*).

10. Hasan ibn Yusuf al-Hilli, *Al-Babu'l-Hadi 'Ashar: A Treatise on the Principles of Shi'ite Theology,* trans. W. M. Miller (London, 1928), p. 62.

11. To avoid terminological confusion a note is in order. Religious leaders in Shi'ism consist of the *'alim* (pl. *ulama*), "scholar," who is learned in religious sciences; the faqih, "jurisprudent," who is expert in *fiqh* (Islamic jurisprudence); and the *mujtahid* who is

Broadly speaking, Shi'i fiqh holds that a velayat may be exercised by jurisprudents over three areas of community life. First is guardianship over the persons and property of those who might otherwise be victimized. These include orphans, foundlings, widows and persons of restricted capacity. Traditionally, this velayat extends to inheritance and empowers the jurisprudent to overrule, dismiss, and replace a dishonest or incompetent executor. Second is guardianship over the property and activities upon which the religious life of the community depends. For example, this velayat extends to administration of pious charitable endowments (*awqaf*), mosques, madrasas, and shrines. It includes the authority to supervise religious education, to arbitrate disputes within the community and to serve as judges in properly constituted Shari'a courts. Third, jurisprudents may exercise a general guardianship over the welfare of the Muslim community, encompassing the responsibility of serving as a social force aimed at carrying out the Qur'anic injunction to "command the good and forbid the reprehensible" (9:112). This velayat may be exercised in such activities as compelling speculators to release scarce goods, publicly admonishing open sinners, and petitioning the secular authorities on behalf of victims of injustice and oppression.[12] Some Shi'i authorities hold that this velayat empowers jurisprudents to carry out the Qur'anic penalties (*hadd*, pl. *hudud*) even in the absence of properly constituted Shari'a courts.[13] The existence of a jurisprudential velayat

---

licensed (possesses the *'ijaza*) to exercise ijtihad. These distinctions are not to be confused with the hierarchy of *mujtahids*, based both on erudition and size of following: *hujjat al-Islam, hujjat al-Islam wa al-muslimin, ayatollah fi al-'alamin*, and *ayatollah al-ozma fi al-'alamin*.

12. Viz. Hamid Algar, *Religion and State in Iran, 1785–1906: The Role of the 'Ulama in the Qajar Period* (Berkeley, 1969), for numerous examples of such petitioning. Similarly, Nikki R. Keddie, *Religion and Rebellion in Iran: The Tobacco Protest of 1891–1892* (London, 1966), provides a useful account of ulama political activity aimed at redressing social grievances.

13. W. Madelung, "A Treatise of the Sharif al-Murtada on the Legality of Working for the Government (*Mas'ala fi'l-'Amal ma'a'l-Sultan*)," *Bulletin of the School of Oriental and African Studies* 43, pt. 1 (1980) [hereafter cited as "Treatise"]: 26. As Madelung indicates, the question of whether or not the *hudud* could be carried out in the absence of properly constituted Shari'a courts is a matter of some dispute. Shaikh al-Hurr al-Amili reports in *Wasa'il al-Shi'a* (IX:1, 338) that Shaikh al-Mufid (d. A.H. 413/1022 C.E.) held it obligatory for jurisprudents to carry out the hudud if an opportunity presented itself. Shaikh al-Ta'ifa al-Tusi (d. A.H. 460/1067 C.E.) concurred (*Kitab al-nihaya fi mujarrad al-fiqh*, p. 301), arguing that a jurisprudent could execute the hudud on behalf of an oppressive ruler if he could follow the requirements of the Shari'a. 'Allama al-Hilli (d. A.H. 726/1325 C.E.) is reported to have held that jurisprudents were obligated to execute the hudud during the occultation (viz. Muhammad Sadiq Mahdi al-Husaini, *Sharh tabsirat al-muta'allimin*, I:300).

Conversely, Muhammad ibn Idris al-Hilli (d. A.H. 598/1201 C.E.) argued in his *Kitab al-sara'ir al-hawi fi tahrir fatawi* (p. 161) that only the imam or his directly appointed deputy could apply the *hudud*. Muhaqqiq al-Hilli (d. A.H. 676/1277 C.E.), in his *Shara'i al-Islam*

over these areas of community life is a matter of virtually unanimous agreement among Shi'i authorities. However, no such unanimity exists with respect to a fourth claim put forward by some Shi'i scholars, namely, that jurisprudents enjoy a velayat empowering them to exercise direct political authority—to conduct the day-to-day operations of the government—particularly in times of danger or impending chaos, on behalf of the hidden Twelfth Imam.[14] There has been little disagreement over the right of jurisprudents to engage in political activities, especially those aimed at redressing injustices or protecting the religious and moral standards of Islam. However, this fourth claim extends beyond this to the actual administration of government and institutional control over political processes, powers which belong to the "universal authority" of the imams.

There was no question of jurisprudents exercising velayat except by direct appointment during the life of the first imam, Ali, who held caliphal power (as did his son Hasan, briefly, in Kufa). Nor was there such a question during the lifetimes of the remaining ten imams, for whom Shi'is claim universal political authority, for, with the exception of Husain, none of the imams sought political power, claiming taqiyya (prudent dissimulation) respecting their political rights and urging their followers to adopt a similar attitude.[15] The specified deputies (nayib al-khass) of the Twelfth Imam during his Lesser Occultation acted by his direct appointment and made no claim to political leadership on his behalf or in his stead.[16]

The question of velayat did arise under the Buyid sultanate.[17] The anomaly of a Shi'i Buyid government governing a predominantly Sunni population in the name of a Sunni Abbasid caliph led Shi'i jurisprudents to discuss the degree to which Shi'i fiqh permitted the faithful to participate

(1:160) and Al-Mukhtasar al-nafi' (p. 146), found the position that only the imams and their direct appointees can carry out the hudud to be the more prudent (ahwat) position.

14. Ayatollah Shariatmadari in an interview with the author (March 1979) described this view as "a possible interpretation, but a matter in much dispute," citing the Afghan invasion of the eighteenth century C.E. as an example of such a period of chaos. However, Shariatmadari emphatically rejected any suggestion that Iran's revolution constituted such a period. He affirmed this view in an interview with Dr. Djamchid Darvich in January 1980. The claim for a full political velayat—along lines similar to those of Khomeini—is made by Shaikh Ali Tehrani', an influential clerical thinker; however, Tehrani treats this velayat as a collective responsibility of the ulama, criticizing Khomeini's claim for a single faqih as bi'da (heretical innovation).

15. Viz. S. Husayn M. Jafri, Origins and Early Development of Shi'a Islam (London, 1979), pp. 281–83, 297–98.

16. Viz. Abdulaziz Sachedina, Islamic Messianism (Albany, 1981), pp. 86–99.

17. Two articles by M. Kabir throw considerable light on this period: "The function of the Khalifah during the Buwayhid Period (949–1055 A.D.)," Journal of the Asiatic Society of Pakistan 2 (1957):174–80; and "The Assumption of the Title of Shahanshah by the Buwayhid Rulers," Journal of the Asiatic Society of Pakistan 4 (1959):141–48.

in an illegitimate (*mubtil*), oppressive government. There could be no question in the Shi'i mind that the rightful (*muhiqq*) ruler was the Twelfth Imam, then in occultation, not the Abbasid caliph. Indeed, no matter how fervently Shi'i the Buyids might be in their faith, doctrine held that any government—no matter how necessary or just—was oppressive and illegitimate if it was not that of the imam. This discussion led to a theory of deputation of believers by the imams to participate in government activities: in the case at hand, to serve as administrators and Shari'a court judges. This theory significantly foreshadowed the claim for a political velayat-e faqih and can be seen clearly in a treatise by Sharif al-Murtaza (d. A.H. 436/1044 C.E.)[18]

Al-Murtaza's treatise "Concerning the tenure of office on behalf of the oppressor and the nature of the doctrine about its propriety or impropriety" assumes that the Twelfth Imam is the only rightful ruler of the Muslim community.[19] However, he finds that service in the government of an oppressive, illegitimate ruler is obligatory (*wajib*) under the Shari'a if the potential officeholder has prudent reasons to believe that acceptance of the office would enable him "to support a right and to reject a false claim or to order what is proper and to forbid what is reprehensible, and if it were not for this tenure, nothing of this would be accomplished."[20] Such service becomes compulsory (*farz*) if the life of the potential officeholder would be threatened by refusal.[21] However, it is forbidden (*haram*) to accept such an office if it involves the unjust spilling of blood.[22] Furthermore, al-Murtaza predicates these judgments on a theory of deputation by the imams:

The tenure of office on behalf of an unjust ruler is, when there is something of the aforementioned in it that makes it good, only in appearance on behalf of the unjust ruler. Intrinsically, it is on behalf of the true Imams—peace be upon them— because they have given permission for the tenure of office under the conditions which we have mentioned. The officeholder thus took it on their order and is in reality holding office on their behalf and acting in accordance with their command.[23]

He strengthens this judgment by asserting that the "rule concerning someone hindering and resisting [one holding such an office] is the same

---

18. Madelung, "Treatise." It is interesting to note that this document was occasioned by a discussion conducted under the patronage of Abu'l-Qasem al-Husain al-Maghribi, a prominent Shi'i who served as *wazir* under the Buyid Sultan Musharrif ad-Daula.
19. Ibid., p. 24.
20. Ibid., p. 25.
21. Ibid.
22. Ibid., p. 27.
23. Ibid., p. 26.

as the rule concerning someone hindering the tenure of office of the person appointed by the just imam."[24] That rule authorizes the use of coercion, even mortal force, to prevent such hindering.[25]

Al-Murtaza provides no clear-cut criteria for recognizing such an officeholder, but suggests that those who "habitually . . . [act] in accordance with religion and respectability and . . . [refrain] from forbidden matters" should be so regarded.[26] Al-Murtaza's student, Shaikh al-Ta'ifa Muhammad ibn Hasan al-Tusi (d. A.H. 460/1067 C.E.), amplified these criteria to include one who "enjoins the good and forbids the reprehensible," recognizes the authority of the imams, is willing to surrender power to the Twelfth Imam on his return from occultation, and who pays the religious taxes (*zakat* and *khums*) to the appropriate heads of expenditure.[27]

It is important to examine carefully the issues that al-Murtaza addresses. The specific question is the Shari'a permissibility of accepting office from an illegitimate ruler *(al-sultan al-mubtil)*—either that of an administrator or a Shari'a court judge—particularly where such office empowers the holder to impose the death penalty. Al-Murtaza finds that it is obligatory to accept such office if the potential officeholder believes on the basis of "clear indications" that (a) he will be able to carry out his duties justly (and, thus, preserve his *'adalat* [justice]); (b) he will be able to observe the norms set out in the Qur'an and the Sunna, (c) any other likely appointees would not observe (a) and (b). Al-Murtaza bases this judgment on the principle that "the acceptance of the office is obligatory for him because of the obligatoriness of that for which it is a means and an expedient for its accomplishment."[29]

The obligation to do justice and to observe Islamic norms are generally imposed on the faithful by the Qur'an and the Sunna of the Prophet and the imams. It is in this sense that they are "general deputies" *(nayib al-'amm)* of the imam: it is a legal formula expressing an ethical imperative. However, it is not precisely this to which al-Murtaza alludes when claiming that such officeholding is "on behalf of the true imams . . . [and] on their order."[29] In this he builds on a distinction between the *zahiri* (exoteric) appearance of service to an oppressor and the *batini* (esoteric) reality of service to the true imam. It is this batini reality which permits al-Murtaza to rule that such an officeholder enjoys the same legal protec-

24. Ibid., pp. 27–28.
25. Ibid., p. 28.
26. Ibid.
27. Shaikh al-Ta'ifa Muhammad ibn Hasan al-Tusi, *Kitab al-nihaya fi mujarrad al-fiqh* (Beirut, A.H. 1390), pp. 356, 357.
28. Madelung, "Treatise," p. 25.
29. Ibid., p. 26.

tions as one appointed by the imam directly. However, this is not to say that one holding office on the basis of this batini reality has the same status as an officeholder openly and directly appointed by the imam. Al-Murtaza is careful to retain these distinctions: the same rule applies to both—indeed to one "as if" it were the other—but they are not the same thing. This seems, perhaps, a technicality, but it underscores al-Murtaza's recognition of the basis in law for officeholding: the direct, open, unquestionable appointment of the imam has a self-evident authority; the implicit appointment, hidden from zahiri perception, which underlies the batini reality of service paid on behalf of the imam, is known only by an inferential process. The problem is not whether the faithful are licensed to act justly and carry out the norms of the Qur'an and Sunna (general deputation); rather, it is whether an otherwise-forbidden activity may be used to further justice and these norms. That it may be so used results from a judgment of reason that the importance of a result licenses the means of its attainment. This is a matter of implicit deputation, for it rests on a rational judgment that the imam has implicitly licensed an activity. About explicit deputation one may be certain, but about implicit deputation one must be prudent (viz. al-Murtaza's insistence that a judgment about any particular officeholder under an oppressor must be a matter of prudence, cautioning the faithful to give such a person, in effect, the benefit of the doubt[30]). It would appear that this implicit deputation could be held by any faithful Muslim (certainly the criteria proposed by al-Murtaza and al-Tusi would support this interpretation);[31] however, it is clear that those to whom the cases in question apply are those learned in fiqh, that is, jurisprudents. The official joining of religious education and training for state positions (viz. the program of the Sunni Nizam al-Mulk) could only intensify this tendency.

Notice in particular that the implicit deputation presupposed by this theory in no way challenged the Shi'i doctrine that the imam alone was the rightful ruler of the community, and such deputation by no means extended to the full complement of the imam's powers. It was, as al-Murtaza pithily noted, an "expedient" to the accomplishment of certain objectives licensed by the imams.

Put forward in its strongest form by al-Murtaza, this view was almost immediately weakened by Shaikh al-Ta'ifa al-Tusi and Shaikh Ja'far ibn Hasan Muhaqqiq al-Hilli (d. A.H. 676/1277 C.E.). Al-Tusi held that acceptance of office under an oppressor with the conditions outlined by al-

---

30. Ibid., p. 28.
31. It is interesting that this notion of general deputation is picked up by Abol Hasan Bani Sadr in his treatment of *Imamat* in his *The Fundamental Principles and Precepts of Islamic Government,* trans. Muhammad Ghanoonparvar (Lexington, Ky., 1981), pp. 47–48.

Murtaza was merely desirable *(mustahabb)*, not wajib.[32] Indeed, unless the life or property of the potential officeholder were threatened, he holds it preferable to accept the unpleasant consequences of refusal. Muhaqqiq al-Hilli regards acceptance of such office as permissible but reprehensible *(ja'iz 'ala karahiya)*.[33] This was the view held by the majority of Shi'i jurisprudents until the early nineteenth century C.E., when Shaikh Mortaza Ansari reasserted al-Murtaza's judgment. It must be emphasized that the traditional view simply legitimized participation in government service under restricted circumstances; the traditional velayat of jurisprudents to intervene in political situations to secure Islamic moral standards and redress injustice remained unaffected.

It is difficult to trace the development of the claim for a full-blown political velayat for jurisprudents. While a full account of that development is outside the scope of this study, it is possible to suggest here that this process was connected to political-religious developments during the Safavi period (A.H. 908–1134/1503–1722 C.E.) and came to the fore in the *usuli* reaction to events following the Afghan invasion (A.H. 1134/1722 C.E.). Some indications of this may be seen in the selection and editing of *hadiths* in the collections of such late Safavi scholars as Mohammad Baqer Majlesi (d. A.H. 1111/1699 C.E.) and Shaikh al-Hurr al-Amili (d. A.H. 1104/1693 C.E.). For example, there are subtle shifts in meaning, such as that pointed out by Abdulaziz Sachedina, comparing a passage in a hadith as reported by al-Tusi and Majlesi. Al-Tusi reports that the Twelfth Imam said, "I am the *hujja* [proof] to you all" *(Kitab al-Ghaibah*, 231), clearly meaning the community as a whole. Majlesi reports the hadith with the change, "and I am the hujja to them [*'alayhim*]" *(Bihar al-Anwar*, XIII:1251), implying that the mujtahids stand between the imams and the community as a kind of mediator. A similar problem occurs in al-Hurr al-Amili's report of the *maqbulah* of 'Umar ibn Hanzala (a matter of significance for Khomeini's argument for velayat-e faqih, as we shall see). Indications of these clericalizing tendencies can be seen as early as the reign of Shah Tahmasp (A.H. 939–983/1533–1576 C.E.), when Shaikh Ibrahim Qatifi was obliged to write a refutation of Shaikh 'Ali al-Karaki, who argued that Friday Prayer is wajib even in the occultation of the imam if a knowledgeable faqih is available to lead it.[34] While Majlesi exhibits these clericalizing tendencies, he is careful to preserve those aspects of the imam's authority which may not be implicitly delegated, for example, only the imam or his explicit deputy may declare an offensive

32. Shaikh al-Ta'ifa al-Tusi, *Kitab al-nihaya*, p. 356.
33. Shaikh Ja'far ibn Hasan Muhaqqiq al-Hilli, *Shara'i al-Islam* (Beirut, n.d.), I:164.
34. Maulana al-Sayyid I'jaz Husain al-Nisaburi al-Kanturi, *Kashf al-Hujub wa'l-Astar 'an Asma' al-Kutub wa'l-Asfar* (Calcutta, A.H. 1330), no. 1364, p. 258. I am indebted to Juan Cole for calling my attention to this material.

jihad, as he argues at length in *Bihar al-Anwar*.[35] These clericalizing tendencies were accentuated in Muhammad Baqer Vahed Behbehani's (d. A.H. 1208/1793 C.E.) exposition of usuli jurisprudence.[36] It is uncertain how popular the claim for a political velayat-e faqih became in this period, but it was sufficiently strong to compel Shaikh Mortaza Ansari (d. A.H. 1281/1864 C.E.) to mount a refutation of the arguments for the existence of such a velayat in his monumental *Kitab al-Makasib*.[37] It may be thought ironical that the strongest advocate of *marja'iyyat*—the doctrine which holds that a believer must follow (give *taqlid* to) a qualified legal scholar (mujtahid) in matters of religious practice if the believer is not himself a mujtahid—should deny the jurisprudent an institutional political role. However, Ansari's finding that the traditional evidence for such a role is weak is simply more evidence of his careful scholarship and a jealous guarding of the imam's prerogatives from encroachment. Ansari's judgment that the political activity of jurisprudents should be limited to intervention to secure justice and Islamic morality were endorsed by Ayatollah Mohammad Hasan Shirazi, who regarded his *fatva* compelling repudiation of the British Tobacco Concession in Iran in A.H. 1309/1892 C.E. as an intervention to secure justice for Iran's peasants and to prevent the spread of *kafir* influence in the Muslim community.[38] The case of Ayatollah Mohammad Na'ini, the mujtahid who became a leading theoretician of the constitutionalist revolution, is more complex. Na'ini indicates "it is true that the ulama's responsibility as General Agents of the *Imam* in all other offices, i.e., rulership, is not unquestionably recognized."[39] However, he conceives of the political role of the jurisprudent as more than simply intervention to secure justice and Islamic norms. He describes this role by analogy to the process of *pak kardan* (to make

---

35. Mohammad Baqer Majlesi, *Bihar al-Anwar* (Tehran, A.H. 1384), XXI:91–117.

36. Viz. Ali Davvani's excellent *Ostad-e Koll Mohammad Baqer ibn Muhammad Akmal Ma'ruf bi Vahed-e Behbehani* (Qom, A.H. 1377) for much otherwise inaccessible material on this author and his period.

37. Shaikh Mortaza Ansari, *Kitab al-Makasib* (Tabriz, A.H. 1375), pp. 56–61.

38. The background to Shirazi's *fatva* may be seen in a telegram he sent to Naser ad-Din Shah some months prior to issuing the fatva. Nikki Keddie provides a translation of the text (*Religion and Rebellion in Iran*, p. 89):

Up to the present I have only addressed myself to His Majesty with wishes of happiness, but because of the various news which has reached me and which is against the rights of Religion and Government I ask permission to say: The entry of foreigners into the interior affairs of the country, their relations and trade with Muslims, the concessions such as the Bank, Tobacco Regie, Railroads, and others are, for many reasons, against the exact sense of the Koran and God's orders. These acts weaken the power of the Government and are the cause of the ruin of order in the country, and they oppress the subjects.

39. Abdul-Hadi Hairi, *Shi'ism and Constitutionalism in Iran: A Study of the Role Played by the Persian Residents of Iraq in Iranian Politics* (Leiden, 1977), p. 193.

clean), whereby a mujtahid may make the questionable ownership of property licit:

> In order to remove the oppression done to the *Imam,* there is one solution. As we said before, the function of the ruler in the new regime is like that of the supervisor of *awqaf.* The person in charge of the *awqaf,* even though he may have illegally occupied the office, can seek the sanction of the lawful authority, i.e., the *'ulama,* to make his own function lawful. If he gains the *'ulama's* approval, then there will remain no usurpation and no oppression of the *Imam.*[40]

Na'ini's view, however, in no way involves actual administration of the government by jurisprudents.

This brief historical excursus confirms the original suggestion that any velayat-e faqih in political matters is extremely limited in Shi'i tradition. With the exception of the eighteenth century C.E., in no period has direct political authority been claimed for jurisprudents by any significant number of Shi'i authorities. Rather, the appropriate political velayat of jurisprudents was defined in terms of occasional intervention into political affairs to redress grievous wrongs and safeguard the religious and moral standards of Muslim society. Judged against this standard, Khomeini's concept of velayat-e faqih appears radical. However, the practical and doctrinal limitation of the political velayat in Shi'i tradition did not prevent Shi'i religious authorities from generating an extensive speculative literature describing the ideal imamic government,[41] and while Khomeini's views tend to regard velayat-e faqih as licensing jurisprudents to rule in the imam's place with his full powers during the occultation, they are not altogether outside this tradition.[42]

II

> *The calamity is that many long years will be needed for these Westernized people to return to a state of normalcy, let alone the state of an advanced human being.*[43]

Khomeini's most systematic presentation of his views on Islamic government and the velayat-e faqih may be found in a series of lectures in Najaf

40. Ibid., p. 194.

41. One should, however, take care with this literature, as it is characterized by a considerable reliance on *taqiyya.* For example, it is possible to read Shaikh al-Ta'ifa al-Tusi's remarks on the government of *al-sultan al-'adil* (the just sultan) as an endorsement of non-imamic government. However, a careful analysis indicates that al-Tusi never uses the term *al-sultan al-'adil* except to refer to the person of the rightful imam. The usage is dictated by taqiyya.

42. The author is indebted to Abdulaziz Sachedina for pointing out the similarity between Khomeini's writings and this genre of Shi'i speculative literature.

43. FBIS, 16 July 1979, p. 11.

in A.H. 1389/1970 C.E. These lectures, collected from students' notes, were published in A.H. 1391/1971 C.E. in Persian and Arabic. In A.H. 1399/1979 C.E. another Arabic edition was published in Beirut with Khomeini's approval.[44]

The lectures on velayat-e faqih originated in a dispute between Khomeini's students and those of Ayatollah Abol-Qasem Kho'i, one of the leading *maraji'-e taqlid* in Najaf. In answer to a student's question, Kho'i had responded that no direct political velayat-e faqih existed. When this pronouncement was reported to Khomeini, he devoted two weeks of the traditional curriculum to an exposition of the maximalist claims for such a velayat.[45]

Khomeini's exposition is interesting in a number of respects. First, he explicitly claims that a jurisprudent "has the same authority that the Most Noble Messenger and the Imams had,"[46] except that his authority does not extend to other jurisprudents,[47] despite the fact "that no particular individual has been appointed by God, Exalted and Almighty, to assume the function of government in the time of Occultation."[48] However, Khomeini unquestionably denies that "the status [*manzaleh*] of the faqih is identical to that of the Imams and the Prophet,"[49] asserting that the velayat "is a rational and extrinsic [*e'tebari*] matter"[50] likened to the appointment of a guardian over a minor. While careful to distinguish the ontological status of the faqih from that of the *ma'sumin* (the Immaculate Imams), he is emphatic in asserting that the faqih enjoys the extrinsic— that is, political—powers of the Imam.

Second, while Khomeini is clearly convinced that this velayat is best

---

44. Hamid Algar's translation of *Hokumat-e Islami*, in *IAR*, pp. 25–166, is an excellent English rendering. It is based on the third Persian edition, published in Najaf in 1971. There are, however, some significant variants to be found in the Arabic text, *al-Hukumat al-Islamiyyah* (Beirut, A.H. 1399), and a comparison would prove useful. Algar seems to be under the impression that the lectures were delivered in Persian; however, persons present during the lectures, including Sayyid Ahmad Khomeini, indicate that they were delivered in Arabic, as one might expect in the *dars al-kharij* (external studies, the advanced course of lectures in fiqh). The English translation published by the United States government's Joint Publications and Research Service is a crude endeavor that is virtually useless for any serious study.

45. The circumstances surrounding the lectures' delivery were described to me in 1979 by several persons who attended the lectures, including Sayyid Ahmad Khomeini. One can see a certain veiled sarcasm directed at the learned Kho'i, an author of several treatises on *taharat* (ritual purity), in Khomeini's scorn for *akhund*s "sitting in some corner in Najaf or Qom, studying the questions of menstruation and parturition instead of concerning themselves with politics" (*IAR*, p. 38).

46. *IAR*, p. 63.

47. Ibid., p. 64.

48. Ibid., p. 61.

49. Ibid., p. 62.

50. Ibid., p. 63.

supported by arguments from reason, he is careful to devote an extraordinary amount of time to arguments from tradition. This concern leads to a convoluted exercise in hadith criticism, arguing that a sentence crucial to his analysis which is reported in *Wasa'il al-Shi'a,* but dropped from the earlier account in Shaikh as-Saduq's *Jami' al-Akhbar* was dropped by mistake.[51] More disturbing is his tendency to cite hadiths in versions given in comparatively recent collections and which show a bias toward the position he is advocating. The case of the maqbulah of 'Umar ibn Hanzala is indicative of the problem. Khomeini cites the version reported in al-Hurr al-Amili's *Wasa'il al-Shi'a.*[52] On first glance this is understandable—*Wasa'il* is commonly used as a text for easy citation of hadiths. However, this citation becomes suspicious in light of the care with which he examines the previously mentioned hadith in *Jami' al-Akhbar,* particularly when *Wasa'il*'s version of the maqbulah is compared to that given in the older and more authoritative *Al-Kafi fi 'Ilm ad-Din* of al-Kulaini.[53] *Al-Kafi* dates from the tenth century C.E., *Wasa'il* from the seventeenth.

The version from *Wasa'il* that Khomeini cites is as follows:

'Umar ibn Hanzala says: I asked Imam Sadiq (upon whom be peace) whether it was permissible for two of the Shi'is who had a disagreement concerning a debt or legacy to seek the verdict of the ruler or judge. He replied: Anyone who has recourse to the ruler or judge, whether his case be just or unjust, has in reality had recourse to *taghut* [i.e., the illegitimate ruling power]. Whatever he obtains as a result of their verdict, he will have obtained by forbidden means, even if he has a proven right to it, for he will have obtained it through the verdict and judgment of the taghut, that power which God Almighty had commanded him to disbelieve in. ("They wish to seek justice from illegitimate powers, even though they have been commanded to disbelieve therein" [4:60].) 'Umar ibn Hanzala then asked: What should two Shi'is do then under such circumstances? Imam Sadiq answered: They must seek out one of you who narrates our traditions, who is versed in what is permissible and what is forbidden, who is well acquainted with our laws and ordinances, and accept him as judge and arbiter, for I appoint him as judge over you.[54]

The version given in the *Kitab al-fazl al-'ilm* section of *Usul al-Kafi* is more extensive:

'Umar ibn Hanzala to Ja'far as-Sadiq: Two men of our community dispute about a

51. Ibid., pp. 68–75.
52. Shaikh Muhammad Hasan al-Hurr al-Amili, *Wasa'il al-Shi'a* (Beirut, A.H. 1391), XVIII:98.
53. Abu Ja'far Muhammad ibn Ya'qub al-Kulaini, *Al-Kafi fi 'Ilm al-Din* (Tehran, A.H. 1375), I:67–68.
54. *IAR,* pp. 92–93.

debt or legacy and they ask the sultan and the judges for a judgment. Is that permissible?

The Imam: Whosoever asks them for a judgment in a matter in which his claim is true or false, he is asking the taghut to give judgment, and whatever judgment is given to him, truly it is taken as forbidden, even if he was entitled to it, for he obtains it through the judgment of the taghut and God has commanded that they should not believe in the taghut. God, the Most High, said: They desire to take their dispute to the taghut, yet they were commanded to disbelieve in them.

Ibn Hanzala: What should they do then?

The Imam: They look for him among you who has related our traditions, has examined what is permissible and what is forbidden according to us, and has known our commands. They should accept him as a judge, for I appointed him a judge over you. If he would judge according to our ruling and his judgment would not be accepted, truly it is contempt for the ruling of God and rejection of us, and he who rejects us rejects God and is subject to the penalty for the attributing of partners to God.

Ibn Hanzala: If each of the two men would choose a man of our community and they both would agree to look at their grievance but they would differ in their judgment and would differ over your hadith?

The Imam: The ruling is to judge according to the judgment of the more just, the better acquainted with the law, the more truthful in relating traditions, and the more pious of the two. And no attention should be paid to the judgment of the other.

Ibn Hanzala: What if both are equally just and equally accepted by our community and neither of the two is more virtuous than the other?

The Imam: Then the tradition related on our authority by each of them and according to which they would judge should be examined. That which is agreed upon by your people should be accepted as our ruling and that which is exceptional and unknown among your community should be abandoned, for that which is agreed upon is not subject to doubt.

Ibn Hanzala: What if both traditions are on your authority and on the authority of the Imam Muhammad al-Baqir and are well-known and have been related by trustworthy narrators?

The Imam: They should be examined. The ruling of the one which accords with the ruling of the Book and the Sunna and contradicts the Sunnis [al-'amma] must be followed. On the other hand, the ruling which contradicts the ruling of the Book and the Sunna and agrees with the Sunnis must be abandoned.

Ibn Hanzala: May I be your sacrifice! If it happens that both jurisprudents proved its [the tradition's] ruling on the ground of a proof of the Book and the Sunna but we find that one of the two traditions accords with the Sunnis and the other contradicts them, which one should be followed?

The Imam: That which contradicts the Sunnis, and right guidance lies with it.

Ibn Hanzala: May I be your sacrifice! What if both traditions accord with the Sunnis?

The Imam: That which is preferred by their rulers and judges must be abandoned and the other must be followed.

Ibn Hanzala: If their judges accept both traditions?
The Imam: Then postpone judgment until you meet your Imam. It is better to stop
over doubtful things than to rush blindly into destruction.[55]

Khomeini employs his citation from *Wasa'il* to argue that "Imam Sadiq
(upon whom be peace), holding absolute authority and empowered to rule
over all the ulama, the fuqaha, and the people at large, was able to appoint
rulers and judges not only for his own lifetime, but also for subsequent
ages. This indeed he did, naming the fuqaha as 'rulers,' so that no one
might presume that their function was restricted to judicial affairs and
divorced from the other concerns of government."[56] The citation from
Wasa'il might give that impression, but the fuller—and more authoritative—version given in *al-Kafi*, with its assiduous concern for rules of
adjudication, in no way supports Khomeini's claim of a *nass* (direct
appointment) for jurisprudential rulership from Imam Ja'far as-Sadiq.
Furthermore, Khomeini is simply too learned a scholar to be unaware of
the disagreement between these versions and the questionable use he
makes of *Wasa'il*. Indeed, he cites the same volume of *al-Kafi* as that in
which the maqbulah is reported in the same lecture.

Third, Khomeini defines the velayat-e faqih as an institution for ensur-
ing the rigorous application of Shari'a to Muslim society.[57] Fourth,
Khomeini tends to conflate a number of arguments—for the establishment
of an Islamic government, for his interpretation of velayat-e faqih, for a
political revolution against "oppressors and tyrants," for a political
reading of the traditional texts of Shi'ism—in ways which suggest that he
sees a relationship among them which gives them programmatic coherence.[58]

A careful reading of *Hokumat-e Islami* indicates that Khomeini recognizes that the position he advocates is radical by comparison with the
dominant Shi'i view, and he is careful to cast his arguments in terms of a
revival of a tradition he traces to the Prophet and the imams, particularly
Ali and Husain, which, he claims, Shi'ism has largely abandoned. It is this
prophetic-imamic world view that Khomeini contrasts to alienation as the
ideal Islamic identity.

55. Al-Kulaini, pp. 67–68.
56. *IAR,* p. 95.
57. Ibid., 59–64; viz. *IAR,* p. 42, where Khomeini asserts that "without the establishment
of such organs [velayat-e faqih] to ensure that through enactment of the law, all activities of
the individual take place in the framework of a just system, chaos and anarchy will prevail
and social, intellectual, and moral corruption will arise."
58. Viz. W. R. Campbell, Djamchid Darvich, and Gregory Rose, "The Operational Code
of Ayatollah Khomeini," unpublished paper presented to the Midwest Political Science
Association, 17 April 1981, for an elaboration of the question of programmatic coherence.

Khomeini's concern with alienation helps considerably to explain the structural and doctrinal idiosyncracies of his theory of Islamic government. Khomeini's writings and speeches, both before the revolution and after, exhibit a preoccupation with the question of Islamic identity. Khomeini defines Islamic identity, as we have said, in terms of a paradigm (or more properly, an archetype) provided by the activity of the Prophet Muhammad, Imam Ali, and Imam Husain.[59] It is their active pursuit of a revolutionary struggle against oppression *(zulm)*[60] and polytheism *(shirk)*[61] that Khomeini characterizes as genuinely Islamic.[62] Khomeini's writings emphasize their faith *(iman),* and the faith of Muslims who approximate an embodiment of their paradigm;[63] his understanding of the nature of faith in Islam is of crucial importance.

As Wilfred Cantwell Smith has pointed out,[64] faith is defined as *tasdiq,* "the personal making of what is cosmically true come true on earth; the *actualization* of truth. . . . the inner appropriation and outward imple-

---

59. The importance of the Prophet Muhammad, Imam Ali and Imam Husain to Khomeini as paradigms of revolutionary Islamic identity may be seen from the following table, which quantifies the appeals to the sunna made in arguments found in *Hokumat-e Islami.* The frequent citation of the sunna made in arguments found in *Hokumat-e Islami.* The frequent citation of the sunna of the Prophet, Imam Ali and Imam Husain in preference to that of the other imams suggests their paradigmatic role as revolutionary archetypes. The frequent citation of Imam Ja'far al-Sadiq in the latter half of *Hokumat-e Islami* results from a technical argument deriving velayat-e faqih from the *nass* of Imam Ja'far al-Sadiq which Khomeini claims to find in the *maqbulah* of 'Umar ibn Hanzala; the resultant skewing is not a significant indicator.

Sunna	Section of *Hokumat-e Islami*				
	I	II	III	IV	Total
The Prophet Muhammad	8	8	57	7	80
Imam Ali	2	7	25	8	42
Imam Hasan	1	–	–	–	1
Imam Husain	2	–	9	1	12
Imam Muhammad al-Baqir	1	–	–	–	1
Imam Ja'far al-Sadiq	–	–	8	3	11
Imam Musa al-Kazim	–	–	4	1	5
Imam Ali al-Riza	–	1	–	2	3
Imam Muhammad al-Mahdi	–	–	3	1	4

60. Viz. J. S. Ismael and T. Y. Ismael, "Social Change in Islamic Society: The Political Thought of Ayatollah Khomeini," *Social Problems* 27, no. 5 (June 1980): 601–19, for a discussion of Khomeini's views on oppression. Care should be taken with this article, as it fails to locate the ideological trends in Khomeini's thought.

61. Isma'il al-Faruqi's work on Qur'anic ethics is a useful reference for background to Khomeini's views on polytheism.

62. Viz. n. 59, above.

63. *IAR,* p. 28, where Khomeini describes "the belief of the people in Islam" as "the major obstacle" to imperialism.

64. Wilfred Cantwell Smith, "Faith as *Tasdiq,*" in Parviz Morewedge, ed., *Islamic Philosophical Theology* (Albany, 1979), pp. 96–110.

mentation of truth: the process of making or finding true in actual human life, in one's own personal spirit and overt behavior, what God—or Reality—intends for man."[65] For Khomeini this is true with a vengeance: faith is an attitude and behavior that embodies in the world a revolutionary struggle for that state of well-being which God intends for man. Faith, for Khomeini, entails revolutionary activity: "Faith consists of this form of belief that impels man to action. . . . Once faith comes, everything follows."[66] The activities of Muslim life are meaningless ritual without this revolutionary context. For example, he says of the *hajj*: "They do not make an Islamic use of this gathering. They have changed this political center to a center which represents a complete turning away from all the problems of the Muslims."[67]

Khomeini locates the source of alienation from this revolutionary Islamic identity in the "Westoxication" *(gharbzadegi)* of Muslim society.[68] There is a less prevalent theme in Khomeini's writings which suggests that two further causes underlie this alienation: the hostile influence of Jews[69] and the imperial ambitions of the Umayyads and Abbasids.[70] However, it is the problem of Western influence which preoccupies him.

Having located this source of alienation, Khomeini emphasizes two related means of redressing alienation on a global scale. First, he is convinced that the creation of a Shari'a milieu is the necessary precondition of any reconstructive enterprise. Second, he argues that the conversion of society into this Shari'a milieu is predicated on an ideological unity (*yek kalam,* which I have heard in his speeches in place of *yek kalameh*), which he relates to a concept of spiritual power common in 'irfani writings. Velayat-e faqih is the institutional instrument for the realization of this milieu.

Khomeini plainly identifies his vision of the role of Shari'a in Muslim society with that of Shaikh Fazlollah Nuri, who opposed the Western-style constitution of A.H. 1324/1906 C.E. Khomeini writes in *Hokumat-e Islami* of his agreement with this *mashru'eh* (Shari'a-based) constitutionalism:

Islamic government is neither tyrannical nor absolute, but constitutional. It is not constitutional in the current sense of the word, i.e., based on the approval of laws in accordance with the opinion of the majority. It is constitutional in the sense that

65. Ibid., pp. 107–08.
66. *IAR,* p. 374.
67. FBIS, 5 November 1979, p. 23.
68. FBIS: 24 September 1979, p. 3; 25 September 1979, p. 1; 9 October 1979, p. 12; 1 November 1979, p. 4; 24 March 1980, p. 7; *IAR,* pp. 35–36, 137–41.
69. *IAR,* p. 27.
70. Ibid., pp. 31, 47, 57–59.

the rulers are subject to a certain set of conditions in governing and administering the country, conditions that are set forth in the Noble Qur'an and the Sunna of the Most Noble Messenger.[71]

This is paralleled by Khomeini's denunciations of the victorious *mashruteh* (Western-style) constitutionalists as "agents" of British imperialism.[72] Furthermore, he has repeatedly praised Nuri, calling him "one of the two or three leaders of the revolution who truly understood what it meant to be a Muslim."[73] This is not surprising: Khomeini's patron in Arak after his father's death was a family friend, Shaikh Mohsen 'Iraqi, under whom Khomeini first studied. 'Iraqi was closely associated with Nuri and the *mashru'eh* position.[74]

Khomeini views the Shari'a as an instrumentality for molding consciousness through conditioning behavior.[75] Indeed, he regards this as the reason for which the Shari'a was given:

Islam provides laws and instructions for all these matters, aiming, as it does, to produce integrated and virtuous human beings [*ensan-e kamel-e fazl*] who are walking embodiments of the law [*yajsed al-qanun*], or to put it differently, the law's voluntary and instinctive executors. It is obvious, then, how much care Islam devotes to government and the political and economic relations of society, with the goal of creating conditions conducive to the production of morally upright and virtuous human beings [*ensan-e mahzeb-e fazl*].[76]

In this way Khomeini breaks quite radically with Islamic tradition. While there is no question that the Shari'a is traditionally regarded as a means of educating man in his divinely decreed responsibilities, there has rarely been an attempt to use the Shari'a to enforce private doctrinal uniformity. As long as a person conformed externally to the prescripts of the Shari'a, the community had no right to inquire into his private opinions; that was a matter between the Muslim and God. Similarly, there could be no *taqlid* (emulation, imitation) in matters of faith (iman), only in matters of practice *('amal)*. Hypocrisy might well be criticized, but the criteria for proof sufficient to sustain action remained at best ill-defined. However, for Khomeini implementing the Shari'a becomes a process of tightening the perimeters of acceptable behavior in order to prevent Muslims from

71. Ibid., p. 59.
72. Ibid., pp. 30–31.
73. Interview with Ayatollah Mohammad Beheshti (March 1979).
74. Viz. Ahmad Kasravi, *Tarikh-e mashruteh-ye Iran* (Tehran, 1951), pp. 281–85, 409, for a discussion of the role of 'Iraqi in the *mashru'eh* movement. He is a figure almost unknown in the West.
75. *IAR,* pp. 329–32.
76. Ibid., pp. 43–44.

embodying anything but the genuine Islamic revolutionary identity.[77] This helps to explain the rigor of his Shari'a-implementation program. It is here, also, that his conceptualist tendencies become clearest, for Khomeini cannot envision the possibility that a rigorous, global implementation of the Shari'a could produce any result except the limitation of human behavior to tasdiq, behavior actualizing God's truth. Thus, dissent becomes for him formally incomprehensible except as a manifestation of foreign intervention or satanic conspiracy.[78] This has extremely serious implications for Shi'i doctrine. As Abu'l-Fadl 'Izzati points out:

> The Shi'ah hold that, because there is always the possibility of finding and perceiving facts which had wrongly been identified or missed by other jurists, the gate of ijtihad must be kept open. . . . There are no absolutely fixed legal decisions to be followed without question . . . The spirit of the Shi'i legal system refuses to call any justified legal decision a heresy. It allows jurists a wide scope of liberty to establish even conflicting opinions.[79]

Jurisprudential opinions that mandate behavior unacceptable to Khomeini's model of Islamic identity pose an acute problem. It is, to be sure, possible to dismiss some dissenters, as Khomeini has done, as SAVAK agents and pseudo-ulama,[80] but a number of his critics have religious or revolutionary credentials equaling, if not exceeding, his own. The house arrest since A.H. 1400/1980 C.E. of Ayatollah Mohammad Kazem Shariatmadari and the strong-arming of Ayatollah Khaqani suggest one answer to this question,[81] albeit a solution that contradicts Khomeini's principle of jurisprudential independence.[82] Another is the proposal made by the late Ayatollah Mohammad Beheshti to recognize two types of authority: marja'iyyat in matters of religion and marja'iyyat in political matters,[83]

---

77. Ibid., pp. 354–60.

78. It is this philosophical-psychological incapacity upon which rests the deviant logic that explains revolutionary setbacks as invariably a result of foreign agentry and/or satanic intervention. The implications may be seen in Ruhollah Khomeini, "Imam Belittles Terrorists, Asks for Vigilance," *Islamic Republican Party Weekly Bulletin* 1, no. 44 (28 August 1981):23–24. This publication is the official English-language journal of the International Section of the Central Committee Secretariat of the IRP.

79. Abu'l-Fadl 'Izzati, *An Introduction to Shi'a Islamic Law and Jurisprudence* (Lahore, 1976), p. 101.

80. *IAR*, p. 145.

81. Ayatollah Shariatmadari is among the most senior jurisprudents in Qom. Ayatollah Taher al-Sobai Khaqani, an Arab religious leader in Khuzestan, was conveyed to Qom under armed guard, where he suffered a heart attack. Sources in Iran suggest that a similar strong-arming of *Hujjat al-Islam* Hasan Lahuti may have resulted in his death.

82. *IAR*, p. 64.

83. FBIS, 19 February 1980, p. 35. I have received from sources in Iran a copy of an internal Islamic Republican Party document circulated by Beheshti's office, in which

but this is even more doctrinally objectionable. A politically authoritative jurisprudent without religious erudition and authority is a contradiction in Islam. Further, Khomeini's argument for the velayat-e faqih rests on the religious authority of jurisprudents as the justification for their political authority.[84] Without the religious foundation, the political argument disintegrates.

The realization of the Shari'a-informed milieu depends, in Khomeini's view, on mobilizing the spiritual power of the Muslims through ideological unity. While it is true that Khomeini's political theories are not so completely molded by 'irfani influences as those of some other Shi'i authorities,[85] there is a definite 'irfani tone to Khomeini's idea of spiritual power. There are indications of neoplatonic and peripatetic influences as well.[86]

Khomeini's interest in *falsafa* and 'irfan is deep. In madrasa he studied falsafa and hikmat-e ilahi ("theosophy") and Rafi'i Qazvini and 'irfan with Shaikh Muhammad Ali Shahabadi. He taught these subjects, particularly 'irfan and philosophical ethics, in the ensuing years to such students as Mortaza Motahhari and Mohammad Mofatteh, who became professors of these subjects in the Tehran University School of Theology and leading theoreticians in the postrevolutionary Revolutionary Council. It was a common view among some Shi'i ulama that Khomeini's acceptance into the ranks of the seniormost jurisprudents was delayed by his continued interest in falsafa and 'irfan.[87] To be sure, he is rare among Shi'i jurisprudents in according 'irfan and falsafa full equality with fiqh among the religious sciences.[88] It is impossible to read Khomeini's "Lectures on Surat al-Fatiha,"[89] "Lecture on the Supreme Jihad" [*Mubaraza ba Nafs ya Jihad-e Akbar*],[90] and "Search and Find the East"[91] without confirming

---

Beheshti solicited comments on this idea from the religious scholars of the *hauzeh-ye 'ilmiyyeh* (centers of religious education) in Qom, Isfahan, and Shiraz. One of the sources from whom the document was obtained indicated that the Qom scholars disapproved almost unanimously and the idea was dropped.

84. *IAR*, pp. 59–61.

85. Mohammad Hosain Tabataba'i, "Velayat va Za'amat," in Tabataba'i, et al., *Bahsi* (n. 8, above), for an excellent example of a view of velayat derived almost entirely from 'irfani influences.

86. These neoplatonic influences are most clearly seen in the logical structure of Khomeini's arguments. The use of arguments from archetype/embodiment (*IAR*, pp. 43–44) and from a *zahir/batin* distinction (*IAR*, p. 39) are suggestive of this structure.

87. This view was expressed to the author in March 1979 by a leading *Hujjat al-Islam wa muslimin* in Qom; he has requested anonymity.

88. *IAR*, pp. 395, 412–13, 423, 424.

89. Ibid., pp. 363–434.

90. Ibid., pp. 349–62.

91. Ruhollah Khomeini, "Search and Find the East," in David H. Albert, ed., *Tell the American People: Perspectives on the Iranian Revolution* (Philadelphia, 1980).

his continued, profound interest in these areas, displaying the deeply mystical basis of Khomeini's political thought. The 'irfani and falsafi preoccupations of his *Kashf-e Asrar*[92] are unquestionable, but care must be taken, for this early work is frequently contradicted by Khomeini's later works (e.g., Khomeini accepts the Shari'a-permissibility of monarchy in *Kashf-e Asrar*). Of particular relevance is Khomeini's emphasis on the perfectibility of man[93]—a frequent theme in 'irfan—and the spiritual power that underlies the perfecting process. This "power of belief"— ideological unity—is the basis for Iran's revolutionary success[94] and the source of human self-transformation (and is related to the question of martyrdom, the "sign" of faith).[95] Indeed, as Khomeini told an Azerbaijani delegation, creation of the Shari'a milieu is grounded in spiritual power: "Today Islam is confronted with the enemy and blasphemy. We need power. Power can be obtained by turning toward God, the exalted and the blessed, and through unity of expression."[96]

The theme of ideological unity—"unity of expression" is at the least infelicitous[97]—had been the watchword of virtually every Khomeini pronouncement since the revolution, as in his message to the hajj pilgrims in 1979: "You Muslims of the world and you followers of the school of monotheism, the secret of all the problems of the Muslim countries is the difference of expression and lack of coordination. The secret of victory is unity of expression."[98] Among the more interesting formulations of this notion of spiritual power derived from ideological unity is this from Khomeini's speech on the day of Arafah in A.H. 1399/1979 C.E.: "The scent and hue of faith and of Islam, which is the foundation of victory and strength, will be eradicated because of quarrels and siding with carnal desires and ignoring the commandments of the exalted God, while unity in truth and the unity of expression and the expression of God's oneness,

---

92. Khomeini's *Kashf-e Asrar* is hard to find in the West. The copy I have consulted was published underground in Iran in the early 1970s. The text is replete with interest in 'irfani and Neoplatonic philosophical concerns, particularly as they have influenced the notion of the imamate. In another connection, it is worth noting that Khomeini's vocabulary is frequently 'irfani in its overtones, as for example, in his invocation of the Orient, *al-Ishraq*, as the source of Islamic learning and strength. For an elaboration of the 'irfani implications of the term, viz. Henri Corbin, "L'Imam caché et la renovation de l'homme en théologie shi'ite," *Eranos Jahrbuch* 28 (1959):47–108, and *Spiritual Body and Celestial Earth: From Mazdean Iran to Shi'ite Iran* (Princeton, 1977).

93. E.g., *IAR*, pp. 409–10.

94. FBIS, 9 July 1979, p. 7; FBIS, 24 March 1980, p. 8.

95. *IAR*, pp. 332, 336, 353.

96. FBIS, 2 January 1980, p. 32.

97. The FBIS translations render *yek kalam* as "unity of expression." For reasons that this study makes clear, the translation "ideological uniformity" is preferred.

98. FBIS, 1 October 1979, p. 7.

which is the fountainhead of the greatness of the Islamic community, will guarantee victory."[99]

Khomeini has been reluctant to define explicitly what he means by "yek kalam." The phrase, in common parlance, can mean simply "unity." In patriarchal Iranian families, uttered by the head of the household, it can carry the force of "the final word." However, it also calls up connotations of a single, logical direction or orientation of thought, and the more technical uses of *kalam* in Islamic speculative and theological writing. Khomeini's use of this phrase deserves further research to plumb these ambiguities. For our purposes, it is sufficient to note that a careful examination of the contexts in which it arises suggests that it connotes a rigid ideological uniformity, characterized by belief and action aimed at reproducing the prophetic-imamic archetype of revolutionary struggle.[100] It is, further, the popular force capable of initiating human self-transformation and sustaining the Shari'a milieu. In the final analysis, it is also a rubric for the suppression of dissent.[101]

The velayat-e faqih is the linchpin in this revolutionary dynamo. By controlling the basic processes of government, the jurisprudent is positioned to guarantee institutional conformity to the agenda for restructuring consciousness and to articulate by expression and example the content of the genuine Islamic identity sought.[102] It is the jurisprudent who shapes and molds the Shari'a milieu by his exercise of ijtihad and the veridical character of his leadership (hence, the maximalist claim for the velayat *must* be made). It is the jurisprudent who mobilizes the ideological unity and its concomitant spiritual power to bring the Shari'a milieu into existence.

There is, to be sure, a sense in which these functions have been approximated by jurisprudents throughout the history of Shi'ism. They have, in fact, been the locus around which the identity of the devout community has been centered. However, these functions have been formalized and institutionalized in Khomeini's thought to a degree that renders them, frankly, things different from the functions undertaken

99. FBIS, 2 January, 1980, p. 32.

100. Khomeini's remarks in the weeks after the seizure of the U.S. embassy in November 1979 are particularly useful in this regard.

101. Viz. Ayatollah Taleqani's remarks (FBIS, 9 July 1979, pp. 16–17), while calling for an end to divisive debates, highlight the rancor of senior ulama at the suppression of dissent, even on religious issues.

102. Khomeini is straightforward about this responsibility, relating it to the prophetic office: "Our primary task in all these affairs is the education of man. Prophets come to educate people so that potential talents can become characteristic; so that potential man can become active man and have perseverance at work and with his ideology and so that he can walk the straight path" (FBIS, 15 October 1979, p. 2).

traditionally by jurisprudents. They have been, in a word, ideologized. This point is essential.

Khomeini's ideological notion of Shi'ism cannot be simply explained as an excresence of a radical Shi'i doctrine. Khomeini's ideology is an original, creative enterprise. It has phenomenologically a great deal in common with modern Western ideologies. One ought not to press these similarities too far, for there are significant differences, but the essentialism (or conceptualism) which stands behind modern Western ideologies is structurally quite close to that upon which Khomeini's ideological schema is based. While it is highly speculative, one might suggest that Khomeini's close contacts with the Palestinian movement while in exile in Iraq may have contributed to the rhetoric in which this ideology is cast (one thinks particularly of the emphasis in Khomeini on the economic correlates of alienation). There is, however, no question of Khomeini's having borrowed this ideology—it is a natural, logical conclusion of his method, the embodiment of the processes of his mind.

IMAGES OF THE REVOLUTION

CHAPTER TEN

Images of the Great Satan: Representations of the United States in the Iranian Revolution

WILLIAM O. BEEMAN

The Symbolic Structure of Discontent

For American citizens one of the most difficult aspects of the Iranian revolution was comprehending the blanket condemnation leveled against the United States by Iranian officials and revolutionary leaders. The vituperative, accusatory rhetoric seemed to be aimed at indicting all American leaders since World War II for unacceptable interference in Iranian internal affairs, and destruction of the Iranian culture and economy.

Of all the epithets, however, the one that seemed both to fascinate and terrify the American public most was Ayatollah Ruhollah Khomeini's characterization of the United States as "The Great Satan." Few in the West were able to appreciate the full meaning of Khomeini's metaphor, some perhaps equating it with the Judeo-Christian notion of The Devil. In fact, the image of the Great Satan is far richer and more potent as a rhetorical device for Iranians than the Western Mephistopheles figure. Its frequent use by the clerical leaders of the emerging Islamic republic was also far more than just an insult hurled at a distant foe. It was an important device in the reeducation of the Iranian people to the new revolutionary ideology of the Iranian state.

Much of the material on which this discussion is based comes from my most recent period of residence in Iran from August 1976 until April 1979. Revolutionary unrest in Iran throughout 1978 extending into 1979 made exact information gathering extremely difficult. Economic statistics for the period are particularly unreliable. Undoubtedly, the causes for the collapse of the Pahlavi regime will be debated for centuries. My conclusions are based on my recorded diaries, contemporary newspaper accounts, and extensive interviews with Iranians who, like me, lived through the revolution. I am particularly indebted to Nikki R. Keddie and Andrew Whitley for valuable suggestions that have improved the manuscript greatly. I alone am of course responsible for any deficiencies that remain.

The bitter irony for the United States is that the American government, without specifically intending to do so, continued to behave throughout the revolution in ways that could be shown by skillful rhetoricians in the mosques and streets in Iran to be characteristic of The Great Satan.

For most Americans such wide-ranging accusations of their country seemed to lack any basis in fact. Had United States government and industry not been working in Iran for the good of Iran as well as the United States? Had joint economic ventures not benefited the Iranian people? Was not the American interest in developing Iran's military strength in the years preceeding the revolution also in Iran's best interest? From an American standpoint it seems that the United States could be accused of no worse than wanting to make an honest dollar in a fertile market.

The gap between the American view of the United States as benefactor and the Iranian revolutionary view of the Great Satan is not easily bridged without a careful look at both the Iranian economy and America's role in it, and the basic structure of Iranian religious beliefs.

With regard to economics, there appears to be some justification for the views of Iran's revolutionary leaders. By the time of the revolution Iran was left with a demoralized population, an economy sprawling and out of control, and a repressive, autocratic government that allowed its citizens no influence in policies that affected them directly—not even the right to complain.

But by the assessment of its own members, a far more serious development had occurred in Iranian society: the civilization had lost its spiritual core. It had become poisoned—obsessed with materialism and the acquisition of money and consumer goods. For Iranians, hardships can be endured with the help of one's own family and social network and through faith and reliance on the will of God. But to lose one's own sense of inner self—to be a slave to the material world—is to be utterly lost. Clearly this central dilemma involves a mix of economic and ideological factors which, if not entirely foreign to the West, is certainly not often seen as a prime motivating factor in domestic and foreign politics. More important, the significance of this spiritual crisis was not recognized by Western nations until Iran had actually passed the breaking point.

Thus a highly complex but very basic issue became concretized in the complex symbolic image of the Great Satan: the loss of the nation's spiritual core and the assignment of blame for the occurrence to the United States. The effectiveness of this symbolic equation is paradoxically not explained by reference to doctrinaire religion. The sense of despair coupled with anger toward America was widespread during and after the revolution, and not at all confined to people who followed the clergy. It was also experienced by members of the middle and upper classes who cared not a fig for the mollas and Ayatollahs. Even these relatively secularized individuals responded to the image of the Great Satan.

Internal and External—The Moral Dimension

In order to understand this phenomenon fully, it is necessary to delve below the surface forms of religious practice and doctrine and gain an understanding of the base elements, the core symbols of society, upon which formal religion is built. Religious doctrine often serves as a concretization of these core symbols, both making statements about the truth of the conceptual world in which society exists, and prescribing for society's members what they should and should not do. Furthermore, religion helps people regulate their lives by placing certain aspects of the range of ideological attitudes available in their cultural system at the center of their personal value and action system, and relegating other aspects to the periphery. Religious systems are not static but dynamic, and occasionally they make their dynamic nature explicit. Such is the case with Iran.

Although generalizations about national character are prone to error,[1] some widespread trends may be suggested. The central symbolic pattern in Iran, which renders human actions both great and small meaningful for many Iranians, is the struggle of the inside, the internal, the core, to conquer the outside, the external, the periphery.

The contrast between the pure inner core and the corrupt external sphere in Iranian ideology is explored in depth in a recent study by M. C. Bateson et al.[2] It discusses the differences between the exemplary traits of *safa-ye batin,* "inner purity," and the bad traits of the external world that lead one to become *bad-bin,* "suspicious, cynical, pessimistic." The bad external traits, epitomized in adjectives such as *zerang* "shrewd," *forsattalab* "opportunistic," *do-ru* "hypocritical," *hesabgar* "calculating," and *charbzaban* "obsequious, insincere," are qualities that many Iranians feel they must combat in themselves as well as in the external world.

Iranians during the Pahlavi era, especially during the final ten years, often expressed regret at behavior they felt conflicted with the good

1. Cf. William O. Beeman, "What Is (Iranian) National Character?" *Iranian Studies* 9, no. 1 (1976):29–43.

2. M. C. Bateson, J. W. Clinton, J. B. M. Kassarjian, H. Safavi, and M. Soraya, "Safa-yi Batin. A Study of the Interrelations of a Set of Iranian Ideal Character Types," in L. Carl Brown and Norman Itzkowitz, eds., *Psychological Dimensions of Near Eastern Studies* (Princeton: The Darwin Press, 1977). pp. 257–73.

qualities desirable for one with a pure and uncorrupted inner core. A doctor I knew in a village outside Shiraz once went into a long disquisition on the difficulties of living in what he assessed as a corrupt world:

They are all corrupt, all of my superiors. They are stealing all the time, and not just from the government—they also steal from the poor people who come to them for medicine and treatment. God help me, in this system they *force* me to be dishonest as well. They will give me medical supplies, but only if I pay them some bribe. When I ask them how I am to get the money, they tell me to charge the patients. So you see I have no choice, I must steal too if I want to carry out this job. I hate myself every day of my life for being dishonest, and I wish I didn't have to be, but I can't help it.

Iranian concern with this problem is reflected extensively in expressive culture. Iranian literature, films, and popular drama often show characters caught between the drive toward inner morality and the external pull of the corrupting world. This is also a central concern in the doctrine and practice of Sufism, where the killing of one's "passions" (*nafs*), is one of the prerequisites to achieving mystic enlightenment.

As Bateson et al. point out, display of one's concern for the depth of feeling that accompanies the drive toward the pure inner life is highly valued throughout Iranian society. One of the highest compliments one can pay another person is to say: "his/her inside and outside are the same."[3]

Internal, External, and the Great Satan in Shi'ism

In Iranian religious doctrine the notions of the internal (*batin*) and the external (*zahir*) have likewise played a central role. Both Ithna 'Ashari ("Twelver") Shi'ism and Isma'ilism incorporate this basic opposition as a central tenet in their belief systems. Keddie shows the role distinctions between "exoteric (*zahir*)" and "esoteric (*batin*)" knowledge played in forming leadership styles in the community of believers:

. . . there early arose the idea that in addition to the obvious, literal meaning of the scripture, there was a more profound, inner meaning open only to the initiate. Among the Shi'i sects the idea became common that this meaning had been handed over secretly by the Prophet to Ali, and by him to his descendants, in whatever line the particular sect happened to believe. . . . And the philosophers' approach to *zahir* and *batin* was also attuned to their intellectual and political position. According to them, the Qur'an contained crude religious notions for the masses, and at the same time had deliberate obscurities and ambiguities which

3. Ibid.

would lead the philosophically minded to contemplate and to achieve a true rational understanding of religion.[4]

That the Great Satan might come to be located at the edges of the external in popular Shi'i belief systems is not surprising, given Iran's religious history. Even though there seems little doubt that Shi'ism involves syncretic incorporation of pre-Islamic beliefs, surprisingly little has been written on the exact nature of that syncretism. Seyyed Hossein Nasr argues that the Zoroastrian cosmology was effectively taken over by Iranian Islamic philosophers, geographers, and writers throughout the Safavid and Qajar periods, and Henry Corbin has analyzed the influence of Mazdean concepts of time on Isma'ilism.[5]

The topic that seems most controversial in assessing Zoroastrian influences on Islam is dualism—the notion of the existence of matched forces of good and evil. This is of course incompatible with strict monotheistic doctrine. Gustav von Grunebaum offers astute observations concerning Ferdausi's treatment of Iranian mythical history in the *Shahnameh,* which suggest that the incorporation of Zoroastrian dualism in popular Islam may have come through sources outside of strict orthodoxy: "Without entering into theological disquisitions regarding the fundamental conflict between dualistic Zoroastrianism and monistic Islam, or regarding the individual tenets of the old religion, he allows mythical events to retain their significance in terms of the dualistic conflict between good and evil, Ormizd and Ahriman. . . . The fight of Good and Evil is real to (Ferdausi), but as a Muslim he identifies the Good Principle, or Ormizd with Allah, the One, the Creator, and reduces the stature of Ahriman to that of a *div* or of the Koranic Iblis."[6]

Iblis is the Great Satan of the Qur'an—the *Shaitan al-Rajim.* In Qur'anic tradition, Iblis was the tempter of Adam and was cast out of God's grace for disobeying his command to bow down before Adam.

4. Nikki R. Keddie, "Symbol and Sincerity in Islam," *Studia Islamica* 19 (1963):53. Keddie's treatment of the notion of zahir and batin suggests that the zahir in religious doctrine need not be identified merely as the locus of evil. It can also be seen as a zone which contains and excludes those evil forces that may attempt to intrude on the pure batin, which should not be open to outsiders. Cf. also Seyyed Hossein Nasr, *Ideals and Realities of Islam* (New York: Praeger, 1967), pp. 160–63; M. S. G. Hodgson, "Batiniya," *Encyclopaedia of Islam,* 2nd ed., vol. 1.

5. Cf. Seyyed Hossein Nasr, "Cosmographie en l'Iran pré-islamique et islamique, le problème de la continuité dans la civilization Iranienne," in George Makdisi, ed., *Arabic and Islamic Studies in Honor of Hamilton A. R. Gibb* (Leiden: E. J. Brill, 1965), pp. 507–24; Henry Corbin, "Le temps cyclique dans le mazdéisme et dans l'ismaélism," *Eranos Jahrbuch* 21 (1951).

6. Gustav von Grunebaum, *Islam: Essays in the Nature and Growth of a Cultural Tradition* (London: Routledge & Kegan Paul, 1955), pp. 171–72.

Here the Qur'an makes a distinction. In his fall he is referred to as Iblis, but as the tempter, he is called *al-Shaitan*.

In popular Islam it is in the role as tempter that the Great Satan is best known. His principal task is to draw men from the path of God and into the path of sin and destruction. His connection with man is intimate; the locus of his activities is the everyday, external world—the zahir. A. S. Tritton cites this tale in his article on the *Shaitan* for the first edition of the *Encyclopaedia of Islam:* "[Shaitan] complained to God of the privileges granted to men and was thereupon given similar ones. Diviners were his prophets; tatoo marks his sacred books; lies his traditions; poetry his religious reading; musical instruments his muezzins; the market his mosque; the baths his home; his food was everything on which the name of God was not invoked; his drink all intoxicating liquors and the object of his hunting, women."[7]

In popular Iranian pre-Islamic belief, the locus of various *div*s was outside Iran. The great White Div of the Shahnameh lived in the North, and similar figures were located on the periphery of the civilized world.[8] This, too, is another kind of zahir—a place external to Iranian core civilization, and a likely locus for the figure of the Great Satan.

Internal and External—The Legacy of History

The struggle between the pure forces of the internal and the corruption of the external exists not only in the ideals of individual morality; it is also a principal theme in the popular view of the history of Iranian civilization.

For ordinary Iranians the waves of external conquest of their land over the centuries—Alexander and the Greeks, the Arabs, Jenghiz Khan, and the Mongols—are as alive as if they happened yesterday. The British-Russian partition of the country into spheres of influence in 1907 continued the pattern of cycles of conquest. Finally, the economic domination of Iran by the United States in the post–World War II period seemed to continue the age-old pattern.

Nevertheless, every time Iran was conquered by one of these great external powers, the nation rose like a phoenix from the ashes and

7. A. S. Tritton, "Shaitan," *Encyclopaedia of Islam,* 1st ed., vol. 3, p. 286.

8. According to anthropologist Victor Turner it is natural to expect that the forces of evil and disorder should have their locus in the marginal areas of human society. Such areas are known as *liminal,* and a good deal of man's energy in ritual and ceremony is devoted either to preventing these corrupting forces from entering the core arenas of society, or expelling them once they make such an entrance. Clearly, if the equation between the United States and the Great Satan is believed, then many of the street demonstrations in Tehran that villified the former can be easily understood as ritual purging of deeply felt forces of corruption. Cf. Victor Turner, *The Ritual Process* (Chicago: Aldine, 1969); Turner, *Dramas, Fields, and Metaphors* (Ithaca, N.Y.: Cornell University Press, 1974).

reestablished itself. The times between these conquests were often peak periods in Iranian culture. Thus the historical struggle between internal and external is seen as a struggle between the destructive forces of invading conquerers and the reproductive growing forces of the internal core of Iranian civilization.

The struggle between inside and outside is also encapsulated in the central myth of Shi'i Islam—the martyrdom of Imam Husain. Husain's father Ali was the only caliph to be recognized both by Shi'is and Sunnis. Following his death, his son Hasan was convinced to resign his claim to leadership by Sunnis, who followed Mu'awiya. On his death, the caliphate passed to his son Yazid.

Husain refused to recognize the leadership of the caliphs of Damascus, and thus set the stage for his martyrdom. In this act of refusal, Husain came to represent for Shi'i Muslims the verification of the leadership of Ali and his bloodline, through his willingness to be martyred when his own right to lead the faithful was challenged. Husain has continued to be for Iranians a manifestation of the struggle between internal and external forces. In death, he became an eternal symbol of the uncompromising struggle against external forces of tyranny, the defender of the faith, the possessor of inner purity and strength, the great martyr in the name of truth.[9]

Yazid and his henchmen, by contrast, become the supreme symbols of corruption. Not only are they murderers, but they also represent false doctrine, imposed from without. The sufferings of those in Husain's family who survived the slaughter of their patriarch are blamed on Yazid as are, by extension, the sufferings of later Shi'i leaders. To this day, a cruel, corrupt individual who brings ruin to others is labeled "Yazid."

From this exposition, it should be clear that to many Iranians the source of corruption is external to the individual and to the society. If civilization or individuals become corrupt it may be because they do not have the strength to resist forces from without that are always impinging on them. This gives a bias to Iranian political psychology. As internal conditions become more and more difficult, the tendency is to search for external conspiracy. This was a feature of the Pahlavis, who saw opposition to the central government as a Marxist-inspired plot. A similar bias inspired the oppositionist forces, who saw central government policies as controlled by non-Iranian considerations. The confrontations that led to the Revolution of 1978–79 and the ouster of the shah took place in an ironic context: both the shah and the opposition viewed themselves as

9. Cf. Michael M. J. Fischer, *Iran: From Religious Dispute to Revolution* (Cambridge: Harvard University Press, 1980), pp. 147–56, for an account of the meaning of the figures of Husain and his father, Ali, in present-day politico-religious discourse.

defending the core of the civilization against the forces of corruption and destruction. Thus, in one sense, the battle was one of definitions: he who could make his vision of the core valid for Iranians could control the nation.

Superiors and Inferiors

Another dimension of everyday life relevant to understanding Iranian conceptions of America's role in Iranian affairs during the decades following World War II is the dimension of superiority versus inferiority in human relations. Status in Iran, as in many countries, is largely relative. The highest official may be placed in an inferior position by one who can claim higher status, superior wisdom, or greater acclaim from those around him. Even the lowest street sweeper is, in contrary fashion, able to claim superiority to younger street sweepers. Consequently, adroit individuals in society must be capable of operating at different levels, knowing both the proper and the effective ways to act. It may be this quality of behavior that has prompted some foreign visitors like Lord Curzon to observe that in Iran: "The same individual is at different moments haughty and cringing."[10]

Status positions within the stream of social life are likewise strategic positions with complementary rights and duties. Persons in a "high" status position are expected to (1) dispense favors; (2) dispense rewards; (3) give orders. This can easily be seen as a set of obligations that involve taking action on another's behalf, dispensing material goods, and issuing a stimulus for either action or goods. In a pure state, these expectations are an absolute characteristic of the high-status position and are obligatory. The implied ethic is one of noblesse oblige.

Low to high status is likewise defined by orientation to action, goods, and stimulus for both parties, in a fashion complementary to the ethic of noblesse oblige above. Low-status persons are expected to (1) render service; (2) pay tribute; (3) make petitions. The ethic implied here is one of *duty*.

It can be seen that the status obligations incumbent on social actors within Iran may in many cases be differentiated only in symbolic terms. A person defined as taking an inferior role may pay rent to a landlord, or a bribe to an official. The landlord may give his tenant a present at the new year, and officials may reward their retainers and dependents. The absolute value of the goods exchanging hands in both downward and upward directions may be the same, but the meaning attached to the exchange is different.

---

10. Lord N. Curzon, *Persia and the Persian Question* (London: Frank Cass, 1892), p. 15.

Much of this exchange involves intangible dealings. Inferiors are expected to praise and defer to superiors. Superiors are allowed to make grand gestures, and be identified as benefactors of others through their actions. Some of the strongest social and emotional bonds in Iranian society obtain between superiors and inferiors. In affective psychological testing, great affection is seen to be expressed by Iranians toward figures whom they revere and respect.[11]

Relations of equality are no less complex. Equality relationships are highly unstable and demanding. Parties in equal status relations must adhere to a bond of reciprocity and loyalty. One is rarely able to achieve this sort of understanding with another person, and usually only for short periods of time. For this reason one's best friends are often family members. Same-age, same-sex cousins are likely candidates for equality relationships, as well as schoolmates and childhood playmates.[12]

The relationship between respect and affection is highly complex in Iran. One rarely exists without the other. Relationships of equality as well as inequality are continually tested for sincerity, and are often broken after years of endurance on the basis of a single small incident.

A relationship of equality or inequality may be forced upon a person, but if the rights and obligations of the position are not observed the respect that is necessary to cement the relationship cannot be established. An illegitimate claimant to a position of superiority will soon be undermined by those whom he expects to serve him. Likewise, a person not accepted as worthy to serve in an inferior position will be betrayed, cast off, or sacrificed.[13]

The question of relative status and the obligations of different social positions is intimately tied to the notion of inner purity. Those who

11. In a study carried out at Harvard University in 1972, James Prior (personal communication) maintained that the highest degree of correlation between vocabulary terms on a list of affective dimensions presented to Iranian students for matching was between *dust dashtan*, "to like, love," and *ehteram gozardan*, "to respect." Lorand B. Szalay, Elahe Mir-Djalali, Jean Bryson Strohl, and Hossein Moftakhar report similar findings in their study *Iranian and American Perceptions and Cultural Frames of Reference: A Communication Lexicon for Cultural Understanding* (Washington, D.C.: Institute of Comparative Social and Cultural Studies, 1979).

12. It is reported that the son of the former shah, ex-Crown Prince Reza, counseled his high-school companions to seek out the best foreign universities for their higher education "since," he reportedly said, "you will all have important positions in my government, and it is important that you get the best training possible." Likewise, the former shah was grief-stricken at the fact that many of those who had betrayed him in the downfall of his regime were army officers whom he had known and trusted since they had gone to school together as boys.

13. For further discussion on superior-inferior and equality relationships, particularly as they relate to language usage, see William O. Beeman, "Status, Style and Strategy in Iranian Interaction," *Anthropological Linguistics* 18 (October 1976):305–22.

achieve positions of superiority among men should ideally do so because of the superiority of their knowledge, understanding, and character. Those who attain their position dishonestly or through the use of brute force are illegitimate. Within Islam supreme authority comes only from God. This authority is transmitted to his representatives on earth. In Shi'i theology this line of authority becomes invested in the imamate. Anything that disturbs the legitimate exercise of authority can, by the exercise of religious doctrine, be declared to constitute corruption. Failing the presence of the imams among men, some Shi'i theologians have argued since the seventeenth century that those individuals who are wisest, purest, and most knowledgeable in the law of God should play a leading role in society. Although for some present-day theologians the *velayat-e faqih* or "regency of the chief jurisprudent" in place of the "hidden" Twelfth Imam, the Mahdi, now the central feature of the constitution of the Islamic Republic, is too extreme; most would agree that it is at least the duty of religious leaders to admonish the people not to follow corrupt leaders, or submit to corrupting forces. For superior individuals within the framework of Iranian society, to do less would be shirking both one's religious and one's social duties, for it would be tantamount to failing to protect and care for one's legitimate followers.

It is incumbent upon the faithful as part of the cardinal duties within Shi'i Islam to "promote the right and resist the wrong." However, it is to religious authority that one must appeal in order to understand the difference. Moreover, as mentioned, religion has both an exoteric and an esoteric aspect in Shi'ism, and only superior individuals can gain the interior knowledge that allows them to grasp the truth at the core.[14] For those who would know the truth, appeal must be made to those superior individuals who have the knowledge necessary to provide guidance. Since Islam has no formal system of certification of knowledge beyond a certain level, a person becomes known for his superior knowledge by virtue of his reputation. Advancement to the higher ranks of authority within the religious community is determined through consensus.

There has been a curious parallelism between religious and secular authority in Iran on this last point. The secular rulers of Iran have served, to a degree, at the sufferance of the people they govern. The bazaar, the tribal populations, even the rural farmers of the country have often opposed the central rule of the state when they felt too oppressed, or

14. Allameh Tabataba'i makes a clear distinction between levels of knowledge of the Qur'an and the discriminatory ability of the public. Aside from the literal expressions of the Qur'an are the esoteric meanings: "deeper and wider levels of meaning which only the spiritual elite who possess pure hearts can comprehend." Cf. Allameh Tabataba'i, *Shi'ite Islam*, trans. Seyyed Hossein Nasr (London: George Allen & Unwin, 1975), pp. 95–96.

when they felt it would be in their interest to do so. Indeed, the Pahlavi era is noteworthy as perhaps the first time in Iranian history when real central authority has been extended to the entire Iranian nation; it is ironic that just as this control was finally complete, the revolution began. Authority is tolerated as long as it has considerable legitimacy among the population. Any force that preserves an illegitimate authority is seen as corrupting by both religious and secular standards.

Concerning human relations, the rights and obligations obtaining between members of society are the paramount issues. Family members should exercise their duty toward each other; friends should preserve the reciprocity obligatory in their relationship; and superiors and inferiors must likewise fulfill their roles in their social relationship while maintaining mutual respect, and not misuse the power residing in the ethics of noblesse oblige and duty. Any force that can severely disrupt these human relationships is identifiable as one that corrupts society as a whole.

The External Seduces the Internal

Many have commented on the economic difficulties that preceded the revolutionary events of 1978–79 leading to the downfall of the former shah. As serious as these difficulties were, they would not have led to a complete rupture between the monarchy and the people and the rapid destruction of the Pahlavi regime if they had not occurred in a way that could be defined as a betrayal of fundamental tenets of Iranian religious sensibility, social ideology, and morality. The reaction against the shah was not calculated political strategy, it was outrage. The same outrage was directed against the United States both at the time of the Shah's fall and after.

The outrage felt by the Iranian people was heightened by the knowledge, rarely admitted after the revolution, that many Iranians were themselves largely to blame for Iran's economic and social difficulties during the years of Pahlavi rule. As one social scientist in Tehran remarked woefully on surveying an area of the city left in rubble after a confrontation between the people and the army at the beginning of the revolution in October 1978, "The Iranians have done this to themselves. We thought it would be enough to be rich, buy clothes in Paris, and travel to London every year for a good time. In the end we ended up selling our souls for a few rags and a couple of nights in a cabaret."

Many Iranians would reject this assessment, for in the classical cultural formulation described earlier, the ultimate locus of corruption for Iranians could not be internal, it had to come from without. The United States stood out in the minds of Iranians both because of its enormous presence, and because of its naiveté concerning its own public image. American government and business interests acted the role of the exploiter and corrupter in highly visible ways, making it easy for revolutionary leaders to adopt successfully the position that the United States was the cause of all the nation's woes.

The Pahlavi regime wanted to be very strong militarily and economically with little serious concern for the common people. The desire for immediate economic development on a massive scale led the regime to a misguided and simplistic reading of the leading growth theory of the 1960s as promulgated by economists like Barbara Ward and W. W. Rostow. Roughly stated, it promised "economic takeoff" if a nation could increase its Gross National Product by a certain percentage for a sustained period. But simple increases in the GNP, which for Iran actually exceeded 20 percent in some of the last ten prerevolutionary years (without correcting for inflation), only blinded the regime to the folly of its superficial planning.

Stated growth rates in the Iranian economy may differ, depending on the measure one uses. The annual rate of GNP growth averaged 23.55 percent from 1965 to 1974 without adjustment for inflation. Adjusted to 1972 prices, the annual rate of GNP growth was 17.45 percent for the same period. The principal stimulus to GNP growth was the massive oil-price increase imposed by OPEC in 1973, which created a massive increase in GNP (49 percent in 1973 and 71.35 percent in 1974; 34.2 percent and 43 percent, respectively, at 1972 prices). The oil-price increase caused a drastic change in the contribution of the oil sector to the economy. In 1959 the oil sector contributed 9.7 percent of the total GNP; by 1974 it contributed 47 percent.[15]

The role of the United States throughout this period was all too clear. Iran as a major oil-producing country was a prime market for the sale of American technology and services. Iran wanted instant development; the United States was happy to oblige. Iran wanted to become the chief military power in the region; so much the better for the United States and its arms companies. Peacekeeping in this volatile area could be left in the hands of a friendly ally, and that ally would even be paying for the privilege in enormous purchases of arms.

Americans looked upon Iran as an economic gold mine. At the time of the oil-price increase in 1973, self-styled entrepreneurs were descending

---

15. The source for these figures is Firouz Vakil, "Iran's Basic Macroeconomic Problems: A Twenty-Year Horizon," *Economic Development and Cultural Change* 25 (July 1977): 713–30. Similar data based on Iran's GDP are presented in: United Nations, Economic and Social Commission for Asia and the Pacific, Development Planning Division, "The Iranian Economy: Oil and Development in the First Half of the 1970's," *Economic Bulletin for Asia and the Pacific* 29 (December 1978): 37–48.

on the country in droves with no clear business—they just wanted to be on the scene and see if they could make a few million dollars (and many did). Iranians often made out better in these deals than their foreign partners, but it was the foreigners whose profits were most visible for the Iranian public, as they seemed to grow rich at Iranian expense.

During this period, the United States embassy was much less a spy mission (as claimed by the Islamic Republic to justify holding of the fifty-two Americans hostage) than a kind of industrial brokerage firm. Much of the ambassador's business was with one or another American industrial concern. One of the embassy's principal activities during this period was to put wealthy Americans in contact with wealthy Iranians for their mutual benefit. The embassy cocktail-party circuit was a virtual bazaar for business dealings.

As a result, for many Iranians the embassy seemed to be sensitive only to the wants and needs of the upper echelons. No American ambassador since World War II had spoken even minimal Persian, and few embassy activities indicated American appreciation for Iranian culture.

Iranian law required that all business operations be 51 percent Iranian owned. Even with those restrictions, Americans could make a lot of money just by founding businesses. Though Iranians would own 51 percent of the concern, they would also provide 51 percent of the financing through government loans, often a necessary incentive to persuade skittish firms to invest in an untried business climate.

The best people for American investors to do business with were, of course, the royal family and other high government officials who would meet no bureaucratic opposition in their financial ventures. They could easily obtain millions from government-controlled banks on their signature alone, and no one dared question construction standards or business practices of concerns that had connections with the court. Soon Iran was not only awash in money, it was awash in new industry. The country seemed to be booming.

The view that Iran could be persuaded to bankroll the United States for almost any purpose extended to many sectors of American society. Even universities were included. Over two hundred institutions in the United States had cooperative arrangements with Iranian institutions. Most of these educational cooperative ventures provided little benefit for Iran but great financial advantages for beleagured American colleges facing rising costs and shrinking enrollments in the early seventies. One notorious educational exchange program between a major American university and an Iranian institution was funded entirely from Iran, and was designed to provide American faculty to help improve and strengthen the teaching at the Iranian university. In practice, the program was used by the American university as a cheap way to reduce their teaching rolls. The faculty members involved in the program were given full teaching credit toward sabbatical leave for the year spent in Iran, and they tended to treat their tour there as something between a research leave and a vacation. They were often absent from their classes without notice (usually touring archaeological sites in the area) and were lax in classroom preparation and evaluation of student assignments. After 1973, the Iranian university terminated the agreement after enduring several years of this abuse.

One practice that added considerably to Iranian feelings of being exploited concerned wage policies in American companies. Americans working in Iran were generally paid at rates far exceeding those paid to Iranian workers. American industrial concerns often had multiple pay scales: United States citizens received the highest wages, followed by Europeans and Japanese; Asians (Indians, Pakistanis, South Koreans, and Filipinos) came next. Only one group fell below native Iranians on the wage scale—Afghan unskilled laborers. ITT paid its American staff up to seven times what it paid its Iranian staff, even though in some cases the Iranian technicians had received precisely the same educational training as their American counterparts and carried out equivalent duties. Some Iranians had even been classmates of their American coworkers at the same American universities. American salaries for low-level management positions ranged to $50,000 per year, and middle management could count on scales reaching up to twice that amount. One can only imagine what top executives were being paid.

Inequalities were not limited to pay. In the oil fields and other "camp" situations controlled by foreign firms, Iranian technicians were often housed in quarters that were separate from and inferior to those of Americans with equivalent training and experience. The refinery city of Abadan was divided between luxurious air-conditioned housing with manicured lawns for Westerners, and two-room mud-brick dwellings for Iranian workers.

Personal relations between Americans and Iranians were not especially cordial. The vast bulk of Americans living and working in Iran were essentially technicians, often with no experience in living abroad, who were only living and working in Iran "for the money." The second largest group was the American military who, likewise, had very little interest in Iran or Iranians.[16]

Perhaps the greatest source of tension between Americans and Iranians on a day-to-day basis was housing. American companies in Iran usually worked under Iranian government contracts on a "cost-plus" basis. That is, the Iranian government agreed to pay the company a certain percent-

16. Cf. Barry Rubin, *Paved with Good Intentions: The American Experience and Iran* (New York: Oxford 1980), pp. 136–38. Rubin estimates that there were 24,000 American expatriates working in Iran in 1976. By 1978 the number had risen to nearly 50,000.

age over its fixed costs if the project was completed. These companies often would move thousands of employees into a city in the space of a month, all of whom would have to find housing immediately. Working through brokers, the Americans would, en masse, rent every available apartment or house in a given area at whatever price was asked. Since housing costs were "fixed costs," Americans did not care how much they paid—the bill would be picked up by the Iranian government. Naturally, after a short time rental costs were driven up throughout Iran. In the period from 1972 to 1974 they had roughly quadrupled on every class of property. By 1976 they had doubled again. Although the general inflation in the country can be cited as a contributing factor to the rise in rents, they would never have increased to the extent they did if American business had acted more responsibly.

Oppositionist leaders seized on yet another aspect of the special relationship between Iran and the United States—the right of extraterritoriality granted to many American citizens living and working in Iran. The Vienna Convention of 1961 is the major international legal agreement defining the rights of diplomatic personnel stationed in foreign posts. Article I of that convention basically assures rights of extraterritoriality, diplomatic immunity in common parlance, to all accredited diplomats serving on foreign soil.

The United States in 1961, before Iran had actually ratified the Vienna Convention, concluded an agreement for economic assistance signed by both nations, which provided that American members of technical-assistance missions would be treated "as part of the diplomatic mission of the United States of America in Iran for the purpose of enjoying the privileges and immunities accorded to that diplomatic mission."[17]

When the question of ratifying the Vienna Convention finally came before the majles in 1963–64, it sparked a lively debate, since the United States had already made clear that it would consider the terms of the Vienna Convention applicable to the 1961 agreement of economic assistance, thus potentially extending the rights of extraterritoriality to many individuals outside of the embassy staff. The Iranian Parliament was caught in a bind. In joining the international community in ratifying the convention, they would de facto be granting special privileges to many American citizens. Although the ratification passed, one deputy remarked sourly that he would have a hard time replying to someone who said that even a foreign refrigerator repairman or apprentice mechanic in Iran enjoyed the immunity that Iran's ambassador enjoyed abroad.[18]

The historical significance of the majles ratification was not lost on

17. Cf. Roy Parviz Mottahedeh, "Iran's Foreign Devils," *Foreign Policy* 38 (Spring 1980): 25.

18. Ibid., p. 27.

Ayatollah Ruhollah Khomeini, already a major oppositionist figure in Iran. The extraterritorial rights granted American hearkened back to the nineteenth century when Great Britain and tsarist Russia had been able to force Iran to grant them the right to try their citizens resident in Iran in special consular courts. Khomeini issued a violent proclamation condemning the majles action, ending with the judgment, "If the foreigners wish to misuse this filthy vote, the nation's duty will be clearly specified. . . . The misfortunes of Islamic governments have come from the interference of foreigners in their destinies. . . . It is America that considers the Koran and Islam to be harmful to itself and wishes to remove them from its way; it is America that considers Muslim men of religion a thorn in its path."[19]

In October 1964, Khomeini preached the sermon that caused his exile from Iran. In this sermon, condemning the right of extraterritoriality, once again he said, "If the shah should run over an American dog, he would be called to account, but if an American cook should run over the shah, . . . no one has any claim against him. . . . If the men of religion had influence it would not be possible for the nation to be at one moment the prisoner of England, at the next the prisoner of America."[20]

Few Americans in Iran were prepared to understand these undercurrents, for most lived in isolation from Iranian society and culture. When American academics concerned with Iran approached large industrial concerns with offers to set up language and cultural training programs for American employees in Iran these offers were not taken seriously. At best they were considered, as one executive put it, as "a nice way to keep the wives from getting bored."

Internal Culture Shock

Americans also had little perspective on what Western technology and cultural institutions were doing to traditional Iranian patterns of social life. Even as late as 1960, Tehrán was a city where citizens pursued a leisurely, close social life. Visiting friends and relatives was the principal social activity.

By 1978 Tehran's population had quadrupled. Automobiles clogged the streets; smog hung ominously, polluting the mountain air; and the more leisurely pace of life had turned into a frantic struggle for most citizens. It could take an hour to travel any distance in the city, as traffic jams were debilitating. As the city spread, family members became widely separated, and could see each other with far less frequency than before. The gap in human contact could be bridged to a limited extent by the

19. Ibid., p. 28.
20. Ibid., pp. 28–29.

telephone, but obtaining this magical device was expensive and time consuming. Humorous writers commented that if one signed up for a telephone at birth, it might be delivered on the day of one's funeral.[21]

Besides telephones, radios (with tape-cassette recorders), cars, and televisions became the new necessities for the modern Iranian family. Even in rural areas some might possess such things and enter the modern age—even if one's village lacked other necessities, such as electricity or piped water. The rural landscape was dotted with television aerials, often run by gasoline generators.

In this way Iran was plunged directly into the age of sound and visual media without ever achieving literacy for the majority. Although National Iranian Radio-Television attempted to support traditional culture through the revival of classical music and traditional cultural forms, it probably did far more to erode cultural life in the provinces than to encourage it. Traditional storytellers, the chief source of entertainment in provincial teahouses, were replaced by television. Music for weddings was purchased on tape cassettes rather than commissioned from traditional musicians. Young men and women were introduced to styles of life that were completely foreign to them, as Western programming was heavily used in a television schedule that Iranian production crews, lacking well-trained technical personnel and a sufficient number of talented artists, could not fill.[22]

Film-going became the chief pastime of urban youth, despite its being frowned upon by conservative religious officials. An average of seventy Iranian films were produced annually, most being of a low-budget, highly popular variety emphasizing melodrama, song and dance, and soap-opera morality. The public loved them.

Paradoxically, as economic conditions improved for business and government, the Iranian commercial film industry began to suffer a decline. Foreign films began to drive the popular Iranian commercial productions off the market, partly because of favorable import laws. Inflation increased production costs, making it more profitable for investors in the film industry to import their products rather than manufacture them. In the highly inflationary, overheated economy, film production offered too great a risk, and too low a return for most investors: office buildings and apartments were more solid than cellulose.

The result was that, from 1973 on, the proportion of Iranian films seen

21. Cf. Robert Graham, *Iran: The Illusion of Power* (London: Croom Helm, 1978), chap. 11, for an extensive discussion of further aspects of cultural dilemmas created for Iranians by modernization.

22. Parviz Kimiavi's film *The Mongols* (1973) burlesques the effects of the invasion of television in rural Iran by likening it to the Mongol invasions of the twelfth and thirteenth centuries. Ironically, the film was financed by National Iranian Radio-Television itself, and shown on television.

by the public dwindled to a small percentage of the films on the Iranian screen. However low their quality, the Iranian films reflected Iranian cultural values and aesthetic sensibilities. Some so-called "new wave" films were of high cinematic quality, and were socially critical within an Iranian cultural frame. Foreign films were often disturbing and shocking for traditional classes, who opposed them more strenuously than ever.[23]

Education was one priority of the Iranian government under the Pahlavi regime. University education in particular increased tremendously during the post–World War II years. Nevertheless, the ambitious development plans of the shah outstripped the ability of the educational system to produce the expertise needed for the expansion of industry, medicine, construction, and the educational system itself. The public viewed education as a path to success, and insisted that their children enter some program of higher education following high school. Nine times as many students took university entrance examinations each year as there were places for entering students.

With a burgeoning need for expertise at the postgraduate level and inadequate training programs to produce that expertise, and an insatiable public demand for undergraduate education, the only solution for Iran was to export its student population for training abroad. The Iranian student population in the United States alone grew to about 35,000 by 1976, the largest body of foreign students in America. Many smaller United States universities, in deep trouble because of shrinking enrollments after the wane of the post–World War II baby boom, became almost dependent on Iranian students to keep them afloat. France and Great Britain experienced similar influxes of Iranian students; even the Philippines and India offered an important educational resource for lower-middle-class Iranians who could not afford the increasingly high cost of Western education.

The return of these students to Iran after years of foreign education had a massive impact on Iranian society. By 1976, few families with money did not have at least one member who had studied or was studying at a foreign university. Returning students, some of whom who had left home at age seventeen or eighteen, had developed attitudes toward male-female relations that severely disturbed their elders. Moreover, they seemed often to be impervious to the old codes of respect and deference which formed the backbone of Iranian family life. Young Iranian women defied traditional codes of modesty and might date (usually in groups) while pursuing careers as modern, middle-class professionals.

23. Cf. Hamid Naficy, "Film in Iran: A Brief Critical History," in Michael E. Bonine and Nikki R. Keddie, eds., *Modern Iran: The Dialectics of Continuity and Change* (Albany: State University of New York Press, 1981).

Returning foreign-educated students were not only causing consternation at home, they also were proving to be increasingly unsuited for the development and social needs of the Iranian people. It would be harsh to blame these individuals directly. Many, if not most, went abroad hoping to acquire the skills necessary to help their advance. Unfortunately, foreign universities emphasized skills that had nothing to do with Iran. The problems of developing a bazaar economy into an investment capital network were ill-served by American graduate-level econometrics. The difficulty of working with small agriculturists in increasing national grain production had little to do with techniques of Western-style agribusiness. Urban and rural housing construction on the dry and mountainous Iranian plateau was not helped through studying architecture at the Sorbonne. German labor management could not aid in modernizing traditional handicraft industries. The returning graduates came back with titles but with few usable skills. They were increasingly employed in elite branches of the bureaucracy like the Iranian Plan Organization, never to emerge again.

Despite their training and living abroad, this group of young Iranians often felt both alienated and useless. The high hopes of the 1960s, when the first large wave of Iranian students surged abroad, turned to cynicism and a bitter feeling of helplessness by the 1970s. Many of these students took up permanent residence abroad; others stayed in Iran and made the best of their condition. Most, however, harbored a lingering resentment against the United States and the other Western nations that had hosted them—not for anything that had been done to them, but for their education, which was to be their salvation yet became a hollow fulfillment of the promise it had offered.

The upper-middle and upper classes, growing ever larger, began to frequent Europe and the United States in increasing numbers every year. By the mid-1970s flights between Tehran and the West were solidly booked at all times. Many of the trips were simply for shopping. Many women bragged that they bought all of their wardrobe in Paris or London—down to the underwear. Boutiques began to open in Tehran and other cities, which specialized in Western luxury items and even advertised, "Did you miss something on your last trip to Paris?—then buy it at our boutique!" Young children from these families began to summer at camps in Switzerland. Many could boast that they had toured all the capitals of Europe, though they had never seen the classical Iranian cities of Isfahan or Shiraz.

For the bulk of the population the foreign orientation of everything around them—television, architecture, film, clothing, social attitudes, educational goals, and economic development aims—seemed to resemble a strange, alien growth on the society that was sapping it of all its former values and worth. Middle-aged people bemoaned the crassness and bustle of modern life, and openly longed for older, quieter times when life was harder but stability reigned; where one could count on other people's attitudes and not expect to be shocked, outraged, or disoriented every time one went out of doors or read a newspaper.

For the religious community the new social orientation was nothing short of directly sinful. Dancing, music, and especially the cinema were singled out for harsh attacks from the mosque and religious schools. In the smaller towns and villages where the religious climate was considerably more conservative than in the cities, residents would explain their ownership of a radio by asserting that they only listened to the news (and not the likes of popular singers Gugush and Dariush). Television was somehow considered less dangerous than the dark city moviehouses; even after the revolution it was declared to be a useful device by Ayatollah Khomeini, provided it was supervised properly by religious authorities.

Of perhaps greater concern to religious authorities than the devices of corruption in social life was the increasing emphasis of the state on the secularization of society. In all areas of daily living, religious guidance seemed to be ignored in public policy-making. Some activities, such as gambling in several casinos around the country, and the manufacture and consumption of liquor, were directly and indirectly supported by the state (as in state-run hotels). There seemed to be a clear attempt by the Pahlavi dynasty somehow to circumvent Islam in the definition of the Iranian state. The self-coronation of the shah and the elaborate 2,500-anniversary celebration of the Iranian monarchy in 1969 and 1972, respectively, both adopted pre-Islamic themes. The predominance of symbols referring to Iran's civilizational glories under the Achaemenian and Sassanian Empires were to be seen everywhere in the years immediately preceding the revolution. In 1976, it was widely rumored that a number of young men in Khuzistan had "converted" to Zoroastrianism (which formally does not accept converts), claiming that their ancestors had been forcibly converted to Islam centuries before. One of the men reportedly took a Zoroastrian bride from Yazd, thus sealing community acceptance of his theoretically impossible act. In that same year, the shah announced a change in the official Iranian calendar. The year would henceforth be reckoned, not according to the hijra of Muhammad, but rather to the supposed date of the establishment of the Achaemenian dynasty. This even caught the attention of the Zoroastrians, who could not fail to notice the similarity between their traditional calendar and the new official one, to the point where some speculated that the shah would reveal that he, too, was actually a Zoroastrian, and would soon declare Iran to be a Zoroastrian state once more.

As silly as these speculations were, the seeming pre-Islamic orientation of the state was viewed by the clergy as yet another attempt by the throne to undermine religious institutions and morality. Some of the first actions taken by the new government of the Islamic Republic were to eliminate official glorification of the pre-Islamic empires. Indeed, Ayatollah Dastghaib of Shiraz is reported to have sent a group to destroy the monuments at Persepolis and Pasargadae in the summer of 1979, an action supposedly thwarted by Shiraz's other religious leader, Ayatollah Mahallati.

The Internal Rises Up

By 1976 a series of altercations involving Americans began to suggest to the American embassy and American business personnel that something was dreadfully wrong. A well-publicized street brawl between American and Iranian workers in the city of Isfahan caused alarm among expatriate companies working there. In response an American compound was created at a far remove from the city where workers could live in splendid isolation. Far from helping the situation, this compound became a local symbol of American imperiousness.

Sadly, even Americans who were aware of these problems tended to take a sanguine view of them. American presence and profits were rationalized by thoughts such as, "Really, Iranians are benefiting from our presence here—they now have cars, televisions, and refrigerators, and a better telephone system than they did before." Buoyed by high GNP growth figures,[24] American officials pointed with pride to the economic boom they had helped to create.

The boom was superficial, however. The quickest way to create instant industrialization is to set up manufacturing operations for which the basic parts are fabricated elsewhere, and only assembled in the country of sale. Iranian industry in the 1970s placed heavy emphasis on turnkey assembly operations with many firms concentrating on consumer goods.

Heavy emphasis on the assembly of consumer goods,[25] elements of which were produced elsewhere, created disincentives for other kinds of investment. Iranian entrepreneurs, finding lucrative consumer markets within Iran, but no potential for export, faced limited outlets for their profits. They could either work backward from the assembly industries toward establishing basic industries that would not yield income for a decade if, indeed, they would ever be profitable; or they could put their money into shorter-term, less productive investments like real estate.

24. Cf. n. 15, above.
25. Cf. Gail Cook Johnson, *High-Level Manpower in Iran: From Hidden Conflict to Crisis* (New York: Praeger, 1980), pp. 11–23.

Large-scale industrial investment became impossible for all but the very wealthy, or the very well connected. Bazaar merchants and middle-class citizens found that they had no access to investment capital through normal channels. The subsidized development loans available to industrialists at 6 percent interest were a far cry from the rates offered by private moneylenders to small businessmen, ranging from 20 to 50 percent.[26] Small merchants had another problem to face in government-subsidized department stores, which severely challenged both their livelihood and the normal pricing structure of the free bazaar.

Nevertheless, bazaar merchants and middle-class citizens retained two areas where they, too, could make a great deal of money rather quickly. Those areas were land speculation and construction, and the distribution of foodstuffs, both imported and locally produced.

Land speculation and construction could be financed on the basis of capital raised by using an existing business as collateral, or through a system of discounted promissory notes, which constitute the chief form of credit transaction used in the bazaar. When housing prices were doubling in a year, the 20 percent interest rates mattered little. The sale of foodstuffs could be manipulated by holding goods off the market, until the price rose, and then flooding the market at the higher price.

The central government was outraged at these developments because they could not be controlled easily. Government officials were cut in quickly on the most lucrative schemes, and speculation continued unabated. The sector of the public that suffered the most were those with no investment capital and no access to any. For these hapless people, life became worse as the cost of food and housing soared to astronomical heights.

Following the oil-price increase in 1973–74 the country was awash in money with no place for the cash to go. The natural result was tremendous inflation, reaching 50 percent per annum by 1976. By 1977 inflation had begun to affect even the wealthy of the country. Complaints about prices were the chief source of public discontent, and soon the shah moved to gain control over the economy.

The first stage of controls was a "campaign against profiteering" instituted by Prime Minister Amir Abbas Hoveida in 1975–76. His actions consisted of establishing draconian price controls for foodstuffs, along with strict penalties for violators, including the jailing of neighborhood grocers who overcharged or undercut government price standards. Ten thousand inspectors were sent to examine store accounts. Guild courts

26. Ervand Abrahamian, "Structural Causes of the Iranian Revolution," *MERIP Reports, no. 87* (May 1980): 25.

eventually imprisoned 8,000 merchants, exiled 23,000 others from their home towns, and fined as many as 200,000 more.[27]

Still, inflation continued unabated, while industrial and agricultural productivity suffered additional declines. In a dramatic change of government, Jamshid Amuzegar, the former oil minister and OPEC representative, was made prime minister in August 1977. He enacted further measures to bring the economy into line. He announced slower economic growth for the immediate future. Tight new regulations were placed on credit and the transfer of land; stringent new taxes were also imposed on real-estate transactions in order to stop the speculation spiral. The overheated land market began to tremble. As a final blow, the new government cut substantial subsidies to the clergy and religious institutions that had been paid by the central government for years. It is noteworthy that the shah in exile identified this act as the mistake that caused his downfall.

Whether directly attributable to Amuzegar's executive actions or to the bursting of an already dangerously inflated real-estate bubble, the Iranian land market collapsed overnight, and with it the construction industry. Within a month, most unskilled construction laborers were laid off. Although figures for this confused period are inexact, those thrown out of work numbered in the hundreds of thousands. The government matched the jailing of small merchants for overcharging by importing food from abroad at approximately twice the domestic wholesale cost to make up for the shortfalls. Through all the economic chaos that resulted, factory owners and manufacturers of assembly-line goods were largely untouched. Prices for their goods actually rose during this period, unchecked by the government. Prices for kerosene and gasoline—a government monopoly—also were increased.

To the man on the street, the message was clear: the government was going to control inflation by cracking down on those few areas of the economy in which government officials, the royal family, and foreign investors had little financial interest. The few ventures that had allowed ordinary citizens to participate in the vast wealth of the country would be wiped out.

Frustration yielded to outright protest. Merchants began refusing to pay bank loans and promissory notes, and the banking system began to feel the pinch. Ringleaders of the financial protest and other prominent merchants in the bazaar began to be hàrassed and jailed. Unemployed construction workers, largely country residents attracted to the cities by

27. J. Kendeli, "The Tehran Bazaar," *New York Times,* 29 June 1979. Cited in Abrahamian, "Structural Causes," p. 25.

wages that seemed high, but which were eroded by inflation, also were restive. After the collapse of the construction industry, they were trapped in the cities with no place to turn.[28]

The Internal Conquers The External

In this climate of discontent, the incendiary exhortations of Ayatollah Khomeini began to be heeded. Opposition to the shah's regime had been increasing for years. In 1975 the presence of the United States reached a critical level. Assassinations of American military personnel and advisers occurred in 1973 and 1975. In August 1976, just three months before the election of Jimmy Carter, three employees of Rockwell International were waylaid in Tehran and killed by a terrorist group. The police and SAVAK[29] stepped up their efforts against the guerillas, who only redoubled their efforts. The guerrillas were giving a clear message: from their standpoint, the United States was clearly implicated in the domestic policy of the shah's government and would be subject to further attacks because of it.

With Jimmy Carter's accession to the presidency, the United States began to preach a policy of human rights. Although the principal thrust of the policy was aimed at Communist states, Carter felt that he had concomitantly to encourage authoritarian ally states to liberalize their policies toward dissident political expression. The shah complied and announced a new policy of liberalization, but according to James Bill, it seemed hollow: "with the beginning of Jimmy Carter's presidency, the shah set forth a new policy, a program of liberalization that was to include an end to torture, a selective release of political prisoners, an attempt to introduce legal reform, and a loosening of tight censorship controls. As 1977 moved into 1978, the people of Iran quietly watched the exchange of visits between President Carter and the shah. When no new policies finally emerged, the violence began."[30]

The beginning of the end came on 9 January 1978 when theology students in Qom began a protest against an article published in the newspaper *Ettela'at,* accusing Ayatollah Khomeini of licentious behavior and other crimes. The article was published under a pseudonym, but indications are that it emanated from the shah. It was submitted to the paper by then Minister of Information Dariush Homayun. The demon-

28. Cf. Farhad Kazemi, *Poverty and Revolution in Iran: The Migrant Poor, Urban Marginality and Politics* (New York: New York University Press, 1980), for additional information concerning the plight of the urban poor before and during the revolution.

29. The well-known Iranian secret police force. SAVAK is an acronym for "Sazeman-e Amniat va Ettela'at-e Keshvar" Organization (for) National Security and Intelligence.

30. James Bill, "Iran and the Crisis of '78," *Foreign Affairs* 57 (Winter 1978/79): 329.

stration met with violence from the police, and started the cycle of violence and death that led to the shah's departure a year later. Predictably, most of the protestors were drawn from the young unemployed males in the large cities, and the protests were underwritten and financed from the bazaar.

At first, even hard-line opponents of the United States could not believe that the American president would support the Iranian government's violence against its own people. Ayatollah Hosain Montazeri was quoted as saying, "We didn't expect Carter to defend the shah, for he is a religious man who has raised the slogan of defending human rights. How can Carter, the devout Christian, defend the shah?"[31]

Nevertheless President Carter's support for the shah continued unabated. To an Iranian public already bitter about American economic activity in their country, the Carter human-rights doctrine seemed to be another form of cruel exploitation: at best a propagandistic sham, at worst a ploy rumored to be designed to encourage popular dissent, only to set the protestors up for massacre.

The Great Satan

Iranian rejection of the United States and the former shah is perhaps too easy to interpret in material terms alone. This view is deceptive, however. The protests that toppled the Pahlavi regime touched every stratum of society in the end and spread through all regions of the country. The rage that caused thousands to burn public buildings, topple statues, and march into live rounds of ammunition touched something far deeper than a mere desire for a larger piece of Iran's wealth.

The principal theme of the revolution might well be thought of as righteous indignation resulting from betrayal. The shah had betrayed his trust as a leader to his people by failing to protect their economic and spiritual interests, eventually resorting to violent attacks against them when no other mechanism existed. In violating the obligations of a superior, he relinquished all rights to the respect due a person in that position. Just as in everyday interpersonal relationships, which can rupture in an instant of ill-faith, the shah lost his standing with the public very quickly. This came as a great shock to him: "Driving through the city of Meshed in an open car only four months before the situation became desperate, . . . I was acclaimed by 300,000 people. Just after the troubles in Tabriz [in February, 1978] my prime minister went there and had an overwhelming reception. I can recall nothing in the history of the

31. Interview in *Al Nahar Al-'Arabi wa al-Duwali* (Paris), 24-30 December 1979. Cited in Rubin, *Paved with Good Intentions*, p. 195.

world—not even the French Revolution—to compare with what happened subsequently."[32]

The view of the United States was in some ways more serious. The shah could be seen to have fallen into corruption, but it was the United States that was identified as the ultimate source of that corruption. The United States was well situated to play the role of an outside corrupting force. It shared a historical legacy with Iran's old nemesis, Great Britain. More important, the United States repeated the old political patterns that the British had employed: strong-arm tactics in the oil market, demands for diplomatic immunity, undue influence on the throne and elsewhere, business and trade concessions, and an imperious attitude toward Iranians and Iranian institutions. Americans were isolated from the Iranian public, and it was easy to associate them with the imperial power of the shah, since most Americans were working in Iran under contracts associated with the throne.

Subsequent revolutionary symbolism bears out the thesis that the United States had indeed become associated with external forces of corruption. Carter was referred to as Yazid (the caliph responsible for the death of Imam Husain). In this formulation, the shah is depicted as Shimr, the general of Yazid. Another series of street drawings from the revolution shows the shah in the role of the pharaoh of Egypt with the Ayatollah Khomeini as Moses. Jimmy Carter is depicted as the false idol worshiped by the pharaoh/shah.

From these depictions and others the symbolic position of the United States vis-à-vis the Iranian people in the context of the revolution becomes clear. The United States is the ultimate supporter of illegitimate authority, in this case the shah. In this it joins the others in history who have supported illegitimate rule. In the Iranian symbolic universe, this is the ultimate external corrupting force, which must be resisted at all costs.

In the writings of Ayatollah Khomeini, colonial Western powers are treated as projections of a single force opposed to Islam. Facing this force are the Islamic *ulama,* who are projections of the legitimate rulers, the imams. The jurisprudents, *faqihs,* derive their charge from the Prophet himself: "His words 'because the faithful jurisprudents are the strongholds of Islam . . .' is an assignment to the jurisprudents to preserve Islam with its creeds, laws, and systems."[33] The colonial powers are the enemies of this legitimate system:

The colonialists have spread in school curricula the need to separate church from the state and have deluded people into believing that the ulama of Islam are not

32. Rubin, *Paved with Good Intentions,* p. 203.
33. Ayatollah Ruhollah Khomeini, *Islamic Government* (New York: Manor, 1979), p. 49.

qualified to interfere in the political and social affairs. . . . The colonialists and their lackeys have made these statements to isolate religion from the affairs of life and society and to tacitly keep the ulama of Islam away from the people and drive people away from the ulama because the ulama struggle for the liberation and independence of the Muslims. When their wish of separation is realized, the colonialists and their lackeys can take away our resources and rule us.[34]

The United States is only the latest of the foreign forces that destroyed the Ottoman sultanate, divided up the Middle East into "illegitimate states," and installed puppet rulers to do their bidding. Thus all the great external usurpers of history are linked, and opposed in a single process to the representatives of inner truth.

The Iranian public already felt that it was being exploited in its dealings with the United States in the first half of the 1970s. Still, as long as the economy continued to expand, the public was willing to put up with the relationship. The economic difficulties of 1975–77 changed the picture. Expectations continued to rise and benefits began to fall. The stern economic measures imposed under Amuzegar made it clear that the masses of Iran could now expect little from the government.[35] The American defense of the shah once the public had abandoned him only confirmed the view of America's worst detractors that the United States was indeed interested only in exploitation, and would do anything to maintain its minions even when they were rejected by their own people.

The history of the United States and Iran during the years leading up to the revolution is a sad chronicle of wrong policies, misunderstanding, and cultural misperception. The United States became the "Great Satan" not in a sudden stroke at the taking of the hostages, but through a slow and steady process. In a myopic manner, America persisted in digging itself into a ready-made villain's role. The great external corrupter, supporter of illegitimate power, and destroyer of the natural bonds that bind men together in beneficial relationships; such is the nature of the beast.

34. Ibid., pp. 15–16.
35. Note James Davies's now classic "J-Curve" theory to describe a revolution of rising expectations: "When a long period of rising expectations and gratifications is followed by a short period during which expectations continue to rise while gratifications fall off sharply, the probability of civil violence against the government rises rapidly." James C. Davies, "The J-Curve Theory," *American Political Science Review* 72 (December 1978): 1357–58. Cf. also Sepehr Zabih, *Iran's Revolutionary Upheaval* (San Francisco: Alchemy Press, 1979), p. 76.

CHAPTER ELEVEN

Two Images of Husain: Accommodation and Revolution in an Iranian Village

MARY HEGLAND

In academic circles, a common explanation for the success of the Iranian revolution has been the powerful effect of Shi'i religion and ritual on Iranians. Iranians are pictured as almost instinctively responding to the call of religious revolution. Supposedly, they present themselves for martyrdom almost as a reflex. The 1978 'ashura rituals mourning the death of Imam Husain are thought to have been especially compelling in sweeping Iranians into revolutionary action for this reason; emotions evoked through participation in the traditional 'ashura rituals automatically drew Iranians into the process of revolution. Singlehandedly, Shi'i world view and ritual were supposedly instrumental in changing Iranians into a nation of revolutionary activists. I will argue that such is not the case, but that rather a transformation in the understanding of the central meaning of Shi'i Islam among the Iranian masses coinciding with changing economic and political conditions was instrumental in bringing about the success of the Iranian revolution.

Several lines of argument can be used to question the purely cultural explanation of the revolution. First, Iranians who are not Shi'i Muslims were involved in the revolution. In fact, there is hardly a religious, tribal, or ethnic minority that was not represented. During a visit to Mahabad, a Kurdish town, in the fall of 1979, I heard detailed descriptions of revolutionary activities among Sunni Kurds. Some 180 persons in the Mahabad area were reportedly killed during the revolution. In Shiraz, members of the large Jewish minority participated in marches and demonstrations, often organized in their own groups and shouting their own slogans. Reflecting the unity of all religious groups in the effort was the slogan "Musalman, yahudi, masihi: Begu marg bar shah!" (Muslim, Jew, Christian: Shout down with the shah!). From all over the country reports came through word of mouth, press, and radio and TV of the revolutionary activities among all types of religious, ethnic, and tribal groups—many of whom are Sunni Muslim.[1]

Shi'i Muslims were not the only persons participating in the revolution, nor was Shi'i ideology the only ideology prompting revolutionary action. Leftists, liberals, and nationalists of a whole range of political persuasions were active, on the basis of secular ideologies alone or in conjunction with religious ideas. Even within the Shi'i Muslim community, the approach to Islam and to politics was hardly monolithic. Some Shi'i Muslims did not participate in the revolution at all, in fact were active in opposing revolutionary tendencies. In the village where I lived and conducted research during the revolution, whole groups of people stayed out of the conflict; peasants, the political elite, opium smugglers, and policemen in general either kept quiet or even attempted to quell the movement, often in brutal fashion. Yet all these people considered themselves Muslims in as good standing as, if not better than, those taking part in the revolution.

It thus seems apparent that Shi'i Islam alone cannot explain the revolution. Many non-Shi'is *did* participate and many Shi'i Muslims *refrained* from participation. In order to understand more fully the forces behind the revolution, one must remember that Islam does not mean the same thing to all its adherents.[2] Most important for this chapter—and, to a degree, for the course of the Iranian revolution—are the variations in Shi'ism at the popular level. The success of the revolution followed a transformation in the understanding of the central meaning of Shi'i Islam among the Iranian masses. Leaders of the revolution from religious, educational, and bazaari groups were successful in their advocacy of revolution because they presented an ideology appealing to large numbers of both Shi'i Muslims and non-Shi'is. This ideology appealed to many non-Shi'i Muslims because its social and political implications were similar to those implied by their own ideologies, or at the least, because they agreed with the goals and means suggested by this ideology.

In the Shi'i Muslim community, the months leading up to the revolution

1. This chapter is based on an eighteen-month period of research in Iran that was made possible by a fellowship granted by the Social Science Research Council and the American Council of Learned Societies. The conclusions, opinions, and other statements in this article are those of the author. Field research was conducted throughout the course of the Iranian revolution, from June 1978 until December 1979. The research site was the village of "Aliabad," with a population of three to four thousand, located half an hour by bus from the outskirts of Shiraz, capital of the southwestern province of Fars. A great debt is owed many kind and open-minded Iranians who offered me their friendship and assistance during tense times, and especially to two individuals well educated in religious matters. I am grateful to Richard Antoun, Kurt Greussing, Nikki Keddie, and Bruce Lincoln for reading and providing helpful comments on this article.

2. Nikki Keddie has recently discussed the variations in Shi'i Islam. See Nikki R. Keddie, "Iran: Change in Islam; Islam and Change," *International Journal of Middle East Studies* 11 (1980):527–42.

saw a struggle between the adherents of two opposing ideologies to gain support for their respective ideologies and thereby for their political stances also. These opposing ideologies—which I will call "Imam Husain as Intercessor," with the allied political stance of accommodation; and "Imam Husain as Example," with its corresponding political stance of revolution—are both based upon the same central event or myth: the martyrdom of Imam Husain, along with some seventy of his family and supporters, on the plains of Kerbala in A.D. 680.

During the course of the revolution, people evaluated "Imam Husain as Intercessor" in light of economic and political conditions and their own position in society, and began to judge it lacking. As they sensed that it no longer accurately explained society nor provided a practical program for behavior, many people began to lose interest in the ideology and in the rituals connected with it. The intercessor interpretation of Shi'i Islam therefore began to lose ground in the conflict between ideologies and supporters of ideologies. In contrast, "Imam Husain as Example" continued to gain adherents as ongoing events supported its world view, persuading people that the political stance it proposed was the right policy to follow. I would argue that people were persuaded to take part in the revolution by ideology and an assessment of observable conditions and events. The decision by individuals to join the revolution was conscious and not based on unthinking religious emotions. As both sides of the struggle sought to legitimize their position and actions in terms of a different version of Islamic ideology, adherence to Shi'i Islam in itself was not sufficient reason for a person to change his views and support the revolutionary version of Shi'i Islam. Although it is true that participation in rituals, such as the important marches on the main days mourning Husain, tasu'a and 'ashura (10 and 11 Dec.), 1978, reinforced commitment to the revolution and inspired further political opposition, a decision had to be made in the first place to take part in such rituals. Participation was not automatic, even for Shi'i Muslims. Persons had to choose between participation in the old forms of rituals commemorating the martyrdom of Imam Husain and participation in the previously unheard of, relatively secular marches and the practice of raising fists and shouting "Down with the shah" as a new form of commemoration.

In supporting the argument, I will first discuss the opposing popular ideologies, their implications for social and political organization, and how their respective action platforms are actually practiced by persons in political activity. I will briefly discuss how changes in material conditions, such as the increase in employment opportunities, gave many people the option of turning to the ideology of revolution. Finally, I will point out how "Imam Husain as Example" was successful in attracting non-Shi'is to the revolutionary movement.

Imam Husain as Intercessor: Political Accommodation

According to this view of Shi'i Islam, Imam Husain, because he was martyred and therefore beloved of God, is able to serve as an intercessor between God and human beings. Imam Husain is believed to be capable of forgiving sins and granting entrance to Paradise as well as fulfilling more mundane wishes and requests.[3] Weeping and mourning for Husain is supposed to be especially effective in gaining his favor and thereby also assuring the fulfillment of one's desires.[4] Extending to the other eleven imams and to their descendants as well, this intercessory and reciprocal relationship is the main focus of religion for most Shi'i Iranians and provides a complete world view concerning the relationship between human beings and holy figures.

When addressing the imams or *imamzadehs* (descendants of imams), the request is generally made in the form of a vow.[5] For example, a person apprehended and jailed for opium smuggling in my research site asked Imam Husain to get him released, promising that if he did so, the asker would provide three public meals to honor Imam Husain during Moharram, the month of his martyrdom. In this view of Islam, a main focus of the believer is concern for himself and his own interests and problems. He hopes that through devotion to the imams he will improve his own standing in society, solve his troubles, and be admitted to Paradise. The believer concentrates on the dyadic, hierarchical relationship between himself and the imam. He strives to show his repsect and devotion to the imam in every way possible, hoping thereby to become close to him, that the imam will then feel disposed to provide assistance. During Moharram especially, Muslims attempt to weep as loud and long as possible, to engage in the most arduous and painful demonstrations of mourning during the ritual processions, and to provide refreshments in the name of Imam Husain in accord with financial ability.

In this interpretation of Islam, the behavior of Imam Husain and his accomplishments, ideals, and values are far less important than his connection with God and the resulting power at his disposal. In making this assertion, I am not denying the very real love and devotion that many Iranians hold for Husain. But it does seem that for many, Imam Husain was loved more for his position—beloved of God and thus able to grant requests—than for his personal qualities. Perhaps acquaintance with the

3. See Mahmoud Ayoub, *Redemptive Suffering in Islam: A Study of the Devotional Aspects of 'Ashura in Twelver Shi'ism* (The Hague: Mouton Publishers, 1978), pp. 142–43.

4. Gustav Thaiss, "Religious Symbolism and Social Change: The Drama of Husain," Ph.D. dissertation, Washington University, St. Louis, 1973, p. 165.

5. See also Anne Betteridge, "The Controversial Vows of Urban Muslim Women in Iran," in *Unspoken Worlds: Women's Religious Lives in Non-Western Cultures,* ed. Nancy Falk and Rita Gross (New York: Harper & Row, 1980), pp. 144–45.

imam as a person is not relevant, because a true admiration and respect are not the most important requirements for the relationship between him and believers. In the end, the relationship is an instrumental one and requires only outward, public deference and honor.[6] In the eyes of the believer, the main aim is to get on good terms with the imams or imamzadehs so as to increase the chances of receiving assistance from them when it is needed.

In this scheme of things, the individual believer is relegated to a position of dependency. He is incapable of attaining his goals through his own efforts; his only hope is to modify his behavior to seek the approval and favor of those in power.

The message concerning political policy found in this version of Islam is: The preferable political action is to try to connect yourself with the powerful so they will protect and assist you. Accept and tolerate the status quo and look to your own interests. Do not fight or struggle; just stay out of trouble and do your best to stay afloat or get ahead. Use the powerful—do not resist them. It is useless to resist because you will only meet with defeat and, in any case, you are dependent upon the powerful and the hope of their assistance.

Indeed, it appears that the teachings regarding the relationship between humans and holy figures provided by this version of Shi'i Islam are applied in attitudes toward political activity in the world of humans as well. In comments made to me by informants in Aliabad, the use of this transactional, dyadic relationship between superior and subordinate both as a way to explain reality and as practical advice for political strategy is apparent. One perceptive villager described this outlook as follows: "The small ones help the bigger one so when the little ones have problems, the big one will help. Like when the shah left, they executed his assistants— like [ex-Prime Minister] Hoveida. Now if the shah were here would they have executed his assistants? Those people [the shah's assistants] helped the shah for the sake of their own interests and for the protection of their own lives."

Reflecting the hopeless and dependent state many persons believed themselves to be in, forcing them to accept their status of dependency rather than revolt against it, are the following comments by the same informant: "It's not that Sayyed Ibn Ali [the head of the kin group of this informant, upon whom he felt dependent] has given me anything to eat or a job or anything. He really doesn't do anything for me these days. But if he has a fight with someone, I'll help him out. I have to help him out. Because if he goes, my fate is sealed."

6. See also Anne Betteridge, "Ziarat: Pilgrimage in Iran," paper presented at the Tenth Annual Meeting of the Middle East Studies Association, Los Angeles, California (1976), p. 11.

In the view of many villagers, the best course of action was to connect themselves with a powerful person who could defend and assist them against possible attacks or incursions by others. Such people felt themselves to be quite at the mercy of the powerful, forced to tolerate any perceived mistreatment from such patrons, forced to spend time, effort, and resources vying for their favor. There seemed to be no alternative to protect themselves, their families, and their livelihoods. The behavior suggested by this framework was actually practiced in the village and was especially apparent in *taifeh* (kin group) organization and in the activities of peasants in relation to the village political elite. Although visible in the behavior of all taifeh members toward the influential head of their respective taifehs, displays of deference were especially striking in the Askari taifeh. The two Askari brothers were the wealthiest and most powerful people connected with the village. As it happens, many of the relatives of these two brothers were quite poor. Perceiving themselves to be dependent on the two brothers for economic reasons and for political protection, the poor relations tried to curry their favor and avoid offending them in any way. Through such behavior, the Askari relatives hoped to present themselves to the brothers as steadfast and dependable supporters, aiming thereby to earn the protection and assistance of these powerful persons along with their affection and trust.

Providing a parallel case is the perceived situation of the peasants and other landowners in Aliabad in relation to the village elite, Sayyed Ibn Ali Askari and his closest supporters. Bitter experience had taught the small landowners that Sayyed Ibn Ali could encroach on their land at will, taking it over as his own. Any attempts to take their case to court resulted in failure because of bribes and the close friendships between Sayyed Ibn Ali and influential members of the court system in Shiraz. They thus concluded that acquiescence to the power structure and demonstrated deference to the Askaris was their only hope of maintaining their access to their land and livelihood.[7] By paying homage to the Askari brothers, the peasants hoped to convey the message that they accepted the brothers' sovereignty, the predominant position of the Askari taifeh, and even the legitimacy of the whole political system on which their power rested. Through catering to the wishes of the Askari brothers, the peasants aimed to get in return some degree of protection. At the very least, they hoped to dissuade the Askaris from taking away their resources.

Peasants did not seem to be aware of the political content of the

7. I deal in greater detail with the dependency of the peasants in Mary Hooglund, "Peasants and the Process of Revolution: An Iranian Case Study," paper presented at the Second Annual Conference of AMESS (Alternative Middle East Studies Seminar), Washington, D.C. (1980). See also Mary Hooglund, "One Village in the Revolution," *MERIP Reports* 9 (1980): 7–12. (In works prior to this one I used the name Hooglund.)

religious ideology and ritual relating to Imam Husain as Intercessor. Villagers did not explicitly state that the expected behavior toward the imams taught them how they should behave toward political superiors in real life. I would suggest that it is precisely because these political messages are disguised in religious symbolism that they are so effective. Because the realm of the sacred is almost by definition unquestionable and unquestioned, political "realities" and messages couched in religious terms are all the more persuasive and powerful.[8] I would argue that the "Imam Husain as Intercessor" ideology and its corresponding rituals both reflect political and economic realities and mold political behavior.[9] The art of pleasing[10]—the strategy of forming connections with the powerful and of modifying one's behavior to please them—practiced in relations with the imams, is also applied to political dealings in the real world.

The above discussion of the "Imam Husain as Intercessor" ideology should demonstrate one reason why ideology is such an effective tool in political conflict. If a political elite can succeed in imposing its own ideology and world view on a people, either through persuading them of the validity of this world view or by forcing them to accept the ideology in a conscious or unconscious exchange for needed resources, people will be encouraged to act in ways that perpetuate the superior position enjoyed by the political elite. The behavior of the peasants in showing deference to the Askaris, accepting the power structure rather than resisting it, and exchanging compliance for protection out of fear and lack of independence was useful to the Askaris in helping them maintain control with a minimum in expenditure of effort and resources.

In teaching acquiescence to the power structure, this ideology was instrumental in maintaining control over local populations, the aim of both central-government officials and local-level elites. As long as most Iranians continued to accept the validity of this world view as an accurate assessment of the social structure and their position in it and a guide to political tactics and maneuvering, the level of opposition required for revolution was not attainable. However, an alternative version of Shi'i Islam presented an ideology and world view that encouraged Iranians to

8. See Abner Cohen, *Two-Dimensional Man: An Essay on the Anthropology of Power and Symbolism in Complex Society* (Berkeley: University of California Press, 1976), p. 53; James Peacock, *Rites of Modernization: Symbolic and Social Aspects of Indonesian Proletarian Drama* (Chicago: The University of Chicago Press, 1968), p. 244; and David Kertzer, "The Role of Ritual in Political Change," paper presented at the Annual Meeting of the American Political Science Association, Washington, D.C. (1980), p. 13.

9. See Peacock, *Rites,* pp. 236–39. Richard Antoun and Bruce Lincoln have also discussed this in personal communication.

10. I am indebted to Richard Antoun for his suggestion of this phrase.

revolt rather than to acquiesce to unjust power. An important reason for the rapid success of the revolution was that leaders of the opposition effectively persuaded masses of Iranians of the validity of this world view and the merit of acting in accordance with it.

Imam Husain as Example: Political Revolution

There are two main reasons why, in the past, residents of Aliabad continued to accept the accuracy and usefulness of the Imam Husain as Intercessor ideology as a means of interpreting reality and a guide for action. First, no aspect of economic or political reality contradicted the ideology. Second, the religious symbolism connected with Imam Husain surrounded both the ideology and the corresponding political structure and behavior with an aura of naturalness and inevitability. But in the years and months preceding the revolution, the ideology of accommodation was called into question along both economic and ideological lines.

Previously, peasants were entirely dependent upon the landlord for access to land. As no other lines of employment were open, they were forced to follow the landlord's wishes in exchange for access to their means of livelihood. However, after the land reform of the 1960s, agriculture deteriorated. Fortunately, while agriculture declined, the oil-boom economy of the seventies opened up a whole new range of job opportunities, in factories built a few kilometers from the village and in nearby Shiraz. For men working outside the village and no longer dependent on the village political elite for access to land and livelihood, the ideology and world view of dependency lost its reliability. No longer could they be forced to accept an ideology and behavior as an unspoken condition for access to a livelihood. If a boss in Shiraz required more submission than they were willing to tolerate, they felt free to move to another job on the plentiful job market. For many of them, religion, as they had previously understood it, began to lose its appeal and central position in their lives and thoughts. Other ideas and ideologies were available and proved intriguing to some of the men commuting to Shiraz for work or school. Marxist books were read clandestinely. Ideas of democracy and representative government were discussed.

The commuters perceived themselves to be economically—and therefore, to a much greater degree, politically as well—independent. Popularized in large part by the teachings of Dr. Ali Shariati, the opposite interpretation of Islam, the ideology of self-reliance and resistance to unjust authority, gained credence. It was a more accurate model of the situation of the commuters and a better representation of the actions they felt like performing. As the revolution escalated, this was increasingly true. With each brutal crackdown perpetrated by government forces against the opposition, the Husain-Yazid model seemed more applicable to the shah's regime. Because of their own economic and political situation and because of the cruel political oppression they more and more observed taking place around them, the ideology of resistance increasingly reflected their own attitudes and view of the world. The Shi'i revolutionary ideology provided a unifying symbolic system around which groups of varying intellectual approaches could rally.

In the alternative view of Shi'i Islam, the martyrdom of Imam Husain serves as an example for the behavior of other believers. In the past, people told me, Iranians did not even know why Husain was martyred. According to one informant, "Only in the last ten years have we begun to learn the real story of Husain." Imam Husain died because he refused to acknowledge the sovereignty of the Umayyad caliph Mu'awiya, whom he considered to be a godless tyrant. Because of his refusal to compromise, Husain and his followers were killed on the plains of Karbala in an extremely uneven battle against many thousands of soldiers led by Yazid. Knowing what the outcome of the battle would be, Husain made the decision to fight anyway, for he believed that his death would, first, demonstrate to all Muslims the godlessness of Mu'awiya and his regime (Husain was the grandson of the Prophet Muhammad and only an extremely evil man would cause the death of such a holy figure). Second, Husain knew that his martyrdom would set an example for all ages, calling Muslims of successive generations to rise up and fight against tyranny and godlessness. Because he actively chose to face death and worldly defeat in order to become a *shahid* (meaning both martyr and witness) of Islam for all times, Husain and his martyrdom on 'ashura, the tenth day of the month of Moharram, have become the central paradigm of Shi'i Islam. In this view of Islam, all human history is pictured as a continuous struggle between the forces of evil and the forces of good. In every age, villagers told me, there is a Husain, a man who fights on the side of God, and a Yazid, who fights against God.

The myth or story of what occurred at Karbala is not one word different according to the two ideologies. But the belief systems based upon the myth and the meaning and significance of the 'ashura events differ considerably when comparing the "Imam Husain as Example" framework with the Intercessor framework. Equally divergent are their implications for the relationship between the believer and Husain; attitudes and behavior toward other persons; self-concept of the believer; and political activity.

In each of the divergent views, Imam Husain is the central figure and his martyrdom at Karbala the central event. But, whereas in the first, his martyrdom mainly serves the purpose of giving him the powers of intercession, in the second view, his martyrdom becomes an example for behavior for all believers. The meaning of life on earth becomes clear; true human existence consists of holding a belief and being prepared to fight and die for it. Here, too, believers strive to become close to Husain. But rather than becoming close to him by forming a transactional relationship with him, they are close to him through emulating him. "Husain's friends . . . are those who are willing to die, like Husain, defending the faith."[22] Believers should be *like* Husain. Just as he "irrigated Islam with his blood," they should be willing to do so as well. Instead of placing primary importance on their own worldly troubles and material advantages, they should concentrate on spiritual progress. Selflessness should replace selfishness. Instead of a bargaining, "commercial"[12] relationship with holy figures, the believer should be ready to give everything for his religion. Gone is the strictly hierarchical nature of the relationship. This is no connection between the all-powerful and the powerless but rather a more egalitarian relationship between companions and coworkers who cooperate in working toward a mutual goal. People perceive themselves to be different from Husain not absolutely but in degrees. Thus, the sister of a young man martyred during the Iranian revolution compared her brother to Husain and herself to Zainab, the sister of Husain: "She gave her Great Husain; I have given my little Husain."

The whole emphasis on a dyadic, instrumental relationship with a powerful figure changes to one of communal cooperation in working toward a goal that will benefit all humanity. One's concern and respect for fellow Muslims grows; other people are both partners in the struggle and the reason for one's self-sacrifice. Likewise, this view sheds more light on the personal qualities of Imam Husain. Greater attention is given to his characteristics, attitudes, and behavior. For it is what he *did* and his reasons for doing it that make him so worthy of esteem and emulation. People love Husain and are devoted to him for his philosophy of life and his actions.

Just as perceptions about the kind of person Husain was changed, the believer's self-concept evolved as well. With the world view provided by the ideology here termed "Imam Husain as Example," the believer no longer views himself as helpless, powerless, and dependent. Because of his perceived companionship on a rather more equal basis with the Imam, and his connection with a large community, both present and long-dead, involved in a cooperative effort, he gains a sense of personal power and worth.[13] He is active rather than passive. He feels himself to be capable of

11. Thaiss, "Religious Symbolism," p. 367.
12. Betteridge, "Controversial Vows," p. 145.
13. In their study of movements, Gerlach and Hine also found a "sense of personal power" and a "radically changed self-image" in new converts both to the Pentecostal

working toward his goals in life and of seeking his own salvation, rather than depending on others to do it for him. He believes that individual initiatives and efforts *do* have an effect so that his own decisions and actions *can* make a difference. Rather than modifying his behavior to please someone else in an indirect effort to obtain his needs, he actively and directly pursues what he wants.

During the months leading up to the Iranian revolution, the political admonition of this alternative Islamic world view was to throw caution to the winds. "Staying out of trouble" was tantamount to joining Yazid; the meaning of life is not to get along or get ahead, to try to connect oneself with power, but to revolt against unjust power. Specifically, practical advice for political behavior included the following points:

1. Revolt rather than accommodating yourself to unjust power. Do not accept a political leader just because he has power.[14] De facto power, position, and connections should count for less than what a person *is* and what he *does*. Resist tyranny and accept only a leader who is concerned about others and not himself, who is a righteous and God-fearing person. Do not compromise and do what others want you to do in exchange for your own safety, well-being, comfort, and material advantages.

2. Forget about your personal, materialistic, this-worldly interests. Practice altruism rather than selfishness. Instead of advancing yourself in society, aim to improve society. Recognize the intrinsic worth of each individual in the community, not only those with power and connections, and cooperate with others on an equal basis to strive toward goals benefiting the whole society. Instead of competing with others over access to scarce goods and close relations with the powerful, join with others in a similar position to overturn the powerful.

3. Forget caution and fear; find courage and confidence. Don't hide what you really think and feel out of fear for your life and livelihood. Live your beliefs no matter what the consequences. Get involved personally instead of staying on the sidelines to stay out of trouble. For individuals and their efforts *do* have political impact. Even if you should die in the attempt, your death will not be without effect; you will have reached the highest spiritual level attainable by conquering self and the material world. And your martyrdom can serve as an example, inspiring others to action, thus escalating the conflict against tyranny.

Such attitudes were continuously applied in the political struggle

movement and the Black Power movement. Luther Gerlach and Virginia Hine, *People, Power, Change: Movements of Social Transformation* (Indianapolis: Bobbs-Merrill Educational Publishing, 1970), p. 143.

14. As an example of the opposite attitude, very prevalent before the revolution, one of the Askari brothers explained his defense of the shah's regime to me thus, "It doesn't matter whether the shah's good or bad—he's the one who has the power."

against the shah by persons supporting the revolution. Among religious activists, endless conversations compared the good-evil, Husain-Yazid dichotomy to the revolutionary effort against the shah's regime and discussed the implications for political action fostered by this revolutionary Shi'i world view. Calling for cohesion and cooperation were such often-heard phrases as "brother," "sister," "unity," "*ham-e ba ham*" (all together). People asserted, "I'd rather die with dignity than live in shame and submission." To reprove those merely standing and watching, demonstrators would shout a phrase from the writings of Dr. Ali Shariati: "Those martyred are doing the work of Husain, those who remain are doing the work of Zainab [Husain's sister who survived to tell his story, thus also contributing to the cause]—and if not, they're doing the work of Yazid." Another slogan carried the same message: "There were no spectators at the martyrdom of Husain." (In other words, if you are not for him, you are against him, so do not stay neutral.) Especially when the serious strikes began in the fall of 1978, and there were shortages of food, fuel, and other necessities, people often proclaimed their confidence in the eventual outcome of the movement and their courage in the face of difficulty. "We don't care if we don't have cooking oil or dishwashing soap or kerosene. We can go cold and hungry. We'll sacrifice our sons and daughters. They can kill as many people as they want, but we'll never give in. It may go on like this for years, but in the end we'll succeed, because we have faith."

As hardly needs stating, the cooperative and fearless behavior urged by the revolutionary Shi'i ideology was very prevalent during the revolution in such activities as the strikes, demonstrations, marches, and in the final months, the bare-handed attacks on statues of the shah, SAVAK offices, and finally government strongholds such as garrisons, city police stations, gendarmerie stations, and military bases.

In the eyes of many involved Iranians, the changing understanding of the meaning of Shi'i Islam was at least in part responsible for the success of the revolution. One Iranian, two days before 'ashura of 1979, described the transformation in the Shi'i world view as follows:

This 'ashura, there'll be mourning but with a big difference. There'll be mourning with victory. Now we are more aware of the teachings of Husain. Now everyone knows *why* Husain went to fight Yazid. Before they didn't know. Three night ago I went to a *rauzeh* [recitation of the passion of Imam Husain], and the *rauzehkhan* [reciter] called Husain "*rahbar-e enqelab*" [leader of revolution]— and he wasn't an educated *rauzehkhan*, just a simple one. He'd never called Husain that before. Before they pitied Husain rather than admiring his courage. Now people are more aware of the whole meaning of religion. It's not something to cling to in order to get better advantages in life, to get your *hajat* [wishes].

Husain, for ordinary Iranian people, because of what he did for God and his
devotion to God, was a hajat giver. He could give them everything they wanted,
fulfil their every wish and desire. The rauzehkhans said, "Just make your request
and he'll give you anything you need." This year we know that his message is—
death. If you can kill, kill. If you can't, die in the attempt. Either kill or get killed,
but like Husain fight against repression and tyranny.

Although the woman quoted possesses a high level of religious knowledge, her attitude is quite representative of many Shi'is at that time.
Indeed, partly because of the very effective communication system
operating before and after the revolution among the activists, a remarkable degree of similarity existed between speeches and ideas of religious
figures disseminated through TV, radio, the press, tapes, and public
appearances and discussion among Iranian villagers.

Accommodation and Revolution: Symbiotic Ideologies

After the revolution, many people continued to condemn "superstitious"
practices, such as asking favors of the imams and giving meals in honor of
the imams in hopes of getting a wish or in gratitude for the fulfillment of a
wish. People railed against talk of Imam Husain as a hajat giver and
discoursed at length on how the shah and his government had hidden the
real meaning of Islam and had taught the people that it only meant
weeping and beating their chests and getting wishes. The government,
they said, involved the people in these things to keep their emotions busy
and to prevent them from knowing *why* Imam Husain was martyred, *why*
he is beloved of God. People complained that the crying and weeping
going on during 'ashuras was useless—crying does not get you anywhere.
It is not following in the way of Husain. One revolutionary-minded
woman told me she had been to a rauzeh given in the name of Imam
Husain recently. The rauzehkhan optimistically commented, "This house
has always been lucky in getting hajat from Imam Husain." My friend
spoke up angrily, "No! Don't talk about Imam Husain as a hajat giver.
Talk about his great courage in facing death. He saw everyone of his
group die before his eyes but he never lost courage. There was hand-to-
hand combat. He was the last to be killed, but he never gave up."
    As the months passed, however, attitudes of people toward the old
practices began to soften. People began to say that weeping, chest
beating, and even devotion to Imam Husain for instrumental reasons have
their place. All these practices had accomplished an important task; they
had kept the memory of Husain and his struggle alive in the hearts and
minds of people, so that when the opportunity presented itself, the
Husain as Example ideology could come to the fore and assist people in
the struggle against tyranny. "Crying for Husain is passive resistance,"
informants explained to me. "We shouldn't continue to think that crying

for Husain is superstition, but it's so that Husain and the just government of Husain won't be forgotten." People credited the custom of crying for Husain with keeping his memory alive through so many centuries, against all odds. "Until," as one informant pointed out, "1360 years after the 'ashura of Karbala, you saw what happened all over Iran during 'ashura of this year, because people found strength to take the place of weeping, went to the street, shook their fists, and screamed, 'Down with the shah!' "

Although the two persons quoted above are well educated in religious matters, these attitudes were present even among illiterate people in the village. A perception that the two divergent ideologies discussed in this article are in actuality two different sides of the same coin seemed to be spreading. People explained to me that Shi'i Islam provides a world view and a guide to its people, no matter what the social and political conditions are during their lifetimes. Islam is a flexible religion that can be adapted to fit all times and problems. It is always relevant. Thus, during times when a strong repressive government controls Shi'is, Islam counsels acquiescence, for survival is of primary importance. During such times, resistance is passive, merely taking the form of weeping.[15] One might add that during such times the Intercessor ideology is useful in providing comfort in the face of life's tribulations, when no hope of ever making a real change in one's situation seems to exist. When, however, conditions allow hope that struggle will not be in vain, Islam provides an inspiration for rising against tyranny and injustice. Each of the two views depends for its existence on the other, and Islam itself can survive only with the help of both world views and strategies. The revolutionary aspect of Islam, which is the true core of Shi'i Islam according to the proponents of this interpretation, depends on the Imam Husain as Intercessor ideology to keep it alive during times of political repression.[16] During such times, people will keep the memory of Husain alive because they believe that weeping and remembering him bring earthly and spiritual rewards. On the other hand, the Intercessor version would soon become a dried-out shell and crumble away without revolutionary Islam, the true living core of the religion. Although sometimes below the surface for the great majority of believers, the true meaning of Islam is kept alive through the passion of Imam Husain and the devotion of a few enlightened believers.

By the time 'ashura of 1979 arrived, this understanding of the signifi-

15. Thaiss also discusses the negative struggle of weeping. Thaiss, "Religious Symbolism," pp. 324, 325, 402.

16. Ayoub also notes that "great emphasis is laid on keeping the memory of this tragic event alive by all possible means, in spite of opposition, hardship, and persecution. From the beginning, the impetus was provided by the Imams themselves, who promised great rewards for the tears of the devotees." Ayoub, *Redemptive Suffering,* p. 148.

cance of traditional practices in relation to Imam Husain was quite widespread. Thus Ayatollah Khomeini could declare, "Whatever you did in past 'ashuras, do the same thing this year too." For these practices had kept the true religion alive and were not to be slighted. So 'ashura saw a return to traditional practices. In fact, people resolved to make 'ashura of 1979 bigger and better than it had even been in the past.

In years preceding the revolution, participants in the mourning rituals of 'ashura had struck their chests and beat their backs with chains while chanting mourning couplets and crying in unison, "Husain, Husain, Husain." In contrast, during the revolutionary processions of 'ashura 1978, marchers raised their fists to beat the air, marking the rhythm of the phrase *Marg bar shah*. (Down with the shah.) Postrevolutionary 'ashura of 1979 saw a combination of these practices, symbolizing a perceived compatibility between the Intercessor and the Example views of Imam Husain. To accompany the swings of the chains and the thump of chains hitting their backs, 'ashura marchers in 1979 chanted both traditional mourning couplets and revolutionary couplets.

Ideology and Non-Shi'is

Ideology was also responsible for recruiting non-Shi'is into the movement. Some such persons were sincerely interested in the progressive ideology presented by movement leaders, judging that such ideology also expressed their own attitudes and needs. They believed that the revolution would bring about the stated goals of these activists. Others were in agreement only with the main and most immediate goal of the movement—to get rid of the shah—and the means by which the movement proposed to do this. Some months after the revolution, a leftist Kurdish activist told me, "From the beginning the Kurds knew what would happen. We knew that a religious government wouldn't allow representative government, that they wouldn't give the Kurds self-determination. But we knew that nothing could ever be done without getting rid of the shah first. That had to be the first step. So we were active in the revolution."

Quite obviously, a characteristic of the Iranian revolutionary ideology was what Gerlach and Hine call the "split-level" nature of movement ideology. According to these researchers, "On one level of the ideology of any movement are those few basic concepts in which all participants find agreement. . . . At the 'lower level' of ideology an almost infinite variety of ideological emphases, interpretations, adaptations and exegetical detours can be found in any movement."[17]

In the Iranian case, the slogan *Marg bar shah* expressed sentiments

17. Gerlach and Hine, *People, Power, Change*, p. 165.

upon which all in the movement could agree—anti-shah, antityranny and anti-injustice, self-sufficiency, and national pride. But below this level of agreement existed many other levels of ideology, providing cohesion among fewer and fewer people at succeedingly lower levels. Concentrating a few important concepts in a number of different belief systems, the slogan "Down with the shah" was able to express the commonly held sentiments of great masses of people, among whom there were in fact great ideological differences, in a concerted effort resulting in the dramatic overthrow of the shah.

The antityranny and antirepression concept in the Imam Husain as Example ideology of Shi'i Islam appealed to non-Shi'is as well as Shi'is. Ideology, then, was the drawing card for both Shi'i and non-Shi'i, although there was disagreement about what should happen after the accomplishment of the immediate goal of ridding themselves of the tyranny of the shah's regime.

Both Shi'is and non-Shi'is were drawn into the revolutionary process through ideology and observation of real conditions and events. Likewise, both groups experienced other aspects of the revolution in similar ways. Among both Shi'is and non-Shi'is, the revolutionary ideology was disseminated through networks of association, through literature, tapes, speeches, and endless discussion among friends and associates. Once having been persuaded by argument, information, and reasoning, of the accuracy and relevancy of revolutionary ideology, converts to the movement were drawn into involvement in the revolution by forces also not specifically Shi'i. Expressing the attitude and emotions making it impossible for an Iranian to stand idly by, forcing him rather to throw himself into the fray, is the Persian phrase *az khod gozashteh* or *az jan gozashteh*. This phrase was used when people were describing to me what prompted them or others to participate in a certain revolutionary event; it refers to a person who is willing to give up his life and no longer makes decisions on the basis of what will preserve his life. One villager explained the concept as follows:

One must calculate. Otherwise something bad might happen. When you don't care about life anymore, then you no longer calculate. When you want your own life you have to calculate. You must think about the final results of your actions. Can you tolerate the end result or not? But when you are *so* unhappy at the hands of someone that you don't care about life any more, then, even if you don't have the hope that victory will be certain, you'll struggle as much as possible, no matter what happens. Like when people become so unhappy under the shah that they're no longer afraid of machine guns. When I no longer care about my own life, when I've given up on my own life, I don't need you any more. When I no longer want my own life, I don't need your help. If I know I'm going to die, I will shoot at the person who is making me unhappy. It doesn't matter if he hits me back, because I'm going to die anyway.

People felt this emotion and gained this attitude through hearing about
or participating in events in which government forces treated people with
violence and injustice. Most active villagers could tell me at least one
story about their involvement in a terrible event, such as the massacre at
Shah Mosque or Habib Mosque, in Shiraz; attacks by police on high
schools or teacher training schools; and confrontations with armed forces
in the streets, complete with tear gas and police clubbing men and
women. In addition to the numerous events in which villagers were
actually involved, in the village, in Shiraz, or in surrounding towns, there
was a constant stream of news about such terrible events elsewhere in the
country, during which people were killed or maimed under horrible
circumstances. To mention just a few: the deadly fire at Cinema Rex in
Abadan, the government attack on unarmed demonstrators in Tehran's
Maidan-e Zhaleh and at the Kerman Mosque, and the reports of government forces attacking a hospital in Mashhad and killing doctors, patients,
and young children. One such occasion followed another in close succession and they were the object of continuous discussion. Villagers reported
to me their horror, fury, and frustration upon hearing about such events,
as well as their resolve that they would never rest until the shah and the
government that did such inhuman things to their fellow Iranians no
longer existed. Hearing about the death of a friend or relative could also
cause such emotions, as could learning about a previously unknown
martyr, about what kind of a person he or she was and the circumstances
of his or her death. Experienced by Shi'i and non-Shi'i alike, these
emotions caused Iranians to abandon all caution and participate in
revolutionary activities, such as the demonstrations and marches which
became the rituals of revolution.

Likewise, the emotions and attitudes evoked by participation in
marches and demonstrations affected all, no matter what their ideological
or religious affiliation. The same terrific outpouring of hate and anger—
long hidden out of fear—toward a repressive dictatorship; the joy, elation,
and pride; and the intensified commitment and confidence were experienced by everyone, not only Shi'i Muslims who had taken part in the
traditional 'ashura processions and rituals of previous years.

Conclusion

Rituals, especially the rituals of marches and demonstrations and specifically the demonstrations of tasu'a and 'ashura of 1978, played a significant
role in the Iranian revolution. Such rituals provided confidence and faith
in an eventual victory, helped recruit new members to the movement,
inspired feelings of unity and cohesion, instilled stronger commitment and
determination, and presented such an overwhelming show of strength in

the war of nerves and morale that unarmed masses decimated a military giant. But participation in the rituals of revolution—demonstrations and marches—and in the revolution itself was not an automatic, unthinking response from the depths of Shi'i hearts to a primordial religious force. Quite the contrary, for Shi'i Muslims, participation in the tasu'a and 'ashura marches called for a break from traditional religious practices and traditional rituals commemorating the death of Imam Husain. Indeed, many sincere Shi'is were shocked at this behavior and dismayed that people could sully the holiness of these two religious days with matters of a political secular nature. People took part in the alternative form of ritual, the marches and demonstrations, only after they had already made some decision and had reached a degree of commitment to the cause.

Rational reevaluation, embedded in ideology, of real political, economic, and social conditions, not an unreflective emotional attachment to traditional rituals, was instrumental in pulling a people together to revolt. For assessing the world and individual attitudes toward it, Shi'i thought provides two central possibilities. Both of them are closely related to Imam Husain's martyrdom: Husain as Intercessor—the quietist ideology of adaptation to the existing relations of power; Husain as Example—the revolutionary ideology of struggle against tyranny. Overall social oppression as well as a change of economic and social relations in the village itself have favored a weakening of the traditional Husain as Intercessor ideology. The revolutionary version of the concept of Husain transformed the Shi'i masses' perception of their religion, and, for many, caused a revival of their Islamic heritage and identity. For others, the progressive ideology of revolutionary Islam provided an incentive for their involvement in the hope of furthering their own goals and political interests. In any case, this ideology, by appealing to the least common denominator of groups otherwise quite divergent in their ideas and beliefs, was able to unite social action of a great number of people—at least until their common goal, the overthrow of the shah's regime, was achieved.

Select Western-Language Bibliography: Shi'ism and Politics, with Special Reference to Iran

Books

Akhavi, Shahrough. *Religion and Politics in Contemporary Iran: Clergy-State Relations in the Pahlavi Period.* Albany: State University of New York Press, 1980.

Algar, Hamid. *Religion and State in Iran, 1785–1906: The Role of the Ulama in the Qajar Period.* Berkeley and Los Angeles: University of California Press, 1969.

Bausani, A. *Persia religiosa.* Milan: Saggiatore, 1959.

Bayat, Mangol. *Mysticism and Dissent: Socioreligious Thought in Qajar Iran.* Syracuse: Syracuse University Press, 1982.

Bonine, Michael E., and Nikki R. Keddie, eds. *Modern Iran: The Dialectics of Continuity and Change.* Albany: State University of New York Press, 1981. See especially articles by M. Bayat, W. Beeman, and N. Keddie.

Bosworth, C. E., ed. *Iran and Islam: In Memory of the Late Vladimir Minorsky.* Edinburgh: Edinburgh University Press, 1971.

Browne, Edward G. *Materials for the Study of the Babi Religion.* Cambridge: Cambridge University Press, 1918.

———. *The Persian Revolution, 1905–1909.* Cambridge: Cambridge University Press, 1910.

———. *A Year Amongst the Persians.* London: A. and C. Black, 1893.

Calder, Norman. "The Structure of Authority in Imami Shi'i Jurisprudence." Ph.D. dissertation, University of London, 1979.

The Cambridge History of Iran. Cambridge: Cambridge University Press, vol. 5, 1968; vol. 4, 1975.

Chardin, Jean. *Voyages de Monsieur le Chevalier Chardin en Perse et autres lieux de l'Orient.* 2 vols. Amsterdam, 1711.

Chelkowski, Peter J., ed. *Ta'ziyeh: Ritual and Drama in Iran.* New York: New York University Press, 1979.

Corbin, Henry. *Terre céleste et corps de résurrection, de l'Iran mazdéen a l'Iran shi'ite.* Paris: Buchet, Chastel, Correa, 1961. 2nd ed., *Corps spirituel et Terre céleste.* Paris, 1979.

———. *En Islam iranien.* 4 vols. Paris: Gallimard, 1971–72.

————. *Histoire de la philosophie islamique*. Paris: Gallimard, 1964.

Cottam, Richard W. *Nationalism in Iran: Updated through 1978*. Pittsburgh: University of Pittsburgh Press, 1979.

Donaldson, Dwight Martin. *The Shi'ite Religion*. London: Luzac & Co., 1933.

Doroshenko, Elena Alekseevna. *Shi'itskoe dukhovenstvo v sovremennom Irane*. Moscow: Akademiia Nauk, 1975.

Faghfoory, Mohammad Hasan. "The Role of the Ulama in Twentieth Century Iran, with Particular Reference to Ayatullah Haj Sayyid Abul-Qasim Kashani." Ph.D. dissertation, University of Wisconsin, Madison, 1978.

Fernea, Elizabeth W. *Guests of the Sheik*. Garden City, N.Y.: Doubleday, 1969.

Fischer, Michael M. J. *Iran: From Religious Dispute to Revolution*. Cambridge, Mass.: Harvard University Press, 1980.

————. "Zoroastrian Iran between Myth and Praxis." Ph.D. dissertation, University of Chicago, 1973.

Frye, Richard N. *The Golden Age of Persia*. London: Weidenfeld & Nicolson, 1955.

Garoussian, Vida. "The Ulama and Secularization in Contemporary Iran." Ph.D. dissertation, Southern Illinois University, 1974.

Gibb, H. A. R. *Studies in the Civilization of Islam,* ed. William R. Polk and Stanford Shaw. London: Routledge & Kegan Paul, 1962.

de Gobineau, Comte. *Les religions et les philosophies dans l'Asie Centrale*. 3rd. ed., Paris, 1957.

Greussing, K., ed. *Religion und Politik im Iran*. Frankfurt am Main: Syndikat, 1981.

Hairi, Abdul Hadi, *Shi'ism and Constitutionalism in Iran*. Leiden: E. J. Brill, 1977.

al-Hilli, al Allama al-Hassan ibn Yusuf ibn al-Mutahhar. *Al-Babu'l-Hadi Ashar*. Trans. W. M. Miller. London: Royal Asiatic Society, 1928.

Hodgson, Marshall G. S. *The Order of the Assassins*. The Hague: Mouton, 1955.

————. *The Venture of Islam*. 3 vols. Chicago: University of Chicago Press, 1974.

Holod, Renata, ed. *Studies on Isfahan*. Special issue of *Iranian Studies* 7, nos. 1–2 (1974).

Huart, C. *Textes persans relatifs à la secte des Houroufis*. Leiden: E. J. Brill, 1909.

Ibn Babuya, Muhammad ibn 'Ali. *A Shi'ite Creed*. Trans. A. A. Fyzee. London: Oxford University Press, 1942.

Iran in der Krise. Bonn: Verlag Neue Gesellschaft, 1980. Includes 8 articles in English.

Islam and Revolution: Writings and Declarations of Imam Khomeini. Trans. and annotated by Hamid Algar. Berkeley: Mizan Press, 1981.

Ivanov, Mikhail Sergeevich. *Babidski vosstaniia v Irane: 1848–52*. Moscow: Akademiia Nauk USSR, 1939.

Ivanow, W. *Studies in Early Persian Ismailism*. Leiden: E. J. Brill, 1948.

————, ed. and trans. *The Truth-Worshippers of Kurdistan: Ahl-e Haqq Texts*. Leiden: E. J. Brill, 1953.

Kazemi, Farhad, ed. *The Iranian Revolution in Perspective*. Special edition of *Iranian Studies* 13, nos. 1–4, (1980). See especially articles by M. Fischer, S. A. Arjomand, G. Nashat, and D. Menashi.

Keddie, Nikki R. *Iran: Religion, Politics and Society*. London: Frank Cass, 1980.

————. *An Islamic Response to Imperialism: Political and Religious Writings of Sayyid Jamal ad-Din "al-Afghani."* Berkeley and Los Angeles: University of California Press, 1968. Paperback with new introduction, 1982.

————. *Religion and Rebellion in Iran: The Tobacco Protest of 1891–1892*. London: Frank Cass, 1966.

————. *Sayyid Jamal ad-Din "al-Afghani": A Political Biography*. Berkeley and Los Angeles: University of California Press, 1972.

————, ed. *Scholars, Saints, and Sufis: Muslim Religious Institutions in the Middle East Since 1500*. Berkeley and Los Angeles: University of California Press, 1972. See chapters by H. Algar, E. W. and R. Fernea, N. Keddie, and G. Thaiss.

Lambton, A. K. S. *Theory and Practice in Medieval Persian Government*. London: Varorium Reprints, 1980.

Laoust, H. *Les schismes dans l'Islam*. Paris: Payot, 1965.

Lewis, Bernard. *Islam in History*. New York: The Library Press, 1973.

————. *The Assassins: A Radical Sect in Islam*. New York: Basic Books, 1968.

————. *The Origins of Isma'ilism*. Cambridge: Cambridge University Press, 1940.

MacEoin, Denis M. "From Shaykhism to Babism." Ph.D. dissertation, Kings College, Cambridge University, 1979.

Makarem, Sami Nasib, ed.' and trans. *The Political Doctrine of the Isma'ilis (the Imamate)*. Delmar, N.Y.: Caravan Books, 1977.

Malcolm, John. *The History of Persia*. Vol. 2. London: J. Murray, 1815.

Massignon, Louis. *La passion d'al-Hallaj*. Paris: Gallimard, 1975.

Mazzaoui, Michel. *The Origins of the Safawids*. Wiesbaden: F. Steiner, 1972.

Minorsky, Vladimir. *Notes sur la secte des Ahle-Haqq*. Paris: E. Leroux, 1921.

————, trans. and ed. *Tadhkirat al-Muluk: A Manual of Safavid Administration*. London: Luzac, 1943.

Mottahedeh, Roy P. *Loyalty and Leadership in an Early Islamic Society*. Princeton: Princeton University Press, 1980.

Nasr, Seyyed Hossein. *Three Muslim Sages: Avicenna—Suhrawardi—Ibn 'Arabi*. Cambridge, Mass.: Harvard University Press, 1964.

Nicolas, A. L. M. *Essai sur le sheikhisme*. 4 vols. Paris: Geuthner, 1910–1914.

Nizam al-Mulk. *The Book of Government or Rules for Kings*. Trans. H. Drake. London: Routledge & Kegan Paul, 1978.

Pakdaman [Nateq], Homa. *Djamal-ed Din Assad Abadi dit Afghani*. Paris: J. Maisonneuve, 1969.

Rafati, Vahid. "The Development of Shaykhi Thought in Shi'i Islam." Ph.D. dissertation, University of California at Los Angeles, 1979.

Richard, Yann. *Le Shi'isme en Iran*. Paris: J. Maisonneuve, 1980.

Sachedina, Abdulaziz A. *Islamic Messianism: The Idea of the Mahdi in Twelver Islam*. Albany: State University of New York Press, 1981.

Sadighi, G. H. *Les mouvements religieux iraniens au IIe et au IIIe siècle de l'hégire*. Paris: Les Presses Modernes, 1938.

Said, Edward. *Covering Islam*. New York: Pantheon, 1981.

Savory, Roger M. *Iran under the Safavids*. Cambridge: Cambridge University Press, 1980.

Shaban, M. A. *The 'Abbasid Revolution.* Cambridge: Cambridge University Press, 1970.

Shariati, Ali. *The Islamic View of Man.* Trans. A. A. Rasti. Bedford, Ohio: Free Islamic Literatures, 1978.

———. *Marxism and Other Western Fallacies: An Islamic Critique.* Trans. R. Campbell. Berkeley: Mizan Press, 1980.

———. *On the Sociology of Islam.* Trans. H. Algar. Berkeley: Mizan Press, 1979.

Sharif, M. M., ed. *A History of Muslim Philosophy.* Vol. 2. Wiesbaden: Otto Harrassowitz, 1966. See especially chapters on Safavid and Qajar philosophy by Seyyed Hossein Nasr.

Le shi'isme imamite. Paris: Presses Universitaires de France, 1970. See especially chapters by W. Madelung, C. Cahen, H. Corbin, G. Lecomte, Y. de Bellefonds, R. Brunschvig, S. H. Nasr, J. Aubin, and A. Lambton.

Tabataba'i, S. Muhammad Husayn. *Shi'ite Islam.* Intro. and trans. S. H. Nasr. Albany: State University of New York Press, 1975.

Watt, W. Montgomery. *The Formative Period of Islamic Thought.* Edinburgh: Edinburgh University Press, 1973.

———. *Islam and the Integration of Society.* London: Routledge & Kegan Paul, 1961.

———. *The Majesty That Was Islam.* London: Sidgwick & Jackson, 1974.

Articles and Chapters

Abbreviations of Journals
IJMES   *International Journal of Middle East Studies*
IS   *Iranian Studies*
JAOS   *Journal of the American Oriental Society*
MEJ   *Middle East Journal*
MES   *Middle Eastern Studies*
SI   *Studia Islamica*

Abrahamian, Ervand. "The Guerilla Movement in Iran, 1963–1977." *MERIP Reports* 86 (March–April 1980): 3–21.

Akhavi, Shahrough. "The Ideology and Praxis of Shi'ism in the Iranian Revolution." *Comparative Studies in Society and History,* forthcoming.

———. "Shi'i Social Thought and Praxis in Recent Iranian History." In C. K. Pullapilly, ed., *Islam in the Contemporary World.* Notre Dame, Ind.: Cross Roads Press, 1980.

Algar, Hamid. "Shi'ism and Iran in the Eighteenth Century." In Thomas Naff and Roger Owen, eds., *Studies in Eighteenth Century Islamic History.* Carbondale and Edwardsville: Southern Illinois University Press, 1977.

Arjomand, Said Amir. "The *Ulama*'s Traditionalist Opposition to Parliamentarianism: 1907–1909." *MES* 17, no. 2 (April 1981): 174–90.

———. "Religion and Ideology in the Constitutional Revolution." *IS* 12, nos. 3–4 (1979): 283–91.

———. "Religion, Political Action and Legitimate Domination in Shi'ite Iran: Fourteenth to Eighteenth Centuries A.D." *Archives Europeennes de Sociologie* 20, no. 1 (1979): 59–109.

Aubin, Jean. "La politique religieuse des Safavides." In *Le shi'isme imamite*. Paris: Presses Universitaires de France, 1970.

Batatu, Hanna. "Iraq's Underground Shi'a Movements: Characteristics, Causes and Prospects." *MEJ* 35, no. 4 (Autumn 1981): 578–94.

Bayat, Mangol. "Islam in Pahlavi and Post-Pahlavi Iran: A Cultural Revolution?" In John L. Esposito, ed., *Islam and Development: Religion and Sociopolitical Change*. Syracuse: Syracuse University Press, 1980.

Bill, James A. "Power and Religion in Revolutionary Iran." *MEJ* 36, no. 1 (Winter 1982): 22–47.

Binder, Leonard. "The Proofs of Islam: Religion and Politics in Iran." In George Makdisi, ed., *Arabic and Islamic Studies in Honor of Hamilton Gibb*. Leiden: E. J. Brill, 1965.

Cahen, Claude. "La changeante portée sociale de quelques doctrines religieuses." In Claude Cahen, ed., *Les peuple musulmans dans l'histoire medievale*. Paris: A. Maisonneuve, 1977.

———. "Points de vue sur la revolution 'abbaside." In Claude Cahen, ed., *Les peuple musulmans dans l'histoire medievale*. Paris: A. Maisonneuve, 1977.

Calder, Norman. "Accommodation and Revolution in Imami Shi'i Jurisprudence: Khumayni and the Classical Tradition." *MES* 18 (January 1982): 3–20.

Calmard, Jean. "Le chiisme imamite en Iran à l'epoque Seldjoukide." *Le monde iranien et l'Islam* 1 (1971): 43–67.

———. "Les mysteres de la passion de Hosseyn (ta'ziya)." In D. Bogdanovic, ed., *L'Iran—les sept elimats*. Paris, 1972.

Corbin, Henry. "L'ecole shaykhie en théologie shi'ite." *Annuaire d'E.P.H.E.*, 1960–61.

———. "Confessions extatiques de Mir Damad, mâitre de théologie à Ispahan (ob. 1041/1631–1632)." *Mélanges Louis Massignon*. Vol. 1. Damascus: Institut Français, 1956.

Eliash, Joseph. "The Ithna'ashari Shii Juristic Theory of Political and Legal Authority." *SI*, no. 29 (1969): 17–30.

———. "Misconceptions Regarding the Juridical Status of the Iranian 'Ulama." *IJMES* 10 (1979): 9–25.

Fischer, Michael M. J. "Islam and the Revolt of the Petit[e] Bourgeoisie." *Daedalus* 111 (Winter 1982): 101–25.

Gallagher, Charles T. "Contemporary Islam: The Plateau of Particularism, Problems of Religion and Nationalism in Iran." *American Universities Field Service Reports*. New York, 1966.

"The Heterodoxies of the Shi'ites in the Presentation of Ibn Hazm." Trans. with a commentary by I. Friedlaender, in *JAOS* 28 (1907): 1–80, and 29 (1909): 1–183.

Hodgson, Marshall. "How Did the Early Shi'a Become Sectarian?" *JAOS* 75, no. 1 (1955): 1–13.

Keddie, Nikki R. "Iran: Change in Islam; Islam and Change." *IJMES* 11 (1980): 527–92.

———. "The Origins of the Religious-Radical Alliance in Iran." *Past and Present* 34 (1966): 70–80.

———. "Religion and Irreligion in Early Iranian Nationalism." *Comparative Studies in Society and History* 4, no. 3 (1962): 265–95.

————, and A. H. Zarrinkub. "Fida'iyyan-i Islam." In *Encyclopaedia of Islam.* New ed., vol. 2.

Lambton, A. K. S. "The Persian Ulama and Constitutional Reform." In *Le shi'isme imamite.* Paris: PUF, 1970.

————. "Quis Custodiet Custodes? Some Reflections on the Persian Theory of Government." *SI,* no. 5 (1955): 125–48, and no. 6 (1956): 125–46.

————. "A Reconsideration of the Position of the Marja' al-Taqlid and the Religious Institution." *SI,* no. 20 (1964): 115–35.

————. "Secret Societies and the Persian Revolution of 1905–6." *St. Antony's Papers* 4 (1958): pp. 43–60.

————. "Some New Trends in Islamic Political Thought in Late 18th and Early 19th Century Persia." *SI,* no. 39 (1974): 95–128.

Madelung, Wilfred. "Imama." In *Encyclopaedia of Islam.* New ed., vol. 3.

Millward, William G. "Aspects of Modernism in Shi'a Islam." *SI,* no. 37 (1973): 111–28.

Minorsky, Vladimir. "Ahl-i Hakk." *Encyclopaedia of Islam.* New ed., vol. 1.

————. "Iran: Opposition, Martyrdom and Revolt." In G. E. von Grunebaum, ed., *Unity and Variety in Muslim Civilization.* Chicago: University of Chicago Press, 1955.

————. "The Poetry of Shah Isma'il I." *Bulletin of the School of Oriental and African Studies* 10, no. 4 (1942): 1006a–53a.

Mirjafari, Hossein. "The Haydari-Nitmati Conflicts in Iran." Trans. and adapted by J. R. Perry. *IS* 12 (Summer–Autumn 1979): 135–62.

Molé, M. "Les Kubrawiyya entre sunnisme et shi'isme aux huitième et neuvième siècles de l'Hegire." *Revue des Etudes Islamiques* 29 (1961): 61–142.

Mottahedeh, Roy Parviz. "Iran's Foreign Devils." *Foreign Policy* 38 (Spring 1980): 19–34.

Nouraie, Fereshteh M. "The Constitutional Ideas of a Shi'ite Mujtahid: Muhammad Husayn Na'ini." *IS* 8, no. 4 (Autumn 1975): 234–47.

Ramazani, R. K. "Church and State in Modernizing Society: The Case of Iran." *The American Behavioral Scientist* 7, no. 5 (1964): 26–28.

Savory, R. M. "The Principal Offices of the Safawid State during the Reign of Ismai'il I." *Bulletin of the School of Oriental and African Studies* 23, no. 1 (1960): 91–105.

Scarcia, Gianroberto. "Intorno alle controversie tra ahbari e usuli presso gli imamiti di Persia." *Rivista degli Studi Orientali* 33 (December 1958): 211–50.

————. "Kerman 1905: La guerra tra Seihi e Balasari." *Annali del Instituto Universitario Orientale di Napoli,* N.S. 13 (1963): 195–238.

————. "Stato e dottrine attuali della setta sciita imamita degli *Shaikhi* in Persia." *Studi e Materiali di Storia delle Religioni* 29, no. 2 (1958): 215–41.

Sepsis, A. "Quelques mots sur l'etat religieux actuel de la Perse." *Revue de l'Orient* 3 (1844): 96–105.

Sohrweide, Hanna. "Der Sieg der Safaviden in Persien und seine Ruckwirkungen auf de Schiiten Anatoliens im 16 Jahrhundert." *Der Islam* 41 (1965): 95–223.

Spooner, Brian. "The Function of Religion in Persian Society." *Iran* 1 (1963): 83–95.

Stern, S. M. "Isma'ilis and Qarmatians." In *L'elaboration de l'Islam.* Paris: Presses Universitaires de France, 1961.

Thaiss, Gustav. "The Bazaar as a Case Study of Religion and Social Change." In
Ehsan Yar-Shater, ed., *Iran Faces the Seventies*. New York: Praeger, 1971.
———. "Unity and Discord: The Symbol of Husayn in Iran." In Charles J.
Adams, ed., *Iranian Civilization and Culture*. Montreal: McGill University,
1972.
Watt, W. Montgomery. "The Rafidites: A Preliminary Study." *Oriens* 16 (1963):
110–21.
———. "The Reappraisal of 'Abbasid Shi'ism.' " In G. Makdisi, ed., *Arabic and
Islamic Studies in Honor of Hamilton A. R. Gibb*. Leiden: E. J. Brill, 1965.

INDEX

LIST OF CONTRIBUTORS

Shahrough Akhavi is associate professor of government and international studies at the University of South Carolina, book review editor for *Iranian Studies,* and the author of *Religion and Politics in Contemporary Iran: Clergy-State Relations in the Pahlavi Period.*

William O. Beeman is assistant professor of anthropology at Brown University and the author of *Culture, Performance and Communication in Iran* and the forthcoming *Iranian Interaction Styles.*

Juan R. Cole is a Ph.D. candidate at the University of California, Los Angeles, and is preparing a dissertation under an SSRC fellowship on Shi'i Islam in pre-British North India. He has published several articles on modern Islamic society and thought.

Willem Floor works in the Hague and has published many articles on the socio-economic and political history of Safavid, Qajar, and Pahlavi Iran in *International Journal of Middle East Studies, Persica, Welt des Islams,* and elsewhere. With Wolfgang Behn, he published the *Bibliography of Iranian Political Periodicals,* and he has forthcoming studies on the labor movement in Iran and industrialization under Reza Shah.

Mary Elaine Hegland is a Ph.D. candidate in anthropology at the State University of New York, Binghamton, and is writing a dissertation on religion and politics in the Iranian revolution, based on field work done in Iran under an SSRC fellowship. She has published several articles.

Homa Katouzian is senior lecturer in economics at the University of Kent at Canterbury, England. His English and Persian books include *The Political Economy of Modern Iran, Ideology and Method in Economics,* and *Khaterat-e Siyasi-ye Khalil Maleki.*

Nikki R. Keddie is professor of history at the University of California, Los Angeles, and past president of the Middle East Studies Association. Among her most recent books are *Roots of Revolution: An Interpretive History of Modern Iran; Modern Iran: The Dialectics of Continuity and Change* (edited with Michael Bonine); and *Women in the Muslim World* (edited with Lois Beck).

Yann Richard is a researcher at the Centre National de la Recherche Scientifique, Paris, a past fellow of the Institut Français d'Iranologie de Téhéran, and author of *Le Shi'isme en Iran.* He wrote a section on modern Iranian political thought for Nikki Keddie's *Roots of Revolution* and contributes regularly to *Abstracta Iranica.*

Gregory Rose, a former journalist, is a graduate student in religion at Miami University, Oxford, Ohio.

Azar Tabari, a Ph.D. candidate at the University of Manchester, England, has published several articles, is writing a dissertation on the Iranian land reform, and is co-author of the forthcoming book, *Under the Shadow of Islam: the Women's Movement in Iran*.

William Montgomery Watt is professor emeritus of Arabic and Islamic studies at the University of Edinburgh and the author of numerous books and articles. He is internationally recognized as an authority on early Islam and the early history of Islamic theology.